GOLF'S STRANGEST ROUNDS

ANDREW WARD

Robson Books

Special edition for PAST TIMES

GOLF'S STRANGEST ROUNDS
text © Andrew Ward

9 8 7 6 5 4 3 2 1

PAST TIMES

Contents

INTRODUCTION

Golf's strangest stories have many themes. There are tales of tragedy ('Boy Kills his Father'), interference from wild life ('The Goose Incident') and odd tactical ploys ('With a Handkerchief Over His Eyes'). There are others of weird weather ('A Gale at the British Open'), bizarre betting ('A Plantation at Stake') and recondite rules ('How to Win with the Wrapping Still on the Ball'). From the world of professional golf, there are stories of remarkable recoveries ('Player and Lema'), record rounds ('Mr 59') and controversy ('Sportsmanship at Risk').

Other strange stories defy categorization. There's the one about the star golfer who refused to compete in tournaments ('Mysterious Montague — "the Best Golfer in the World"'), another about a mysterious pacesetter ('The Woman who Played in Trousers') and several concerning sensational shots that dogged Greg Norman in the late 1980s and early 1990s ('Greg Norman's Novel Ways to Finish Second - Lessons One to Six').

Inevitably, the stories in this book are a personal choice. I opted to omit thematic team matches, like 'Admirals' against 'Generals', and decided that some tales were too silly for inclusion. These include one about a player who threw the ball round (left-handed from bunkers of course) and another about a man who regularly went round in the low 70s by firing the ball from a sling-shot. In some cases my choice has been governed by what information was available. Almost all of these tales come from Britain and the United States, with a few from

Australia. To be sure, strange events have happened in other countries, but I had enough for the moment.

My research practice has been to return to original sources, in particular contemporary local newspapers and the golfing press. The *Golfer's Handbook* was an important starting-place, and other leads were discovered from friends, newspaper and magazine indexes, and golf's rich literature; Mark McCormack's annual, *The World of Professional Golf*, was especially valuable.

Much of the research was done in five libraries – the Bodleian (Oxford), the British Library Newspaper Library (London), the Library of Congress (Washington DC), and specialist golf libraries at St Andrews, Scotland, and Far Hills, New Jersey. I am grateful for the assistance of the staff of these libraries, and I also acknowledge help from Kim Banner, Bobby Burnet, Jack Daniels, Mike Lean, Karen MacDowell, Colin May and Brenda Stones.

HOLED IN ONE ... BUT LOST THE HOLE

MUSSELBURGH, 1870

It was all-square in a foursome at Musselburgh, and almost dark, when Robert Clark played his tee-shot at the short eighteenth hole. The green wasn't visible from the tee, and no one saw where Clark's ball went. The golfers walked forward and started searching.

They looked everywhere. Clark and his partner were particularly concerned, given the balanced state of the match. Eventually, they admitted their ball was lost, conceded the hole and with it the match.

Yes, you've guessed. Clark's ball was in the hole. They never thought of looking there.

Clark, an Edinburgh printer, was the author of an early golfing anthology, and we can assume he was a reliable witness. Since his unsuccessful hole-in-one, I believe the rules have been changed so that the ball is dead and the hole finished the moment the ball goes in the hole. Hence, even if you concede the hole as lost, the position of the ball takes precedence. Worth checking though. You never know when it might happen next.

Golfers have stumbled on other ways to lose a hole with an 'ace'. One method is perhaps more obvious than Clark's. Reverend H. C. Moor gives an example in a letter to *The Times* on 2 February 1940: 'On the Castle Bromwich links, near Birmingham, there was, some 30 years ago, a green set in a hollow, blind from the tee. Two brothers playing together drove to the green and found that they had both holed in one

But it was not a halved hole, for one brother had to give the other a stroke.'

A third possible method of losing a hole with an 'ace' was discovered accidentally by two golfers at Walsall's fourth hole in May 1950. The 182-yard hole was not visible from the tee, concealed by bunkers. Dr E.R.S. Grice and L Watson, playing in a club competition, could see they had put their tee-shots somewhere on the green. When they walked on to the green they discovered one ball in the hole, the other nearby. Unfortunately, on examining the balls, they found that both were brand new and of the same make and number. There were no distinguishing marks on either ball. It was impossible to say which ball was which. All they could do was assume the balls were lost, return to the tee and start again. So the player who holed in one – whoever he was – may, or may not, have won the hole eventually.

No hole is safe. Even if you hole in one.

AT NIGHT WITH
PHOSPHORESCENT BALLS

ST ANDREWS, AUGUST 1871

Professor Peter Guthrie Tait (1831-1901) was not a competitive golfer. He loved the game because it was a source of exercise, amusement and philosophical discussion. When the British Association for the Advancement of Science held its annual meeting of top European scientists, Professor Tait initiated a strange golf match with phosphorescent balls.

He was Professor of Natural Philosophy at Edinburgh University, a 40-year-old fun-loving practical joker, known to play as many as five rounds a day at St Andrews, yet he was also respected for his racy scientific articles in the newly launched *Nature*. Professor Tait was a scientist for the people, as his later work on golf proved.

In 1871, as President of Section A at the Edinburgh meeting of the British Association, Tait gave an address admiring Hamilton's quaternions and Kelvin's dissipation of energy. After the meeting, a number of distinguished scientists accompanied Tait to St Andrews. They included Huxley, Helmholtz, Andrews and Sylvester. Thomas Huxley played a round of golf every afternoon during his stay of two months, but Helmholtz took little interest. Helmholtz, however, makes it clear in one of his letters that golf consumed Professor Tait's interest and spirit of scientific investigation: *'Mr Tait kennt hier nichts anderes als golfing.'*

Professor Tait formulated a hypothesis: if golf balls are

5

coated with phosphorus, they will glow in the dark. Professor Crum Brown, Tait's brother-in-law, gave him every encouragement to experiment.

The match was described by John L Low: 'It is the dinner hour and the Professor proposes to the company that a round may be played with phosphorescent balls. When proper arrangements have been made the party assemble at the first teeing ground. To this match came the Professor and his lady, Huxley, keen on the humour of the thing, Professor Crum Brown and another friend. The idea is a success; the balls glisten in the grass and advertise their situation; the players make strokes that surprise their opponents and apprise themselves of hitherto unknown powers. All goes well until the burn is passed, and Professor Crum Brown's hand is found to be aflame; with difficulty his burning glove is unbuttoned, and the saddened group return to the Professor's rooms, where Huxley dresses the wounds. The pains of the phosphorescent hand having been mitigated by the tender care of the great scientist, it is not difficult to picture the fun which our Professor would derive from the night's adventure.'

Professor Tait's experiments eventually helped him state a more interesting problem: Why did a well-driven golf ball 'carry' so far and remain in the air so long? In the late 1880s, while Tait's second youngest son, Freddie, was developing a career that would bring him two British Amateur Championships, the Professor explored the heart of this new mystery.

As Knott wrote: 'While the son [Freddie] was surprising and delighting the world by his strong straight driving, his remarkable recoveries from almost unplayable "lies", and his brilliant all-round play with every kind of club, the father was applying his mathematical and physical knowledge to explain the prolonged flight of the golf ball. The practical golfer at first smiled in a superior way at this new science of the game; and Tait was scoffed at when he enunciated the truth that underspin was the great secret in long driving.'

In the early 1890s, *Nature* published Tait's series of articles on 'The Physics of Golf'. Sadly, the Boer War affected Tait's career. Lieutenant Freddie Tait was killed at Koodoosberg in February 1900, and Professor Tait's scientific work ended with his son's death. He retired later that year, and died in July 1901.

His spirit for night-time experiment has lived on with all manner of help – moonlight, acetylene flares, candles, flash-lamps, car headlights, rockets, street-lamps, photographers' flash-bulbs and floodlights.

A WALK-OVER WINS THE BRITISH OPEN

ST ANDREWS, SEPTEMBER 1876

In those early years of the British Open Championship, the venue alternated between St Andrews, Prestwick and Musselburgh. The 1876 Open was played at St Andrews on a showery Saturday. The greens were heavy but the links were crowded, not only with 34 Open competitors but also with members. Often the tournament golfers had to wait for the greens to clear, and this was a key factor in the strange result.

Old Tom Morris and Willie Park, Snr, were among the competitors, paired together, but the pre-tournament favourite was Davie Strath, a friend of Young Tom Morris, who had died suddenly the previous Christmas. Strath's first-round 86 was equalled by Bob Martin.

The second – and final – round began at 2 pm. At the fourteenth, Strath must have found it very difficult to decide whether the green was clear of golfers. The crowd was packed around him, and the hole was a long one. When he played his second shot, there was trouble, as we learn from the *St Andrews Citizen:* 'His tee-shot was a fine drive, and his second was also good, but the ball, when he played the latter, struck Mr Hutton, upholsterer, who was playing out, on the forehead, and he fell to the ground. We are glad to say that though Mr Hutton was stunned he was able to walk home. This seemed to shake Davie a little bit, for this hole and also the next he did in six strokes.'

If Strath had any knowledge of the rules, he must have sensed that he now risked disqualification. Watched by hundreds of people, however, he stuck to his task of matching Bob Martin's second round of 90. Before the last two holes, he had 10 to win, 11 for the tie. His third shot at the seventeenth again struck 'some party standing near the hole', but Strath recorded a five. A six at the final hole gave him the tie.

Then came the wrangle.

Did Strath infringe a rule by playing up to the green while others were putting out?

If so, had others done the same during the tournament?

The organizers seemed unable to come to a firm decision. They agreed that Strath and Martin should play-off on the Monday, but the matter was still under dispute. Strath declined to play unless the dispute was decided one way or the other, so Martin played the course alone, and was declared winner of the £10 first prize. Strath, meanwhile, still qualified for the £5 second prize, indicating that he wasn't really disqualified, merely under threat of disqualification had he won the play-off.

Strath had many sympathizers. Either he was disqualified or not, they argued. If not, he was entitled to play-off without any dispute hanging over him. If he was disqualified, he shouldn't have been awarded the second prize. Strath himself was willing to give up the prize and the cup and play Martin for the honour alone.

Some play-offs did take place that Monday. Bob Kirk and Walter Gourlay played a round to decide eighth and ninth place, while Old Tom Morris, Mungo Park and Willie Thomson settled which of them should be fourth, fifth and sixth. Park and Thomson played together, and Old Tom Morris was joined by Willie Park, Snr, for a match within a match. Morris earned fourth prize with a 92 – to Mungo Park's 94 and Thomson's 96 – but Willie Park, Snr, matched him with the same score. They halved the last six holes.

9

'A CASE WILL BE DRAWN, AND THE MATTER REFERRED'

WESTWARD HO!, SEPTEMBER 1877

At 5.20 on a September morning Captain Molesworth set out for a busy day at the Royal North Devon Golf Course. To win his match, he had to walk three miles to the links and play six rounds of golf under 660 strokes.

The outcome was a dispute that lasted several days.

In the 1870s it was fairly common for sportsmen to bet on such feats of stamina. One of the most famous was W G Bloxsam's attempt to play twelve rounds of the Aberdeen Links and walk ten miles home to Schoolhill within 24 hours. He won his bet between 6 am on Tuesday 6 July 1875 and 1.15 am the following morning. 'During the day he kept up his strength by copious libations of Liebig's Extract of Meat in a liquid state', we learn from the Aberdeen Golf Club minutes.

Captain Molesworth's match, first agreed at the Whitsun meeting, was a focus for much talk and betting. His opponents were cheered by the moisture in the air that September morning. Having successfully walked 'to work', Molesworth was faced with a thick dew when he started playing at 6.10 am. The conditions were as difficult as playing in heavy rain. The dew not only handicapped his first-round scoring – a 14 at the ninth hole, for instance – but also ruined his wooden clubs. The face of his driver dropped to pieces at the twelfth hole, and he was forced to rely on irons and his putter. His score of 120 was a brave one in the conditions, but it promised little for his supporters, who knew he needed to average less than 110 for his six rounds.

He played his second round immediately, relying solely on iron clubs. He was lifted by a score of 105, but the third round was miserable. A 15 at the ninth hole led to a disastrous score of 122, and Captain Molesworth took his first rest (five minutes) at the end of the round.

Scores of 108 (fourth round) and 102 (fifth) brought him back into contention. He had now played five rounds in 557 strokes, and a second consecutive round of 102 would complete six rounds in the required figure.

His sixth-round score was 105.

662.

Three over.

Had he lost his bet?

He might, at that point of the day, have justifiably felt tired and defeated. He had walked three miles to the course and then played six rounds of golf while carrying his own clubs, each round involving about 100 minutes of hard walking. But Captain Molesworth had a bright idea – he would play another round. He did this seventh round in 104 strokes and argued that he had now done six rounds in 646 strokes, if you didn't count the first round. It was now 5.30 pm. He walked home, arrived at 6.40, and spent part of the evening playing billiards.

The dispute was about whether he was entitled to play the extra round. Some spectators had gone home after the sixth round convinced that the bet had already been decided. The confusion was summarized in *The Field*: 'Captain Molesworth's backers say that the match was to play six rounds in one day, between the hours of daylight and dark: and, therefore, it did not matter how many rounds he played, if six rounds were played in under 660 strokes, and that he was entitled to leave out the first or any other round, so long as six whole rounds were done in under the number. The other side contended that, as six rounds were played, and the number of strokes taken was over 660, the match was lost. A case will be drawn, and the matter referred.'

11

A referee had been agreed when the match was originally made. He now read and assessed the case before him: 'You will observe the first six rounds are 662 strokes, the best six 644, the last consecutive 646. Say whether Captain Molesworth has won or lost the match you made, and give your opinion.'

The referee gave his reply: 'I think Captain Molesworth has won; if, as I understood the match, Captain Molesworth was to do six rounds in the day in 660 strokes, he was entitled to play a dozen rounds (if he could) till he did six within the number.'

So Captain Molesworth won his bet.

A BET AT NIGHT

HOYLAKE, NOVEMBER 1878

Members of the Royal Liverpool Golf Club often sat in the bar parlour of the Royal Hotel, socializing, drinking and making bets. 'Great matches were arranged during these evenings,' wrote Guy Farrar in his history of the famous club, 'matches in which large sums of money were involved.'

The Royal Hotel was the original clubhouse, and its owner, John Ball, Snr, was a legendary figure and the father of a famous amateur golfer. Fond of sporting bets himself, Ball once matched a horse against Hay Gordon, a noted runner, over 100 yards. Most of the money went on the man, punters figuring that the horse would not recover quickly enough from a slow start, but Ball trained his horse to respond to pistol noise and won his bet.

Another of the club's many characters was R.W. Brown, known as 'Pendulum' Brown. On one occasion he backed himself to play the five holes round the out-of-bounds field, known as 'the circus', in less than a certain figure at the dead of night. He won his bet comfortably; indeed, his night-time score was better than his score in daylight the next day.

'Pendulum' Brown's most publicized bet was another night-time match. He vowed that he could start at 11 pm and go round the Hoylake course in less than 150 strokes. The conditions were established, notably that he would be penalized only 'loss of distance' for a lost ball, and spectators were not allowed to help him search for it. The intrepid golfer demanded that the

13

spectators be silent when he played his shots ... so he could hear the ball drop.

Night-time golf is a game for ears rather than eyes. An account in *Golf Illustrated* some years later captures some of the atmosphere of the Hoylake links at night: 'Time was one June night, when Hoylake lay under calm stars, and ghostly moonlight and the beating sea had withdrawn to the great deeps, when we heard the faint sound of a cleek shot some distance away. We at once made a forced march to see who were the brave hearts that were so bold as to play the game when night was over the land. It was a strange but idle venture; time and again we could hear the click of a "driver", or the muffled sound of a niblick in a bunker, but the long level flight of the little white ball we could never see. We attempted to discover the mysterious players by hiding in bunkers, or suddenly appearing out of a waiting hazard, but the quest was fruitless. To this day we have never been able to solve the mystery of the phantom players. Perhaps, it was some of the giants of old, returned to the happy hunting grounds of their previous existence, doomed to play ghostly foursomes at the witching hours, to practise those strokes which handicapped them from the "Great Greens".'

'Pendulum' Brown's round was real enough. His progress over the first three holes was watched by a large crowd. Then most of the spectators retired for the evening; they probably realized how dangerous it was to walk in the dark. Brown was left in the company of Messrs Cullen and John Ball, Snr. These two spectators walked the course and watched as the golfer searched for ball after ball. Brown lost 32 balls in total, and therefore wasted 32 strokes.

Mr Brown's problems can be gauged from one story, which may or may not be true. It is said that, on the fourth hole, faced with a fairway riddled with rabbit-holes, Brown drove off and failed to find his ball. He tried again and lost another one. The two spectators, having stayed forward for the second drive, saw the ball go into a particular rabbit-hole, but the conditions of the match prevented them from informing the golfer. Brown's third drive stopped a foot short of the same rabbit-hole. He found this one himself. When he had played his ball, the spectators showed him where his second ball was. To their surprise they found the first in the same rabbit-hole, and the third had stopped not more than a foot short of it.

His score for the round was 147, and he won his bet by three strokes.

A FEE TO WITHDRAW FROM THE BRITISH OPEN

MUSSELBURGH, NOVEMBER 1889

'It is difficult to realize the almost haphazard manner in which, in the '80s, the great event of the year in golf was encompassed,' wrote William Reid. 'I am told that at one time it was advertised that the [British Open] Championship would be played on such and such a date, and that the competitors simply presented themselves at the first tee at the advertised hour of start and gave in their names.'

The 1889 Championship was the riskiest ever. It consisted of four rounds of a nine-hole course on a gloomy Friday in November. There were 48 competitors, and 22 of these were Musselburgh men. It helped to know the course, because, by the end of the third round, it was almost dark.

The tournament's organizers, the Honourable Company of Edinburgh Golfers, needed to do something desperate to complete the tournament before it was totally dark. The field needed to be thinned, so they offered five shillings to any player who retired from the tournament at the end of the third round. The debate about elimination was beginning. Later we would have 'the cut'.

The last round saw a riveting duel between Willie Park, Jnr, of Musselburgh and Andrew Kirkaldy of St Andrews which took the Championship to a play-off, although Kirkaldy missed a one-inch putt at the fourteenth by casually playing an 'air shot' with one hand. Long before the last couple came in, the street lamps adjoining the course were lit, and scores were checked by candlelight. As the *Scotsman* recorded, it was so dark that 'the markers could scarcely see to mark, far less the players to play'. In these atrocious golfing conditions, Kirkaldy's playing partner, a local amateur called Robertson, produced a stunning cleek shot to hole in one at the eighteenth.

The tournament organizers had a lot to learn. They had warned of strict punishments if players started late, but had caused problems themselves by starting the tournament as late as 10.30 am and limiting it to one day. Everyone agreed that the tournament needed an earlier start, a smaller field or a date when there was more daylight.

The organization of that Open Championship was so haphazard that the play-off could not be played the following day (a Saturday) as it clashed with an amateur tournament at the Braid Hills. Park and Kirkaldy returned to Musselburgh on the Monday, and played a further 36 holes. The play-off was not as interesting as Friday's tie, when both men had scored 155. Willie Park led by four after the first nine holes, and his total of 158 was good enough for a five-stroke victory.

There was a sequel to the play-off story. Willie Park issued a challenge to any golfer for a match over 'four greens' for £100 a side. Andrew Kirkaldy took him up, so Park and Kirkaldy met again.

Kirkaldy found the challenge match difficult on the first course, at Musselburgh, where the home gallery supported Willie Park. 'Bullocks couldna hae behaved much worse,' Kirkaldy reportedly said of the spectators. The match was still close after Prestwick, but, at Troon, Kirkaldy swung it his way and went on to win eight and seven on his home course at St Andrews. A new champion had arrived.

THE BATTLE OF ONE TREE HILL

PECKHAM RYE, LONDON, OCTOBER 1897

Thousands of people stormed the golf-course fence with sticks and stones and brickbats, and 500 policemen fought against them. It was a story to live in history and it was called 'the Battle of One Tree Hill'.

The trouble began much earlier that year. Alfred Stevens leased his land to the newly formed Honor Oak and Forest Hill Golf Club, and local people objected fiercely when the golf club put up a fence. They believed it was common land, with public rights of way, and an enclosure was illegal. A Protest Committee was formed. The committeemen claimed they had evidence that the public had right-of-way across One Tree Hill and the whole area belonged to the people, not the freeholder.

The land in question was on the border of Peckham Rye and Honor Oak. Alfred Stevens was in no doubt that he owned the land, and that the new tenants were within their rights to build the fence. Said Stevens, in a letter to the *South London Observer*: 'May I say once for all that every foot of the land which I and my family hold was paid for either by my late father or by my brother and myself, that we have never enclosed any land or encroached on any parochial or private rights, but have, on the contrary, given to the Camberwell Parish lands to widen roads, and that the public have no rights of way over the property and that none of it is common land.'

This statement did not appease the protestors. Open meetings began in August, and local anger soared when two youngsters were charged with destroying part of the golf-club fence. A confrontation was slowly coming, and the protestors began to form two factions. Those loyal to the Protest Committee believed in collecting money to support peaceful action through the law. The others were growing impatient.

At a routine open meeting, early in October, Fred Polkinghorne captured the mood of the crowd when he appealed for more direct action. Angry with the lack of tangible progress, frustrated with a lack of information from the Protest Committee, he proposed an ultimatum. If the fence didn't come down, the people would take back the hill.

'To the Hill,' people shouted.

The Protest Committee called for calm, but Polkinghorne motioned for an amendment.

'To the Hill,' came the massed shout.

The motion was put to the people, and hands showed the support of the majority.

'To the Hill,' they shouted.

The motion was carried.

If the fence stayed, the hill would be stormed on Sunday 10 October.

At 3 o'clock on the afternoon of Sunday 10 October, a far from passive crowd assembled on the Triangle on the Rye. Polkinghorne told the gathering that his views hadn't changed.

'To the Hill,' they shouted at him.

Other protest meetings were going on, but a crowd of over a thousand moved towards the golf course on One Tree Hill. Around 4.30, a youth climbed the golf-club fence and opened the gate. The crowd raced through, and two policemen on duty could do little except send for support. They were soon joined by a further 30 Constables and Inspectors, but the only person arrested that afternoon was a youth who threw a stone through a clubhouse window.

Several quiet rounds of golf were soon disturbed. Intruders swarmed across the course, shouting and cheering, pulling out flags and damaging putting-greens. 'The crowd, numbering several thousands, was largely composed of roughs and bird-catchers, ready for any scrimmage,' stated *Golf* magazine. The golfers abandoned their game and headed for the clubhouse, accompanied by hoots and hisses from the crowd.

When the roaring mob threatened the clubhouse, some members pointed out that a frightened woman and child were inside. The crowd left them alone, but for two hours that Sunday afternoon, One Tree Hill returned to the public, and the general mood was cheerful and friendly.

It was different the next Sunday.

The protestors were still divided about how best to reclaim the hill. On Saturday 16 October, a group of five men, including Fred Polkinghorne, agreed to be served writs as a test case. At the golf-club gate, they amicably introduced themselves to Major Gilbert of Scotland Yard. While half a dozen golfers were going about a normal week-end round, the gang of five forcibly removed a few planks from the fence and awaited arrest peaceably.

It was a lovely autumnal afternoon the next day, ideal for a battle, and policemen waited in hiding. They were in the clubhouse, concealed by St Augustine's Church, and tucked away in two empty houses near Honor Oak station. There were over 200 police, including about 20 on horseback.

By 3 o'clock, about 5,000 people had gathered on the Honor Oak Rise side of the hill. The golfers had sensibly stayed away from the course. Only journalists and newspaper artists occupied One Tree Hill.

The crowds started demolishing the planks of the fence. One man was arrested, and another defended him by attacking a policeman. He was arrested too, but his friends fought to rescue him. Sticks and flints were used, and the crowd stormed forward. 'Women and children screamed in terror,' stated one report.

The mounted police held the crowd back with a hard-fought struggle. At 4 o'clock the crowd regrouped on the open furze-covered slope at the foot of St Augustine's Church. There must have been about 10,000 of them, angry and intent, armed with sticks and stones and brickbats. They were faced by a solid row of over 200 policemen, shoulder to shoulder. The battle raged. The police held back the rioters, but one Inspector received a serious facial cut when hit by a stone.

At 5.30 a furze bush was set alight. The fire spread so quickly that it must have been helped by paraffin-oil. Other fires were lit, and whin bushes burned freely. The police charged the crowd, and threw people down the slope. By 6 o'clock the rioters had been slowly beaten back, and the fires had died down. The Battle of One Tree Hill was over.

Ten rioters were prosecuted. One of them, George Kilbey, received one month's imprisonment with hard labour for attacking a policeman. The others were either fined or sent to prison.

The next Sunday, 500 policemen were waiting around One Tree Hill. A large crowd of demonstrators turned out, but there was no rioting. Some demonstrators returned on future Sundays, but the crowds dwindled in size.

The Golf Club stayed, and gradually the golfers had better value for the club's £200 a year rent, plus rates and taxes. By June 1898, membership had reached 180, and *Golf* was able to report: 'The club is now established on a sound and satisfactory basis, and is entirely free of debt. The dispute between the public and the club, which culminated in a serious riot one Sunday afternoon in October last year, has happily come to an end; and we are not likely to hear anything more of the alleged right-of-way over One Tree Hill, which nature evidently intended for a golf course.'

CROSS-COUNTRY GOLF

MAIDSTONE TO LITTLESTONE-ON-SEA, APRIL 1898

'Undoubtedly the longest hole ever played at golf is one measuring a distance of no less than 26 miles in a bee-line and 35 in actual play, the tee being at Linton Park, near Maidstone, and the putting-green at Littlestone-on-Sea.'

So started an article in *The Strand Magazine* (July 1913). It was written by T. H. Oyler of Littlestone Golf Club, who played the 26-mile hole, the longest at the time, with A. G. Oyler. The freak match was an outcome of a conversation on Appledore railway station which went something like this.

'How many strokes would it take to cover the distance from Maidstone to Littlestone-on-Sea?'

'One player?'

'No, two men playing alternately.'

'I should say two thousand would be a fair number.'

'Two thousand?' queried a sporting parson in the party. 'I'll wager five pounds that none of you could do it in two thousand.'

The rules were laid down within five minutes: the match should take place within three months; the ordinary rules of golf should be observed; and an umpire should be appointed to keep score. A Cambridge undergraduate, H. M. Wyatt of St Katharine's College, agreed to umpire, not realizing how tedious it would be.

On a beautiful spring day, they set off from Linton Park with two or three of each club – brassie, cleek, niblick and driving-

22

iron – and half a gallon of old balls which were newly painted
and carried in a bag. The first drive, their only tee-shot, played
with a brassie, landed in a rhododendron bush, 'out of which
we dropped with a penalty'.

Progress through the park was slow, but eventually they
reached the River Beult (for 65 and another lost ball). They
stuck to pastured land, where the principal hazards were
hedges and ditches. They ticked off landmarks like Hertsfield
Bridge (for 97), Hawkenbury Bridge (for 158) and Frittenden
Road Bridge (for 201). After 213 strokes, at Headland, they
stuck a stump in the ground to mark the ball, and retired to the
village inn for lunch. It was 2.30.

After lunch, they played along the road rather than across
fields, but anything other than a short putt brought problems as
the ball tended to roll into a ditch either side of the road. They
returned to the fields and woods, although 'one very rough
arable field gave us much trouble,' wrote Oyler, 'and for a time
a heavy niblick was the favourite club.'

Just before 6 o'clock, they stopped play for the day, close
to Crampton House Farm (for 427), between Biddenden and
High Halden. Near there they were met by their carriage and
driven home after 'a fair day's work of 14 miles'.

The next day they were back with their clubs, caddie and
umpire. On they went. Over hedges, into ditches, out of
ditches and into small woods. At Moat Farm they were treated
as trespassers.

'What are you doing on my premises?' the owner demanded
to know.

'We're playing golf.'

'I must request you to leave as quickly as possible.'

Fortunately a capital brassie shot into a rough wheat-field
took them to another farm, and peace was restored, although
another problem remained: 'Here our caddie gave us some
trouble, as he had evidently an old quarrel to settle with some
other lad of his own age, and we had to dismiss him and engage
another.' Altogether they went through six or seven caddies.
The caddies usually gave up when they were worried about

getting lost on the way back home.

Then it was one problem after another. A strong cross-wind made play tiring. A high fence cost them five strokes before they put the ball through it. And several strokes were wasted in a hop-garden where the poles restricted the swing of a club. When they finally reached Ingledon Park (for 500) they celebrated with a rest. On restart, a network of dykes caused them to retrace steps on several occasions. Instead of reaching Appledore for lunch at 2.30, they arrived at 4.25 – for 714, with another ball lost, this one in the Military Canal.

After lunch they headed for Appledore railway station, taking tea at the Railway Hotel at 5.50. Their first attempt to clear the level-crossing gates hit the gate and rebounded on to the rails. They putted over the railway-crossing, then kept to the road for a distance, before losing a couple of balls in dykes and giving up for the night after 844 strokes.

Starting at 8 o'clock the next morning, they persevered along the strange course. After being fortified by a friend's sloe gin at Brenzett, brassie shots were 'far and sure'. 'We now crossed the main sewer which drains Romney Marsh,' wrote Oyler in his account. 'Twice our ball hit a sheep, and we were frequently in small ditches, but could generally play out. After passing the quaint little church of Old Romney, we found many rushes and reeds, and strokes were short.'

They had now played more than a thousand strokes but were almost at their destination. Losing a ball down a rabbit-hole – the seventeenth lost ball of their journey – was barely a setback. A good mashie shot landed them on the first green at Little-stone-on-Sea, a putt rested within four feet of the hole, and another ended the wager after 1,087 strokes.

They learned several lessons from their cross-country feat. One was that golfers often take fewer strokes than first im-agined, as distances on real golf courses include a lot of fairly short putts. However, the emphasis on distance with each cross-country shot acts as a prolonged strain on arms, wrists and hands.

Dry conditions helped them enormously. Cornfields had

been recently rolled, and provided plenty of good lies. Otherwise many of their brassie and cleek shots might have relied on the niblick.

A modern text-book on cross-country golf would refer to many other experiences. Rupert Phillips and Raymond Thomas had to jump over a hedge to escape a bull that chased them during their 20-mile meander from Radyr, near Cardiff, to Southerndown in 1920. They covered the course in 608 strokes, including the proper penalty for 20 lost balls. Another tricky moment came when they had to wade knee-deep through a ford.

In 1927, Doe Grahame set off from the first tee of Mobile Golf Club in an attempt to play 6,160,000 yards to Hollywood, California. It was one of golf's all-time ambitious journeys. In Pearl River, not far up the road, the Sheriff caught him acting suspiciously with a flashlight and golf clubs late at night, so Grahame spent a night in jail. He drove through the countryside, used a brassie in the suburbs and putted along city sidewalks. He completed 850 miles to San Antonio, Texas, in 30,930 strokes, having lost 105 balls. He was so confident that he spent his day off on a local golf course, where he played 36 proper holes. This was what O. B. Keeler referred to as 'the Mad Twenties', the era when golf swept over the United States 'like a prairie fire'.

The Guinness Book of Records notes an even more amazing effort than Grahame's trek – Floyd Rood's journey from Pacific surf to Atlantic coast in the mid-1960s. He covered the 3,398-mile course in 114,737 strokes. He lost 3,511 balls, and was away for a year and 19 days.

Some cross-country matches are competitive, though the prize rarely resembles that of P. G. Wodehouse's short story 'The Long Hole', in which Jukes and Bingham play a 16-mile hole to decide who Amanda Trivett will marry (forgetting that the woman had a choice). In 1892, scores of 114 and 118 were recorded across nearly four and a half miles of Gloucestershire countryside. In July 1931, a foursome from Australia's Port

Pirie Club played a seven-mile hole through bush country. After seven hours, Mallyon and Leahy's 196 was good enough to win by four strokes.

Later that same year, 1931, a masked man golfed 700 miles from Brisbane to Sydney in about 25,000 strokes. He lost 57 balls, and his worst experience came when he was taking a short-cut through a zoo about 48 miles out of Brisbane. His ball rebounded into the leopard's cage for a very difficult lie.

If our cross-country text-book needs chapters on 'Dealing with animals' and 'Choosing your snake-bite kit', it also requires an essential section on 'Playing through towns and cities'. In 1899, William Patton, a member of the Allegheny Golf Club, played nearly five miles through the centre of Pittsburgh. Patton achieved his aim of breaking 150 (by 31 strokes) but broke a few windows too. He won just enough money to settle the bill for damages.

A similar wager took place in London 40 years later. Toby Milbanke bet that Richard Sutton couldn't play from the other side of Tower Bridge to the steps of White's Club, St James's Street, in fewer than 2,000 shots. This is a ridiculously high number, but Milbanke was relying on Sutton being arrested. Sutton was stopped by the police four or five times, but his explanation – 'I'm doing it for a bet' – was accepted each time. Sutton putted the course in 142 strokes and won £5 and a set of golf clubs from his friend.

HOUSE OF COMMONS v INVERALLOCHY FISHERMEN

SANDWICH, APRIL 1905

At 3.35 pm, on Wednesday 29 March, a team of 10 fishermen from the Scottish village of Inverallochy, four miles east of Fraserburgh, set off to fulfil a golfing fantasy – a match against leading British politicians on the Royal St George's course at Sandwich.

Cheered off by hundreds of spectators, they embarked on the longest train journey of their lives. They arrived at King's Cross station, London, 18 hours later.

'I should think we should manage to lick them,' said one of six scratch players in the Inverallochy team, 'but playing the Prime Minister's nae lauchin' maitter.'

The Prime Minister was Arthur Balfour, a regular member of the House of Commons team and no stranger to Scottish golf courses. Balfour would play in the big match, which had been arranged by Mr Maconochie, MP, as a way of binding the north and south. The date of the match – Saturday 1 April – should not fool anyone. This is a true tale, and most of the national newspapers took up the story with gusto. It was said that 45 team photographs were taken before the players set out from Inverallochy.

Having arrived in London at 7.25 on Thursday morning, the fishermen-golfers checked into their hotel, and by 10 o'clock were off on a whirlwind tour of London. They saw the Mansion House, the Royal Exchange, the Tower of London, St Paul's

Cathedral, the National Gallery and Buckingham Palace. And that was only the morning.

In the afternoon they went to the Houses of Parliament. They looked over the premises from the outside, had a smoke on the terrace, and were then ushered to seats in the public gallery, where they were able to see their future opponents in action – debating, that is, not playing golf.

'I've nae idea what they were speakin' aboot,' said one Inverallochy man. 'I kent it wis something aboot the Transvaal, and that wis a.''

'The men saw more in one day than most Londoners themselves have seen during their whole lives,' wrote the *Fraserburgh Herald and Northern Counties Advertiser*.

That evening they were given seats in the front row of the Empire Theatre. The next morning, at 9 o'clock, they were whisked off to Sandwich, where they were booked into the Fleur d'Lys Hotel. They practised over the Royal St George's course in the afternoon.

A big crowd turned up for Saturday's match. The House of Commons team arrived late and kept the Inverallochy men waiting on the tee. Do you think this might have been strategic? The Inverallochy men had already been put through quite an ordeal – a long, tiring journey followed by demanding sightseeing, and now they were subjected to a nervous wait on the course. The presence of spectators, reporters and photographers made them even more nervous.

The fishermen, captained by Captain William Whyte, wore guernsey sweaters rather than the usual golfing jackets. They started nervously but were on their best behaviour. One politician later commented that a fisherman had actually apologized for playing one very bad shot.

They played two sets of foursomes, one in the morning and one in the afternoon. After the first round, luncheon was served, and 'the competitors sat together without social distinction, a fisherman sitting either side of Mr Balfour'. Balfour talked with Joe Buchan about boats, fishing and the herring industry.

A large crowd followed the top match, and fortunes fluctuated in the morning. Balfour and Eric Hambro won the first hole, the fishermen squared it at the third and went ahead at the fourth. The politicians pulled back at the fifth, but the fishermen took the lead again at the Maiden. The two Buchans took the morning game, but it was a rare success for the men from Inverallochy. They lost the overall match convincingly – eight-two.

After the match, each Inverallochy player was presented with a golf club, and Prime Minister Balfour autographed the clubs received by his two direct opponents. All that remained was more sight-seeing – work-related trips to Billingsgate Fish Market and Maconochie's tinning works – and a long journey home. The Inverallochy men were convinced that it would have been a different story on their own course, with its shorter holes.

IT DEPENDS HOW YOU SCORE

HOYLAKE, APRIL 1907

The twenty-ninth annual Oxford-Cambridge University match was comprised of eight 36-hole singles. Oxford won more matches – four to three with one halved – but lost the overall match. Not surprisingly, the scoring system was reconsidered afterwards.

Ever since the inaugural university match, in 1878, the match had been decided on number of holes won rather than number of matches, a common enough method of scoring in club matches. The most staggering result was Oxford's 69-0 win in 1900. Captained by Marshall Hunter, Oxford University had an excellent team, and the best performing Cambridge player, Hill-Thomson, still went down to a two-hole defeat. Oxford led by 44 holes after the morning round, and added a further 25 in the afternoon. The *Oxford Magazine*, not surprisingly, found no excuses for the beaten 1900 Cambridge team: 'The teams on either side were fully representative, the elements were smiling until the very last hole was played, and the greens were in the most perfect condition possible.'

And so to 1907, and the match that started a fanatical debate about scoring methods. It was certainly close, and included an interesting statistic early on, when Robertson-Durham (Oxford) and Barry (Cambridge) halved the first 11 holes of their match. Robertson-Durham was the first to lose a hole, when he hit his ball against himself trying to get out of a bunker, but he won the match by seven holes.

After the morning round, Oxford led 9-6 on holes. They kept

a narrow lead into the final nine, but much depended on the two captains, Hon. C. N. Bruce (Oxford) and Allen (Cambridge). They went out last in the afternoon after playing second in the morning. The Cambridge man led easily, so easily that Bruce received some later criticism for not being in practice. The kindest words were that he was 'off his game'. However, Bruce had been ill in the recent past, and was growing very tired on the last few holes.

When Bruce lost the sixteenth and seventeenth in the final round, he was 13 down on the day's play, and Oxford trailed 23-22 on holes. Oxford needed to win the last hole to halve the match. Bruce and Allen were both left with three-yard putts for fours at the eighteenth. Allen putted two feet short, so Bruce had his three-yarder to make the overall score a 22-22 tie. He made certain he wasn't short, and ran it a yard past. The hole was halved in five.

The final scores looked like this:

J. A. Robertson-Durham	7	A. G. Barry	0
Hon. C. N. Bruce	0	M. T. Allen	13
Lord Maidstone	4	B. Meakin	0
C. V. L. Hooman	0	V. C. H. Longstaffe	3
Hon. D. G. Finch-Hatton	5	J. Martin-Smith	0
Hon. C. T. Mills	0	W. N. Potter	7
G. N. Foster (halved)	0	H. B. Hammond-Chambers (halved)	0
J. H. Gordon	6	C. B. Barry	0
OXFORD UNIVERSITY	22	CAMBRIDGE UNIVERSITY	23

The following year the scoring system was changed to number of matches won rather than number of holes up. But which system was the fairer? Some people argued that at least the old system ensured that everybody played every hole. And why should a match won by, say, 13 and 12, count the same as one won by one hole?

The decisive point seemed to be that the 1907 Oxford University team deserved to win. The odd 1907 result brought the universities level in the series – 14 matches each with one halved – and the time was perhaps right for a fresh start.

BETTER IN THE FOG

HOYLAKE, NOVEMBER 1907

A blanket of fog hung over Merseyside on the morning of the Milligan St Andrew's gold cross medal competition. Nearly a hundred members of the Royal Liverpool Golf Club were entered. As soon as they saw the weather, their hopes dropped.

'Will the fog clear?' they asked themselves. 'Probably not.'

Some stayed at home. Others braved the cold, damp day but soon turned back. The more intrepid continued their journeys, only to be let down by late ferries or delayed trains. Some made it through to the clubhouse, mainly those who lived near the golf course.

Johnny Ball was there that day. His association with Royal Liverpool went right back to the club's formation in 1869 when he was a seven-year-old boy and his father an active member. Three years later he won the children's medal and never looked back. Sixth in the British Open when only 15, he went on to win eight British Amateur Championships between 1888 and 1912, a record unlikely to be beaten, and his victory in the 1890 British Open did much for the prestige of amateur golf and English golfers (for Ball was the first English winner). During his phenomenal career, John Ball also won a staggering 94 medals at the Royal Liverpool club.

When he arrived through the fog that St Andrew's Day – the Saturday did fall on 30 November that year – Johnny Ball learned that the Milligan medal competition had been cancelled. Fog stopped play. We can only imagine the clubhouse scene that followed the decision, the friendly banter about whether he knew the course so well that he could play in the fog, the bravado and camaraderie that went back and forth. Someone bet John Ball that he couldn't go round in the fog in under 90, taking not more than two and a quarter hours and without losing a ball. The star amateur chose to play with a black ball, and went round in 81 with time to spare.

A week after that foggy Saturday, John Ball and the other members were given a second chance at the Milligan gold cross. The result was a three-way tie between Ball, John Graham, Jnr and F. W. H. Weaver. The most surprising thing, however, was that they tied with rounds of 82, scores that were not only astonishingly high for good conditions but phenomenally high when compared with Ball's 81 in the fog. He had actually done better when he was unable to see. If you look at it like that, the course had been fit for play the previous Saturday.

Two weeks later *Golf Illustrated* included a cryptic one-line message: 'A *black ball* on a foggy day does not necessarily imply exclusion from the club.'

Another John Ball story concerns a round he played in the middle of the night. It is said that darkness made little difference to his game; he was slower, but only because he spent so much time looking for his opponent's ball. He was one of golf's great stylists, but a man of mystery and silence, one who avoided publicity and did his talking with golf clubs. In 1907, not long before his foggy round at Hoylake, he was made an honorary member of the Royal and Ancient Golf Club.

GOLF IN THE OLYMPICS

SANDWICH (ALMOST), JUNE 1908

There were problems from the start.

The British Olympic Association claimed to have written to all the relevant golfing bodies in July 1906, inviting them to join a committee that would decide the format for the 1908 Olympic golf competition. The Royal and Ancient Golf Club claimed that no letter had arrived. The two organizations clashed.

That problem wasn't too bad. It could be blamed on the Post Office. The real problems came with the committee's decision on how Olympic golf should be organized. W. Ryder Richardson, secretary of the Royal St George's Golf Club and honorary secretary of the Amateur Championship committee, was in charge of the arrangements. In January 1908 he attempted to explain the complexity of the two competitions – an individual stroke play and a team event.

The individual competition was to consist of three days' solid golf – 36 holes at Royal St George's, 36 holes at Cinque Ports and 36 holes at Prince's. The team event was to run conjointly. Each country would nominate six men in a team, the best four to count, and each country was allowed to send four teams – a device to ensure that England, Scotland, Wales and Ireland could all be represented as separate teams.

British golfers didn't look forward to the Olympics. Not only was a 108-hole competition a daunting prospect, but the timing of the event – the first three days of June – was bad for them. The Olympics would come immediately after three demanding competitions within 10 days of one another – the St George's

Cup at Sandwich, the international match and the British Amateur Championship.

Questions were fired at the British Olympic Association. Why not simply crown the British Amateur Champion twice – the second time for the Olympics? Why not have a much shorter Olympic competition? Why not change the arrangements?

John L. Low was outraged that the Royal and Ancient Golf Club had not been consulted about the Olympic arrangements, even if a letter had gone astray. He protested that many of the proposals were not in the spirit of the game, and he made it clear to 'foreign and American' golfers that the proposed contests were not sanctioned by the Royal and Ancient. It was absurd, someone said, that Belgium could send four teams and Scotland only one, while other golfing folk suggested that the 'medal-hunting' of Olympic competition was also not in the spirit of amateur golf. Was golf an original Olympic sport anyway? Hardly.

The Times caught the mood of the golfing world in January 1908: 'It is difficult to think otherwise than that Olympic golf is a mistake, and foredoomed to at least partial failure.'

It was indeed foredoomed – there was only one entry.

Such a small response made a joke out of one British Olympic Association contingency plan: 'Should the number of entries for the Olympic contest be too great to permit all the players getting round twice one course in a day, there will be a division into three sections, each section playing over one course per day.'

On Saturday 30 May, it was officially announced that the Olympic golf competition was abandoned: 'The explanation of the British Olympic Association is that a number of British golfers sent in their names, but did not conform with the regulations in filling up the entry forms. Their forms were, therefore, returned to the players with a request that the desired particulars be given; but, as they had not been received by the association on Saturday, there was nothing to do but to abandon the fixture.'

The only entry in order was from George Lyon of Toronto, Canada, who had won the 1904 Olympic golf competition in St Louis. In the 1904 final, Lyon beat Chandler Egan at the Glen Echo Country Club. By 1908, Lyon was 50 years old, but a match for British players. Despite a late start to his golfing career, Lyon, an all-round athlete, was eight times Canadian Champion and 10 times Canadian Senior Champion.

So, whereas there were 32 competitors in 1904, all from North America, four years later there was only one Canadian. George Lyon retained his Olympic title without any competition. A gold medal was offered to him but he declined it.

Not a stroke was played in 1908.

Nor in any Olympic Games since.

MAN AGAINST WOMAN

WALTON HEATH AND SUNNINGDALE, OCTOBER 1910

The 1910 General Election loomed, but women were not allowed to vote. Suffragettes, seeking to remedy this inequality, were attracting attention with acts of violence and hunger-strikes in prison. Some even damaged golf courses.

The golf match between a rising female star and a proven top-class male really caught the public's imagination. Miss Cecilia Leitch, only 19, took on Mr Harold Hilton, twice British Open Champion and twice British Amateur Champion. All this at a time when women's golf and men's golf were kept very separate.

It was 72-hole match-play from the men's tees. The first 36 holes would be on the old course at Walton Heath and the last two rounds at Sunningdale. Harold Hilton was to concede a half (nine strokes in 18 holes).

'Seldom has a match been more written about or talked about,' wrote *The Times*, 'and still on the morning of the fray the most extraordinarily divergent opinions prevail as to the probable result.'

Cecilia 'Cecil' Leitch, born of a Scottish father and English mother, had come to prominence as a 17-year-old in 1908 when she reached the semi-final of the Ladies' Championship at St Andrews. Since then she had beaten Tom Ball by one hole on Ball's home course, West Lancashire, in a match which saw the professional concede a half. She also held the course record at her home course of Silloth.

38

The morning of 11 October was perfect. Special trains ran from London, and hundreds of cars converged on Walton Heath. The crowd, estimated at 'fully 3,000', was probably as large as had been seen on a course in the south of England. There was something symbolic about the match. The men backed Hilton, the women backed Leitch.

The golfers arrived at the first tee. Wrote one reporter: 'Miss Leitch turned out in a cream-coloured serge skirt, striped with blue, a white blouse with the collar turned down, and one of those spreading green ties with red in it which were the fashion 10 years ago. It was fastened with a safety-pin halfway with a little brilliant in it. Blue stockings and tan shoes. Her hair was done with a comb or two, securely but artistically fastened.'

Hilton was dressed in plus-fours which gave way to long socks just below the knee. Under his jacket he wore a white shirt and tie. A flat cap covered his head, and a cigarette was in his mouth, even while playing a shot.

Cecil Leitch pulled her first shot. It hit a perambulator with two babies in it. Everyone yelled 'fore', except the two babies, who simply yelled.

At the third she hit a dog with her ball and went one down. She received her strokes at the even holes, but by the thirteenth she was four down anyway. Hilton, driving 20-25 yards farther, was in charge of the match and Leitch seemed in danger of breaking down. The male spectators looked smug.

With the help of her stroke, Cecil Leitch won the fourteenth to pull back to three down. Her first two shots at the fifteenth hit spectators and saved her from the heather, so she halved that hole, and the sixteenth too. She was still three down with two holes of the morning round to play.

A shot on the seventeenth changed the crowd's mood. Cecil Leitch played a brassie from a heavy lie and left the ball close to the flag. She won a very difficult hole with a four to Hilton's five and no stroke to help her. She won the eighteenth too, helped by her stroke. At lunch she was one down, having gone round in 90 to Hilton's 78.

Hilton won the first two holes in the afternoon and then

played badly. Leitch won the fourth, fifth and sixth, and was back to all-square. Fortunes fluctuated but Hilton squared the match on the fifteenth. At the next hole Leitch played a perfect four to win it with her stroke, but Hilton won the next two.

At the end of the day's play at Walton Hall, the man was one up.

In the morning at Sunningdale, in front of another large crowd, Harold Hilton played almost perfect golf through teeming rain and gale-force winds. The two players were soaked to the skin before they reached the first green. Hilton went out in 36 (approximately) but Leitch was only two down. By lunchtime, however, after 54 holes of the 72, Hilton was four up and the match looked decided.

The first hole after lunch, Sunningdale's first, was a long hole of over 500 yards. Cecil Leitch was bravely on the green in two (wind assisted) and won with a four against five. She was still showing that hard hitting and accuracy could be achieved by women as well as men. One reporter looked closely at her driving style: 'She stands with rather a wide stance, the knees very stiff and the ball exceptionally far back near the right foot. In such an attitude the act of swinging throws a tremendous strain on the right knee, which rather gives under her, producing a pronounced "duck". Still, she comes through beautifully, times the stroke well, and has a very great power of picking up the ball with a wooden club.'

But Hilton won the second and third on the final round to go five up with 15 to play. Then Leitch won the fourth, sixth, eighth and, more surprisingly, the ninth. Hilton was one up with nine to play.

At the tenth, Leitch hit three perfect wooden club shots, got her five and won the hole with her stroke.

All-square again.

Leitch won the eleventh and twelfth, and Hilton the thirteenth with a long putt for a two. As the pressure increased, they halved the fourteenth and fifteenth with more moderate play. But Leitch was one up.

The sixteenth was a difficult four. Leitch did it in five and won the hole with her stroke. Dormy two. She was playing very well now – the afternoon's 16 in only 72 – and was showing what was known in those days as fortitude or pluck. Her third shot at the seventeenth demonstrated it best of all. She played her ball beautifully out of a clump of fir trees to the left of the fairway. This was followed by an excellent pitch-and-run shot that left the ball dead. Hilton had a putt of four or five yards to save the match. The ball hit the tin and jumped out.

The woman had won.

Two and one.

WITH A HANDKERCHIEF OVER HIS EYES

SUNNINGDALE, FEBRUARY 1912

He stood on the first tee at Sunningdale and addressed the ball.

'Alright,' he said.

A purple-and-white handkerchief was tied firmly over his eyes.

'Alright,' came the reply.

He let fly at the ball with no preliminary waggles.

As he played the shot he was conscious that his body was stiff down one side. That cursed bicycle accident the other day. He knew he wasn't in tip-top condition. He knew he wasn't at his best. Especially with a handkerchief over his eyes.

His drive was long but slightly sliced.

His opponent then stood on the first tee. This was Mr A. Tindal Atkinson, a good scratch player who knew the course.

Tindal Atkinson pulled his tee-shot. It wasn't as long as the man with the purple-and-white handkerchief.

The match was underway.

Blindfolded professional against the all-seeing amateur.

Alf Toogood against Mr A. Tindal Atkinson.

Guy Livingstone started it all. One wet day, early that month, a *Daily Mail* golf-instruction article had annoyed him. More of that 'keep your eyes on the ball' advice, Livingstone thought. No wonder all my pupils mesmerize themselves. They glue their eyes to the ball, play their shot, the ball moves, their eyes move, their head moves, and the stroke is ruined. It's wrong to keep your eye on the ball. You should keep your eye on the ground underneath the ball, and hold it there till you hear the ball click.

Livingstone believed there was better advice than keeping your eyes on the ball.

'Keep your head still.'

'Keep it in a vice.'

'Don't move it.'

Guy Livingstone had nothing better to do. He sat down at his desk at the Chelsea Golf School, where he was secretary, and wrote a letter to the editor of the *Daily Mail*.

> Sir,
>
> With reference to the first paragraph of your article 'The Golfer's Progress' I venture to make a somewhat startling assertion – viz, it is *not* necessary to keep your eye on the ball.
>
> Given your stance is correct and that your swing is true, you will hit the ball perfectly truly whether you are blindfold or not.

The letter appeared at the bottom right corner of an inside page, but it was spotted by readers.

When people responded to Livingstone's comment, a challenge was issued. Alf Toogood, professional at the Chelsea Golf School and Livingstone's colleague, offered to play any amateur, and Toogood would play blindfolded. He was expecting an average club player to take the challenge. Instead it was Tindal Atkinson. Toogood knew that he would have to be at his best to beat Tindal Atkinson even if he weren't blindfolded.

Meanwhile the letters poured in.

J. H. Taylor doubted whether anything so heretical had ever been said about golf as Livingstone's notion of not keeping your eye on the ball.

Bernard Darwin didn't think it would catch on anyway.

43

Wrote Darwin: 'The prospect of a pause before every stroke, during which the caddie, after the manner of a hangman, slips a white cap over the victim's head, is positively alarming to those who find golf on a crowded course quite slow enough as it is.'

Harold Hilton gave Livingstone's comments some credence. He agreed that a strong, forcing player ceased to focus on the ball at some point. Hilton was certain that, on long shots, he almost closed his eyes during the latter part of the downward swing. On short-range shots, though, Mr Hilton believed that you must look at the ball.

The *Daily Mail*'s correspondent went to watch Alf Toogood at practice and had to admit that the blindfolded professional looked good.

All over Britain, thousands of average golfers and duffers were shutting their eyes in the hope that this was the big breakthrough they wanted.

All would be revealed at Sunningdale.

He addressed the ball for his second shot.

'Alright.'

Guy Livingstone, acting as Toogood's second or bottle-holder, tied on the handkerchief again.

'Alright,' Livingstone said. He stepped back smartly to avoid the swing of the club.

At that moment a photographer knelt to take a daring action picture of the strange golfer with a handkerchief over his face. Toogood snatched at his approach shot and topped and sliced it. The ball whistled past the photographer's ear.

Old-timers in the gallery nodded sagely. Their mouths formed the words, 'Keep your eye on the ball'.

Toogood took seven at the first, Tindal Atkinson five. The amateur was one up.

At the second Toogood reached the green in three excellent shots. The amateur was some distance away.

On the greens, where Toogood didn't swing his club so much, it was safe for Livingstone to hold the handkerchief in front of Toogood's eyes rather than waste time tying it. Unfortunately, on the second green, Livingstone had to do this four times. Another seven on the card. Toogood two down.

It was downhill from there. Toogood continued to outdrive the amateur and occasionally he played an excellent tee-shot. His pitching wasn't quite so good, and his putting was abysmal, not helped by Sunningdale's undulating greens. He persisted in slicing the ball, and, when putting, often sent it four or five yards to the right. But he played some good shots from the rough and on one occasion chipped beautifully out of a bunker.

He halved the third, ninth and tenth, but lost the rest. It was all over by the eleventh. In 85 minutes, the blindfolded professional had lost eight and seven.

The controversy continued. Shortly afterwards, a scratch golfer, receiving a stroke a hole and blindfolded with opaque motor 'goggles', went round in 92 and beat a six-handicap man three and two.

GOLFER PLAYS IN A SUIT OF ARMOUR

BUSHEY HALL, APRIL 1912

The sun shone brightly over the Bushey Hall course and Harry Dearth's resplendent suit of armour glistened and glittered as he clanked and creaked from hole to hole.

'Dear me,' remarked an infirm gentleman as he caught sight of the man in armour. 'I know it's dangerous to go round with golf balls hurtling in all directions, but it would never have occurred to me to take those precautions.'

Dearth's strange, imposing appearance had nothing to do with caution. It had more to do with risk. He was an actor hoping to win a bet that involved playing a nine-hole game of golf in a suit of armour. Dearth had worn the armour on stage when playing St George in a recent Sir Edward Elgar production called *The Crown of India*.

The game was played on 23 April – St George's Day. The correspondent for *The Stage* whimsically commented that Graham Margetson, Dearth's opponent, showed bad form in appearing in ordinary golfing gear. Mr Margetson 'should have completed the matter by disguising himself as Will Shakespeare, whose day it was also'.

'Mr Dearth represented St George,' stated *Golf Illustrated*. 'The opportunity to remark at this point that there was no dragon to be seen except the drag on his putts would cause a professional humorist to pause until the last echoes of the laughter had died away, but we propose to go straight on to make the critical observation that Mr Dearth looked every inch a polished golfer. In fact, he looked better polished than anybody we have ever seen on the links.'

Despite his 'polished' appearance, Harry Dearth was under several disadvantages, not to mention a certain discomfort. His hot and heavy outfit was hardly suited – oh, excuse me – to the distances he had to walk across the course in the heat of the day. At least he was spared having to wear a visor on this occasion. Even so, nine holes at Bushey Hall was not quite the same as the stage at the Coliseum, and Harry Dearth's suit of armour restricted his golf swing to about half its normal arc.

'Notwithstanding these disadvantages, however, Mr Dearth made a gallant fight of it,' summarized one report. 'There was never much to choose between the players and in the end Mr Margetson won the match, which was over nine holes, by two up and one to play. Mr Dearth secured the bye. The contest was on level terms.'

The reporter for *Golf Illustrated*, however, showed some resentment at the interest shown by the public in Harry Dearth's armoured play and Alf Toogood's recent blindfolded appearance. The reporter couldn't resist a facetious gibe at the future: 'It is understood that A.H. Toogood has now offered to play blindfolded against Mr Dearth in armour. The referee will crawl around on his hands and knees; while the caddies will be in chains, and will extract the clubs from the bags with their teeth. After that, semi-comic golf will be given up in despair.'

STROKE-SPEED PLAY

SUGAR HILL, NEW HAMPSHIRE, SEPTEMBER 1912

Sport history is littered with stories of how Americans, pragmatic and inventive, have adapted British games into something more native. Examples include baseball (from rounders) and American football (from soccer). I wonder if there were occasions when golf might have taken a cultural turn, occasions like a club competition at the Sunset Hill Golf Club, for instance.

The nine-hole Sunset Hill course was the scene of a few strange competitions that year. There was a one-hole competition, for example, when golfers played a hole of 1,250 yards – from the top of a nearby hill through underbrush, across two cow pastures and over three barns until they reached the second green of the actual course. One local rule was that balls could be teed at any time with the loss of one stroke. F. C. Long won the hole with a score of 12 (including two extra tee-shots), far less than most people expected.

The second, and perhaps more interesting tournament, was one in which both strokes and speed counted. A golfer's score for the nine holes had to be added to the number of minutes he had taken to complete the 2,100-yard course. It was a competition for athletes and golfers alike, and, like the one-hole competition, it created a lot of debate and interest, as summarized by the American magazine *Golf*: 'The biggest galleries of the year turned out for these contests and as the number of entries

48

in each was large, they furnished the real feature of the golf season at Sugar Hill.'

People in the big galleries faced interesting decisions too. It wasn't easy to follow one golfer. Better to stay by one green and watch them all run through?

The best time for the course was 15 and a half minutes by E. E. Babb Jnr, but it wasn't good enough to win the tournament. Babb took 47 strokes for the nine holes for a combined score of 62 and a half. He finished second to J. D. Standish of Detroit – 41 strokes and 19 minutes for a total of 60.

I presume there was no system of handicapping. It might add an interesting complexity if there was a system of netting the number of minutes by age or previous times.

In case anyone would like to develop the stroke-speed play idea further, here are a few pieces of information that may be relevant. As most speed competitions are played with only one club, it is worth remembering that Thad Daber, with a six-iron, won the 1987 World One-club Championship with a 70 on the 6,037-yard Lochmore course in North Carolina. And, for speed, few can compare with 16-year-old Jim Carville, who took only 27 minutes nine seconds to complete a round of the 6,154-yard Warrenpoint course in Northern Ireland the same year. About 1,000 people watched Carville knock seven seconds off the previous record, and the proceeds of the event went to the local Gateway club to develop premises for handicapped children. The chairman of Gateway presented Carville with a trophy 'to commemorate one of the finest moments in the history of Warrenpoint Golf Club'.

I have heard of other kinds of speed competitions. The craziest was one where the winner was the first to hole out at a long hole. Golfers charged down the fairway like cavalry in an attempt to be the first. It sounds very dangerous. Indeed, all speed competitions sound dangerous. They raise questions about how a golfer can play safely if covering a course at a different time to the person playing ahead, and further questions about whether a golfer is fit enough to do it. But do you think it might become an Olympic event? The 5,000-metre golf handicap for all ages, or the men's downhill golf slalom? Somehow I doubt it, although I'm sure that athletic golfers will continue to make something strange out of the sport.

MASKED ENGLISH GOLFER IN
NEW YORK

NEW YORK CITY, NOVEMBER 1912

'Who is he?' asked Americans when a golfer in disguise appeared on public courses around New York City and attracted attention with his prodigious driving and English accent. His face was covered with a black mask, or occasionally painted white or black, and the mysterious golfer attracted so much interest that he challenged the US Open Champion to a big-money match.

If this is a tale about a good English professional flirting with the American golf scene, it is also a tale about trans-Atlantic communication. Nowadays, it would be relatively straightforward to identify a high-ranking golfer by a wired photograph or faxed description. In 1912 it all took time.

To Americans, the masked man looked like someone in the same class as Harry Vardon and James Braid. A few well-chosen words, dispatched by telegram, showed that Vardon and Braid were busy playing in England. Braid, of course, wasn't even English.

But who could it be?

American reporters camped outside the masked man's room in the hope of seeing him without his disguise. The American public took to the golf courses and watched his confident play. The crowds were so big that it became difficult for him to practise. His style was surely a clue.

Early in November, news reached Britain of a great challenge match. The US Open Champion was 21-year-old Johnny

McDermott, who had also won the title the previous year. However, McDermott had failed to survive the qualifying stage of the British Open at Muirfield that year, and the top American golfers were rated below the best British. The masked man was an ideal player for a challenge match. He was unknown in the United States, but was a golfer of great potential. A round of 73 at Muirfield in the British Open showed what he could do.

'McDermott has accepted Black Mask's challenge for a match for $1,000,' wrote *Golf Illustrated*. 'According to the *Daily Mirror*, the contest will take place this month, and for the first time in history since the days of chivalry the champion will meet a masked unknown.'

Golf Illustrated also took pains to deny the rumour that the masked golfer was a prominent member of the Rules of Golf Committee at St Andrews. 'The secrecy which envelops the lives and doings of these gentlemen probably gave rise to the report,' the magazine said.

The masked man's backers in the United States certainly approached McDermott, but the American didn't agree to the terms of the match.

'Since that time the "black one" has issued several challenges in the columns of the press,' said *The American Golfer*, 'but McDermott very properly intends to ignore him until he comes out from cover and suggests a contest in manner befitting the dignity of the game. American golf is honorable and dignified and anyone who attempts to debase it should be rebuked. Our courses are not three-ring circus tents and our players are not in the habit of appearing in the character of the buffoon. Wash your face my man and come clean!"

The identity of the masked golfer was revealed in the *Daily Mirror* on 12 November. As several newspapers had already suspected, it was Bill Horne, the former professional at Chertsey, who could drive 'like a kicking mule'. His incredible drives included one at North Berwick in 1909 which was claimed to be 388 yards. 'Horne has a rather peculiar swing, somewhat shorter than the ordinary,' stated one account, pleading for a positive identification from the United States. 'He is also a noticeably large person, and anyone who has seen him play should be able to penetrate the disguise.'

'OUIMET IS CHAMPION'

BROOKLINE, MASSACHUSETTS, SEPTEMBER 1913

In 1913, British golfers were considered the best in the world. Top American players had made no impact on the British Open, while the only American to win the US Open, John McDermott, had done so in years when the entry was virtually all-American. Therefore, when two top British golfers, Harry Vardon and Ted Ray, announced they would play in the 1913 US Open, the opposition winced. They thought Vardon or Ray would win. The outcome, however, was something else, and the 1913 US Open was a turning-point in the history of American sport.

The star of the tournament was a 20-year-old American amateur named Francis Ouimet. Vardon and Ray were old enough to be the boy's father, and Vardon had a big reputation before Ouimet knew what a golf club was. Ouimet – pronounced 'we-met' by Americans – was of French-Canadian extraction but born in Brookline, a suburb of Boston. He was raised near the Brookline Country Club, and, as a child, took a short-cut across the fairways on his way home from school, occasionally picking up a lost ball (gutta-percha of course). Later, he caddied on the Brookline course, and then developed as a golfer at the Woodland Golf Club in Auburndale, near where he worked as a shop assistant.

Shortly before the 1913 US Open tournament, Francis Ouimet played two rounds of 88 on the Wellesley Country Club course. It was not championship form, and he seriously considered withdrawing, especially with Vardon and Ray playing. Ray was the 1912 British Open Champion, while Vardon had won the British Open five times (with a sixth to come in 1914). It might be better to watch them play, Ouimet thought, and learn something from such experienced professionals. He made enquiries about withdrawing. 'As long as you have entered, you had better plan to play,' he was told.

The field for the US Open was split into three qualifying sections. Ouimet surprised a few people by finishing second to Vardon in one section, while Ray comfortably led another. 'Great Britain has yet to lose its supremacy in the world of golf, even though now defending that title in the stronghold of the "enemy",' said the *New York Times*.

On the first day of the tournament proper, they played two rounds. Vardon and another Englishman, Wilfred Reid, led the field with 147, with Ted Ray on 149 and Herbert Strong on 150. The Ouimet boy was one of a bunch on 151. Not a real contender, although he had recovered well after starting the day with two sixes.

The next day it rained continuously. It was a day of heavy turf, muddy balls and sopping rubber raincoats, all of which added to the strangeness of the spectacle. After three rounds, Vardon, Ray and Ouimet were all tied on 225. As Ouimet walked out to the first tee for his final round, he watched Ray complete his last round.

'Ray's done a 79,' someone told Ouimet.

It was a good round in such atrocious conditions, but not unassailable.

On his dramatic final round, Ouimet listened to rumours that circulated the swampy course.

'Vardon's tied with Ray – another 79.'

'Barnes has it won.'

'Barnes has blown up.'

'Tellier will win it in a walk.'

'Tellier's in trouble.'

Ouimet went out in 43, and his hopes of winning seemed gone. A five at the par-three tenth made things worse.

'It's too bad, he's blown up,' Ouimet heard a spectator say.

That remark angered the youth. He concentrated harder, and made a par four at the eleventh and a difficult five at the twelfth. If he wanted to equal Ray and Vardon, he must do the last six holes in 22, two under par. Almost impossible in these conditions.

Then he chipped in from 30 feet for a birdie at the thirteenth and did the next two holes in par. He needed another birdie and reckoned that the short sixteenth was his best bet. But he overplayed the hole and was fortunate to escape with a par. He went to the seventeenth feeling slightly deflated.

'The seventeenth was the sensation of this round,' wrote Charles Macdonald a few years later. 'It is a dog-leg hole and it took two fine shots to reach the green. The ball was some 12 yards or more to the right of the hole and Ouimet was left a very ticklish putt. As it was downhill he might easily run two or more yards beyond, but in hitting the ball truly he found the bottom of the cup for a birdie three.'

Ouimet needed a par four at the eighteenth to tie, and 5,000 spectators in his gallery cheered like a baseball or football crowd. It wasn't easy for George Sargeant, his playing partner. It was also making Ouimet tense.

'Keep your eye on the ball and hit it,' said Ouimet's caddie, 10-year-old Eddie Lowery, as he handed over an iron for the second shot at the eighteenth. Ouimet put the ball on the green in two, and, from 35 feet, laid the ball to within four feet of the pin. He sank that putt confidently to ensure a three-way tie, and the gallery closed around him with a uniform yell. They lifted Ouimet shoulder-high and carried him to the clubhouse. They nearly tore his limbs off. Many thrust bills at him, but he refused them politely. He was, after all, only an amateur.

Ouimet had a good night's sleep and arrived fresh and rested for the 18-hole play-off with Ray and Vardon.

'Don't worry about them,' advised John McDermott, who had finished a few strokes behind. 'Play your own game. You're hitting the ball well.'

There was a kerfuffle about who should caddie for Ouimet.

A veteran caddie offered young Lowery money to stand down, and other experienced caddies were available. But Ouimet stuck with the 10-year-old, who was on the verge of tears at the thought of being rejected. It wasn't too arduous for the boy – Ouimet used only seven clubs.

Ouimet drew the longest straw and prepared to drive through the mist and rain.

'Be sure and keep your eye on the ball,' said his caddie, handing over the driver.

After seven holes Vardon had a one-stroke lead over the other two. At the par-four eighth, Ouimet's second shot was a foot from the hole, and Ray sank a 40-footer for a birdie. They were all-square, two experienced English professionals and a young American amateur.

It was so wet that it was difficult to hold the clubs. The course was dripping water. On the tenth green, both Ray and Vardon had to putt or chip over marks made when their balls landed. Ouimet took a lead of one stroke. The excitement was intense.

After 16 holes – only two to play – Ouimet was still one stroke ahead of Vardon, while Ray, five strokes behind, was virtually out of it. Vardon had the honour at the seventeenth but he was feeling the tension and his drive went into a bunker. Ouimet struck a typically straight and steady drive. The cheering was loud and persistent. Ray stopped in the middle of his swing and waited for the noise to subside.

Vardon and Ray had fives; Ouimet a three.

'Ouimet is champion,' the crowd began to shout.

It was confirmed on the eighteenth green.

'It did not enter my head that I was about to become the Open Champion until I stroked my first putt to within eight or nine inches of the hole,' wrote Ouimet in his autobiography. 'Then, as I stepped up to make that short putt, I became very nervous. A veil of something that seemed to have covered me dropped from around my head and shoulders. I was in full control of my faculties for the first time since the match started, but terribly excited. I dropped the putt. Nothing but the most intense concentration brought me victory.'

Ouimet's score was 72, Vardon 77, and Ray 78. The 8,000 crowd swarmed around Ouimet, and he was hoisted on shoulders once again. British golf had been put in its place by a 20-year-old boy, and an amateur at that, the first amateur to win the US Open. He had been helped by a 10-year-old caddie.

Ray and Vardon congratulated the winner and were generous in their praise, but British reporters began to find excuses as time went by: Ray and Vardon didn't know the course; the wet conditions were appalling for 'scientific golf'; Ray and Vardon shouldn't have had to play qualifying rounds; the crowd annoyed Ray and Vardon by cheering at inappropriate times; it was a one-off fluke; a 36-hole play-off might have produced a different result; and Braid, Taylor or Hilton would have beaten Ouimet had they entered.

'Youth has no nerves,' said J.H. Taylor. 'Youngsters playing golf do not realize how difficult it is to play really well. Only when one has made a reputation and understands the dire consequences of failure is one properly thankful if one is playing well. Ouimet is a splendid golfer, endowed with splendid nerves. At the same time my impression is that he had everything to gain and nothing to lose. Vardon and Ray on the other hand knew they carried on their shoulders the golf reputation of this country. That did not make their task any easier. It is much more easy to make a reputation at golf than to maintain it.'

Ouimet gave the United States a reputation in golf that others would maintain, especially in the 1920s, when Americans like Walter Hagen and Robert Tyre Jones, Jnr, began to dominate the British Open. Perhaps the final word on Ouimet's strange success should belong to Charles Macdonald: 'Ouimet's victory was the most dramatic event I have ever known in sport, and it was the biggest win to my mind in golfing history. His finish was amazing.'

The Brookline Club hosted the 1963 and 1988 US Open tournaments, in recognition of the 50th and 75th anniversaries of Ouimet's achievement.

IT WAS ALL ABOUT A BALL

SANDY LODGE GOLF CLUB, MARCH 1914

The rubber-cored Haskell ball had swept through golf and ousted the gutta-percha. A dozen years had passed since the Haskell Revolution. Now Sandy Lodge hosted a strange four-ball match featuring the rubber-cored ball, the guttie and four of the world's best golfers, all of whom held strong opinions on the relative merits of the two balls.

Harry Vardon had made his reputation with a guttie and had won three British Open Championships with it. J. H. Taylor had also managed three British Open victories with a guttie, and he was now almost romantic about playing with one again. The third member of the Great Triumvirate, James Braid, had won only one of his five Opens before 1902, and was a total convert to the Haskell, claiming he could outdrive the guttie by 40 yards. The fourth player, the youngest by far, 21-year-old George Duncan, had grown up on the Haskell and reckoned the guttie's best range was a yard from the hole. Whatever Duncan would do with the guttie, he would do it quickly. His strokes were so fast that it looked like he didn't care, and his later autobiography was appropriately called *Golf at the Gallop*.

The four star golfers played a 36-hole fourball. In the morning Taylor and Braid played with guttie balls, whereas Vardon and Duncan used rubber-cored Haskells. In the afternoon they switched balls, Vardon and Duncan using gutties. The entertainment also included a lunchtime driving competition, each player driving three gutties and three Haskells.

The problem of obtaining guttie balls was overcome with difficulty – the balls were either 12 years old (at least) or specially made and therefore too new – and about 3,000 spectators came to Sandy Lodge to watch. The winners would share £30, the losers £20, prizes provided by the *Daily Mail*.

The guttie ball was exhausting work. It demanded more strength and accuracy in shots. It usually lost about 35-40 yards on drives, except for Braid, who kept it within 25 yards and played a brilliant round with the old ball, compensating for Taylor's difficulties.

Some younger spectators, kidded by tales of the noise made by the impact of the driver on a guttie ball, held hands over their ears as if expecting cannon fire. This was overreacting. Nevertheless, there was a distinctive loud crack as the ball went away down the fairway.

Vardon and Duncan were one up at the turn, but even when holes were halved it was obvious that the guttie-ball players were working far harder. It wasn't until the thirteenth that Taylor bettered his partner's ball, and that was only to rescue the half. At the fourteenth Braid was an inch past Vardon after two shots apiece with wooden clubs. It was the guttie's best achievement of the day.

At lunch, the guttie-ball players were five down, and would have been hopelessly astray had it not been for Braid, who went round in 72.

In the afternoon, Braid and Taylor, now converted to the rubber-cored ball, won the second, fourth and fifth holes to recover to two down. However, the others adjusted to the old ball and Duncan in particular played brilliantly, even when his guttie became distorted near the end of the round. Vardon and Duncan won the overall match by one hole.

The second result was, as anticipated, an easy victory for the Haskell ball, which had won nine holes more than the guttie. The driving competition confirmed the difference, although it was difficult to be certain about distances as the large crowd interfered. Duncan drove farthest with the guttie (240 yards) and Braid with the Haskell (279 yards).

Despite the conclusive results of this experiment, nostalgia for the guttie ball lingered. In 1927, a team of four-handicap golfers with Haskells were beaten 6-3 by a team of leading British players with gutties. The stars included Cyril Tolley, Roger Wethered, J. H. Taylor and Sandy Herd.

As late as 1940, two more guttie-Haskell matches were held, with proceeds going to the Red Cross. At the Mid-Surrey course, Richmond, 70-year-old James Braid played with 72-year-old Sandy Herd, who had won the 1902 Open after switching to a Haskell at the last moment. They used rubber-cored balls, while their opponents, two comparative youngsters, Henry Cotton and Arthur Havers, were compelled to use the guttie. The old-timers won the first and went two up at the sixth, but Cotton and Havers pulled one back at the tenth. Braid won the eleventh for the 'old uns' but the 'young uns' won the twelfth and fourteenth to square the match. Cotton played the fifteenth brilliantly, driving the guttie to within five feet of the 190-yard hole. Herd's putt squared the match again at the sixteenth, but he was so tired by then that he had to rely on his Scottish compatriot for the last two holes. They were halved, and so was the match.

GOLF IN THE SEA

GOODWIN SANDS, JULY 1921

A mysterious, magical golf course, it emerges from the sea for only two or three hours a year, a temporary sandbank six miles from the south-east coast of Britain. It is a submarine course, suitable only for intrepid visionaries, and was first settled by golfers in 1921.

Shortly before his pioneering trip to the Goodwin Sands, Willie Hunter had won the British Amateur Championship, crowning his success with a remarkable 12 and 11 victory against Allan Graham in the final. He had backed himself with 10 shillings (50p) at 33-1, but his wallet was pickpocketed between the final green and the clubhouse.

The soft Goodwin Sands were different from the slick Hoylake greens, but Willie Hunter was willing to experiment. A local Post Office clerk, he was a member of the Walmer and Kingsdown Golf Club, and his father, Harry, was professional at Royal Cinque Ports Golf Club, Deal. He was familiar with the string of excellent courses along the Kent coast, including those at Sandwich, but the Goodwin Sands course provided a charming contrast. At best it extended to three holes.

Shortly after 2 pm, on Sunday 17 July, Hunter and 10 other golfers boarded Harry Meakin's motor-launch *Lady Beatty*. Three children were also aboard. It took 50 minutes to travel six miles to the rising island of the Goodwin Sands, and they arrived when the island was still emerging. The seagulls were so startled at the sound of people and a boat that they took off with a plaintive scream of protest.

The first task was to lay out a course and decide on a few impromptu local rules. They agreed that each player would play out, but what about a pool of water? Could it be called 'casual water' if it was there the whole year? More like casual sand on the rest of the course.

As the tide receded there was space for three holes. One of them relied on the periscope of the sunken German submarine U-48 as a guide-post. The periscope was the only piece of the submarine visible, even when the sands were revealed.

The golfers began, and soon realized that spiked shoes were a handicap. They took off their shoes and socks, and waded through the water.

Later, Willie Hunter responded to a reporter's question about the novel golf course.

'As one takes up one's stance to make a shot, one gradually sinks in,' commented Hunter. 'So the characteristics of a George Duncan, with his lightning rapidity of execution, would be a decided asset on the Goodwins. Another thing that struck me was the tremendous amount of backspin one could obtain on the crisp surface, probably owing to the way one's mashie cut through the sand.'

The pools of water were demanding hazards, but Hunter showed his class by hitting one long soaring drive of 230 yards which struck crisp sand, rose quickly and scattered screaming seagulls when it landed again. When the three-hole competition had ended, the sand drier by now, Hunter gave a demonstration of driving and putting. Later that year Hunter would beat Bobby Jones to reach the semi-final of the US Amateur Championship.

Another party from Deal arrived later in the afternoon for dancing, a picnic and a game or two. In the past, the Goodwin Sands had been the scene of cricket, bowls and cycling, but this was believed to be the first time golf had been played there. The golfers left about 4.50 and landed on Deal beach at 5.40, well satisfied with their adventure.

A HANDICAP OF 150 YARDS

LITTLEHAMPTON, APRIL 1924

Harry Rountree, an artist and scratch amateur golfer, played the better ball of two British Open Champions, George Duncan and Ted Ray. Rountree received '150 yards taken in such quantities and at such points as he preferred'.

The wording was important. Rountree understood golf courses very well – his water-colour drawings of famous courses had appeared in golf magazines – and he knew the value of the wording. He exploited his advantage sensibly and beat the professionals by six and five. He had used only 50 yards and two feet of his handicap.

At the very first hole Rountree used three inches to take his ball out of a bad lie, and a yard to hole a putt. He was one up and still had almost 149 yards to play with. At the 187-yard sixth hole, Rountree drove to within 25 yards of the green. When Ted Ray holed his chip shot for a two, Rountree simply used 25 yards of his handicap for a one. It was a real psychological blow.

The artist found he could use a few inches to improve his lie, a few yards to take the ball out of a bunker, and a few feet to turn a lay-up into a brilliant putt. Only on rare occasions did he hole out, for all putts from six yards downward he took as a matter of course. He lifted his ball at two holes, but his net score for the other 11 was one under an average of threes. It was exasperating for the professionals.

After the novel match, Ted Ray declared that he could win every championship of the world if he was conceded a handicap

64

of one yard. If nothing else, it highlights the number of times a few inches makes all the difference in a game of golf.

TIE AFTER TIE AFTER TIE

GLASGOW AND GLENEAGLES,
APRIL, MAY AND JUNE, 1924

The second annual Glasgow and District Professional Association competition took place on 30 April. It was a stroke competition, played over two rounds at the Pollok course, and a silver trophy donated by Whyte and Mackay was at stake. Early in the final round it developed into a straight competition between two players, and it remained so for several weeks.

The elder player was David Sutherland, the Balmore professional who was captain of the Glasgow and District Professional Association. The younger was John Campbell, a former colleague of Sutherland's at Balmore, now an unattached golfer who was teaching in a sports emporium in Glasgow. Campbell was the holder of the title.

Sutherland and Campbell each had a 75 for the first round of the tournament. They trailed McMinn by one stroke, but the third man soon fell away in the final round. Meanwhile Sutherland and Campbell's capacity for equality was uncanny. They both went out in 35, and all depended on the last nine holes of the tournament.

After his two at the thirteenth, Sutherland had a three-stroke lead, but Campbell immediately pulled back two of them at the next hole and drew level at the eighteenth. Two fine rounds of 70. Both had an overall total of 145, and a play-off was necessary. This was the scoring on the homeward nine.

| Sutherland | 354 | 254 | 435 | — | 35 (70) |
| Campbell | 454 | 434 | 434 | — | 35 (70) |

They went out again that evening. On a dull day, the light was not wonderful, so the play was not as good, but just as exciting. This time Campbell took a commanding lead – five strokes at the eighth – but Sutherland pulled them back by the fourteenth. Campbell gained two strokes at the fifteenth, but lost one at the sixteenth and another at the seventeenth. They went to the eighteenth all-square and halved it in fives. Two rounds of 77, and still no decision.

'It was certainly remarkable that after playing 54 holes there was not a single stroke between the players,' wrote the *Glasgow Herald*.

There was more was to come.

The second play-off, at Pollok, began at 6 pm on Tuesday 13 May. The weather was delightful, the crowd large and the golf brilliant. Campbell was two strokes to the good after three holes, but the two players had identical scores for the next six holes.

| Sutherland | 545 | 443 | 444 | — | 37 |
| Campbell | 444 | 443 | 444 | — | 35 |

Campbell had lost his lead by the twelfth, but played the fourteenth magnificently for three. Sutherland was in a bunker at the same hole, but recovered well for a four. It kept him in the match, and the outcome was almost predictably equal.

| Sutherland | 344 | 344 | 434 | — | 33 (70) |
| Campbell | 355 | 335 | 434 | — | 35 (70) |

The third replay was again at Pollok – at 6 pm on Tuesday 27 May. The weather was poor, but nearly 700 people were curious enough to attend. The first nine holes were typically close, but Sutherland had a slight advantage at the turn.

| Sutherland | 454 | 453 | 535 | — | 38 |
| Campbell | 544 | 453 | 644 | — | 39 |

The 407-yard eleventh was played brilliantly. Both were on the green in two. Both holed fine putts for threes. They played inspired golf, but went to the last hole all-square, after Sutherland had pulled his second shot at the seventeenth on to the road. Campbell needed a long putt on the last green to keep the scores level. Naturally he sank it.

| Sutherland | 335 | 344 | 444 | — | 34 (72) |
| Campbell | 334 | 354 | 434 | — | 33 (72) |

It wasn't easy to arrange a date for the fourth replay. However, they agreed to play a round at Gleneagles on the eve of the *Glasgow Herald* tournament. About 200 spectators followed them round. After only five holes, Campbell had a three-stroke lead, but Sutherland recovered. Campbell three-putted at the eighth, reducing his lead to one, but his six-yard putt at the ninth widened the margin again.

| Sutherland | 545 | 545 | 534 | — | 40 |
| Campbell | 454 | 436 | 543 | — | 38 |

They went to the 170-yard eleventh with Campbell one stroke ahead. Sutherland's tee-shot hit the pin and he made a two. Campbell three-putted for a four. The lead had changed. Not for the first time.

The thirteenth hole at Gleneagles finally settled the tournament. Campbell played two shots from the fairway, while Sutherland's approach drew up three inches from the hole. Sutherland became the new champion, but, in a fitting tribute to one of the most nearly equal contests ever, the two players did the last five holes in identical scores.

| Sutherland | 424 | 345 | 444 | — | 34 (74) |
| Campbell | 544 | 545 | 444 | — | 39 (77) |

After five equal rounds – 75, 70, 77, 70 and 72 – the competition was finally over.

You would think that ended the story, but the next day the *Glasgow Herald* tournament began. After two rounds of stroke play, the leading 32 players would go forward into match-play. Campbell started with a 77, Sutherland an 80, a three-stroke difference which compensated for the previous day, so perhaps it wasn't surprising that they both went round in 75 in the second round of the *Glasgow Herald* tournament.

Sutherland missed the cut with 155, but Campbell's 152 brought him ... yes, you've guessed ... a play-off. Seven players went out in pairs to play-off for the last six places, so obviously one player needed a marker. David Sutherland, the new Glasgow Champion, captain of the Glasgow and District Professionals Association, was an obvious person for the job. He partnered the odd man over the six-hole play-off. So there they were again, Campbell and Sutherland, taking part in a play-off in strange circumstances. Campbell's 26 for the six holes was equal to two other players, but good enough to make the cut as Ockenden had a 29.

ELK AT THE THIRTEENTH

BANFF, ALBERTA, OCTOBER 1925

Gourlay studied the line for a 10-foot putt on the thirteenth. He needed it to win the hole against Leslie, the assistant professional at Banff. The contour of the green demanded the scientific approach of this prominent Banff pharmacist. Satisfied, Gourlay took his stance and addressed the ball.

His concentration was disturbed by a loud crashing noise in the heavy growth nearby. It startled him. He jumped from his crouch, turned and looked. His opponent gazed too. What they saw was a herd of about 75 elk stampeding helter-skelter through the pine and spruce. The elk stumbled across the fairway, watched by the two men. Then a bull detached himself from the herd. He stopped, turned and studied the golfers.

What was he thinking?

Was he wondering if these were the people who had been hitting funny white things near his hide all year?

He was quiet and docile during the summer. Now, in the fall, he was feeling a bit touchy.

Uh, uh. Here he comes.

The bull lowered his head, pawed the ground and broke into a run. He shifted into high gear and charged at the golfers.

Quick! What would the Rules of Golf Committee say about this?

Being golfers, Gourlay and Leslie were good judges of distance. They estimated the bull to be perhaps 60 yards away. They gripped their putters tightly ready to make a gallant stand. Then they had a better idea. They scrambled up nearby trees. Very quickly.

Perched in the branches of the spruce trees flanking the green, they watched the bull as he snorted and stamped the ground at the base of the trees. Minutes passed slowly. Five of them.

A call from the herd attracted the bull's attention. Cheated out of his prey, he set off towards the other elk. The two golfers were in no hurry to come down. They waited 10 minutes, until they convinced each other that the elk were out of sight.

While his opponent kept watch for the elk, Gourlay sank a brave 10-footer to win the hole. Then they set off for the fourteenth and went on to complete the round. Back at the clubhouse, they had a good story for the other golfers. As Gourlay and Leslie warmed themselves by the fire, they told their tale. The others noticed the spruce gum on their trousers, and saw this as reasonable evidence that the story was true.

GOLF AT DUSK

RYE, JANUARY 1926

Darkness creeps up on concentrating golfers. The eyes adjust somehow, the game continues, and only when it is over do they realize how dark it has become. 'We weren't playing in light that bad, were we?' they say to each other from inside the clubhouse.

The last few holes of the 1926 President's Putter final, between Eustace Storey and Roger Wethered, were so exciting that even spectators didn't fully register just how bad it had become. The 18-hole match itself had a strange outcome.

The President's Putter, the annual meeting of the Oxford and Cambridge Society, was the first serious event of the year and was probably one of the top six British tournaments at the time. Roger Wethered had not played much golf that year, and was not in top form in the first round. Fortunately for him, his opponent, Clive Tolley, played surprisingly badly, and Wethered won seven and six. By the semi-final Wethered was at his best, but at the turn trailed by three holes to Ernest Smith. Wethered won seven in a row to go through by four and two.

The final produced two heroes. 'I have never in my life seen a better game of golf on such an occasion,' wrote the correspondent for the *The Illustrated Sporting and Dramatic News*. He also pointed out that it had one of the most extraordinary finishes possible.

None of the first six holes of the 18-hole final was halved, but the players stood level after them. Four of them were won with good figures. Then followed a succession of brilliantly played halved holes, before Storey took the lead at the thirteenth, Wethered topping his second shot from a difficult lie. A two at the fourteenth put Storey two up, and a good second shot at the fifteenth gained him a commanding position. However, Wethered's iron shot at that hole settled two yards from the pin. Storey was now only one up.

They halved the sixteenth, and Wethered squared the match at the seventeenth. When Wethered missed the green with his second at the eighteenth, the odds favoured Storey, but Wethered recovered and sank a good putt for his par. A half. End of round. No result.

It was now 'sudden-death', and spectators must have wished the match would never end. The round had started at 1.30 pm and it was now approaching 5 o'clock. When they went to the nineteenth it was a little dim.

They halved the nineteenth with perfect fours.

Wethered's fourth at the twentieth lay on the lip of the hole. It was not enough to win the hole. Another half. The crowd swelled, night fell, and the players went on and on.

The twenty-first was poorly played but well halved.

Wethered had a chance at the twenty-second but a shortish putt strayed off line. A half again. On they went.

At the twenty-third the chance was Storey's but his putt went down the wrong line. The players were politely informed that unless one of them could win the next hole they would have to stop and try again another day.

At the twenty-fourth they both had putts of about six yards. Each time the ball sneaked by the lip of the hole.

Yet another half.

It was strange that a match that had not produced a half in its first six holes had now produced nothing but halves in the extra six holes. As it was now night, the match had to stop with no definite outcome. The first suggestion was to replay at Sunningdale the following Sunday, but in fact the two golfers agreed to halve the tournament. Normally the winning golfer's ball is attached to a putter presented by A. C. Croome at the tournament's conception. On this occasion two balls were affixed to the putter.

CHOICE OF CLUB DECIDED
BY LOTTERY

ATLANTA, GEORGIA, FEBRUARY 1927

They called it 'the Monkey Tournament'. It was one of the strangest ever. Players didn't choose which club they would use for a shot. Instead they drew a slip of paper out of a hat, and, regardless of the stroke to be played, the slip of paper informed them of the club they had to use. Drivers were used on putting greens, and one woman drove off three times with a putter.

The tournament was organized by the Atlanta Women's Golf Association. It was a nine-hole event, with 10 players on one team and 11 on the other. Besides the strange rule for deciding the club, there was one other violent deviation from the usual rules of golf. While a player was making a shot, her opponents were permitted to distract her with noise and action. Anything except touching an opponent and touching the ball was allowed.

The team captained by Mrs T. T. Williams took a lead at the first of the nine holes, with a four to Mrs Clarence Bradley's team's eight. But the scores shot up when the women realized the opportunities. Players took up their stances with an inappropriate club and then played their shots amidst a glut of distractions. Opponents yelled, screamed, offered advice and criticism, blew police whistles and bashed tin cans together. An alternative distraction was to play practice-shots right next to the player doing the real thing.

Consequently, the Bradley team squared the match at the second hole with a 12 to the Williams 14, and then won the third hole by 13 strokes. The Williams team couldn't really expect to win a hole in 21 shots, even if it were a 'Monkey Tournament'.

The next three holes were very close, but the Bradley team eventually picked up a two-hole lead at the vital seventh. The Williams team kept the match alive but lost by two up. The scores make unusual reading:

Williams team	4, 14, 21, 11, 9, 7, 9, 8, 7 — 90
Bradley team	8, 12, 8, 10, 9, 8, 6, 10, 5 — 76

BOY KILLS HIS FATHER

FOXHILLS, LOS ANGELES, OCTOBER 1927

This is a chilling tale. It is the story of a 12-year-old boy's first golf lesson, normally an event that fosters a lifetime leisure interest, but, on this isolated occasion, a source of tragedy.

Two generations of the Wesley family, father and son, left their Los Feliz house at 11am that fateful Sunday morning. During the week Ben Wesley worked as an auditor at the Western Supply Auto Company, but at the week-end he was a golf devotee. His 12-year-old son, his only child, must have chattered excitedly on the journey to the golf-course. The boy must have realized that his father was a well-known local golfer, and must have cherished the prospect of his first lesson, the first step toward emulation of someone he admired. Perhaps his father looked forward to them spending many hours together on the golf-course.

At the first tee, the father gave clear instructions.

'Keep your eye on the ball,' the father said. 'Don't look up, and swing the club as hard as you can.'

He demonstrated the correct way to drive and then stepped back to give the boy a chance.

The boy drew back the club and swung it heartily, awkwardly, obviously a beginner. The club came forward with a swish and missed the ball completely, continuing on its course until it met with resistance. The club struck the boy's father a hard blow on the neck, and the man fell to the ground without a sound.

Other golfers rushed to the scene. They lifted the victim into a motor-car and started for the clubhouse. The man was dead within minutes. No one dare tell the boy immediately.

Surely the boy was not to blame. Perhaps the instruction he received should have been better, or his father stood too close for safety, or maybe his father moved closer at the last moment to say something he had forgotten. Later examination of the father's body raised other questions. Was it a ruptured artery in the neck and an internal haemorrhage or was death connected to a neck problem for which the father had been receiving treatment? Was it the blow of the club that caused death or the man's collision with the ground? Or perhaps the shock of the blow had caused the heart attack?

The boy's mother collapsed when she heard the news. The following day, the son was told that his father was dead. The boy wasn't to blame, but it was still a huge burden to bear, and now he had no father to teach him golf.

VISIBILITY OF 20 YARDS

WORPLESDON, NOVEMBER 1927

Fog. Thick and thickening. It played havoc with that Saturday's sporting programme, and reports of soccer and rugby games in the *Woking Observer and Weybridge Chronicle* carried a uniform message:

Fog wins at Woking
Beaten by the fog
Fog proves a spoil sport
Clubs find it a bit too thick
Egham v Walton fogged off
Caley Strollers and the fog

In the midst of all this failure, the day's golfers could claim some success. The same newspaper carried a short item on a golf match: 'Worplesdon entertained Oxford University on Saturday, and although the course was enshrouded in thick fog, foursomes were played over 14 holes, each side winning three matches.'

The Times gives us some idea of how bad the fog was: 'The players had the utmost difficulty in finding their way round, and as the morning wore on the conditions became worse and it was impossible to see more than 20 yards ahead.'

Can you play golf with 20-yard vision? These golfers did, and lessons can be learned. First, foggy conditions are to the advantage of people who know the course. In this case, however, the score was halved, three matches apiece. No one knew the course better than Roger Wethered. Playing with G. C. Stokoe, Wethered won the top match against Oppenheimer

79

(Christ Church College) and Bradshaw (Brasenose College) by three and two.

The golfers also learned that they needed to communicate to each other through the fog. They either shouted across the fairways or developed a system of clapping hands. Golfers had been known to lose their partners in the fog, but, if everything went well, they caught sight of each other on the greens, where the damp of the fog had settled and they needed to clean their ball after every shot.

It was not ideal, but they completed six 14-hole matches. Admittedly one went no further than the tenth hole, Baugh (Wadham) and Adam (Brasenose) beating Mead and Frame by six and four.

There was another lesson. Fog strips away some of the anxiety that accompanies a view of hazards ahead. The golfers drove into the great unknown with greater confidence, cavalierish, although there was no telling where they would find their ball, or if they would find it.

Please don't ask me for a report of the play – they probably didn't know themselves. All I can tell you is that the weather showed no sign of clearing after lunch, so the afternoon singles were abandoned.

COMPSTON AND HAGEN

MOOR PARK, LONDON, APRIL 1928

In the 1920s, American golfers began to dominate the British Open. Shortly before the 1928 Open, a challenge match was held over 72 holes at Moor Park, London – a top British golfer (Archie Compston) against one of the best-ever Americans (Walter Hagen).

Hagen was a flamboyant, innovative golfer who usually set the pace, whether it be with cardigans and pullovers rather than jackets, black-and-white golf shoes or simply by taking fewer shots. Hagen once said he never wanted to be a millionaire, just to live like one. At one tournament, where professionals were not allowed in the clubhouse, he changed into golf clothes in a Rolls-Royce parked in front of the building.

In 1926 Hagen had won a similar 72-hole challenge match against top British amateur Abe Mitchell, and the only thing Hagen did wrong was turn up late on the tee. This time, he promised the British public, it would be different.

And it was.

Very, very different.

Unlike Hagen, Compston had yet to win a major title, though he had finished second in the 1925 British Open. He practised hard for this match, however, and prepared meticulously to beat Hagen over 72 holes.

Hagen, meanwhile, was ill-prepared. He had been working on a Hollywood film for two months, and hadn't played any golf during that time. He had a rough journey by train from California to New York, then spent two days getting a new passport because he had left his old one in a Hollywood hotel by mistake. He asked for a short postponement of the match with Compston, but his request was turned down. Hagen's only practice was hitting balls off the *Aquitania* into the Atlantic on the journey across.

The *Aquitania* docked at Southampton a day before the big match. Hagen practised a little at Moor Park that afternoon, but would have liked longer. The next day, up at 6 o'clock, he was on the tee at 9.00, aware of the unfavourable publicity he had received when arriving late to play Mitchell.

'That first round was an amazing one for me,' said Hagen in his autobiography. 'I found myself swamped by a flood of Compston's superb shots. He started by winning four holes of the first six; we halved two.'

Compston, regularly outdriving Hagen by 20 yards or so, went into a five-hole lead at the ninth, before sinking a 10-yard putt at the tenth to go six up. Compston was growing more and more confident, the British public were loving it, and Hagen was wondering what had hit him. At the thirteenth Hagen won his first hole – a five to Compston's six. By the end of the morning round, Compston was four up.

At least 'The Haig' had seen the course now. Surely the second round would be easier for him? It looked possible when Hagen held Compston for the first five holes. Then Compston produced another flood of superb shots to win 10 of the next 13 holes. 'He got greedier as the round progressed,' was the autobiographical comment of Hagen, who was suffering from a blistered hand in the later stages of the afternoon round.

Compston, with rounds of 67 and 66, ended the day 14 ahead, with only 36 to play.

The next morning Hagen trailed by 17 holes at the turn. By the eighteenth green Compston had extended his lead to 18, and Hagen faced a 20-foot putt to keep the match alive. He putted successfully, and at least ensured some afternoon play.

The first hole of the afternoon round, the fifty-fifth of the match, was halved. Compston won the match 18 and 17. It was a record winning margin for professional golf.

'When you are laid out good and flat, you must not squawk,' Hagen told the British press. He responded in the best way possible, going on to Sandwich to win the British Open for the third time. Hagen finished with 292, with Archie Compston in third place, three strokes behind.

AEROPLANE GOLF

LONG ISLAND, MAY 1928

The first game of aerial golf probably took place on and over Long Island's Old Westbury Golf Club. All it needed was four men, two aeroplanes, two cargoes of golf balls and a nine-hole golf course.

It was a curious foursome. William Hammond (on the ground) and M.M. Merrill (in the air) played against William Winston (with clubs) and Arthur Caperton (pilot). The pilot dropped the ball as close to the hole as he could, and the golfer did his best to hole out.

Merrill and Caperton took off from Curtiss Field in two Curtiss planes. They flew across Long Island and attempted to drop balls accurately from very close to the ground.

Ladies and gentlemen, your pilot today is Captain Merrill and he will be flying at around 50 feet, dropping golf balls on Old Westbury Golf Course and we should all be in the clubhouse by lunchtime.

Merrill hit all nine greens with his new variety of 'air shots'. Caperton, however, dropped three in the rough. That was the difference. Hammond and Merrill won by three holes, and a cup was presented to them by Vincent X. McGuire, President of Old Westbury Golf Club.

Little more than a month later, the format was adapted slightly for an aerial golf game at Dunwoodie Golf Course, Yonkers. This time there were two men in each plane and two on each team on the ground. The winning foursome were Representative Fiorella La Guardia and Lieutenant J. P. Maloney (ground) and Captain Elliott White Springs and Cap-

84

tain Bobson (air). They won by one hole against Lieutenant John Dwight Sullivan and Lieutenant D. J. Houlihan (below) and Lieutenant Lester Maitland and Captain Al Sherman (above).

A report of this match suggests that the aviators were becoming even more daring, sometimes flying as close as 10 feet to the ground. Presumably this was safer with two people in the plane, one to fly the plane and the other to concentrate on dropping the golf balls.

Eighteen months later, aerial golf reached England with different rules. It was turned into a direct contest between golfer and aviator. A. J. Young, a professional at Sonning in Berkshire, played a normal round of golf, his 69 being a useful score. The task for his opponent, Captain G. A. R. Pennington, was to fly over the course and drop a ball on each of the 18 greens, the number of balls dropped to count as his 'strokes'. Captain Pennington flew his Moth for 40 minutes and completed the course in 29 strokes, for a very comfortable victory. The balls were wrapped in white cloth to deaden their bounce. Most of the greens were hit in one shot, but Captain Pennington flew over the seventh four times before being successful.

It gave a whole new meaning to the idea of a free drop.

Golf courses have always been symbolic for aviators, perhaps because they resemble aerodromes more closely than other sporting arenas. As early as 1912, a plane made its first scheduled landing on a British golf course, while Littlestone Golf Club historians have documented one odd incident: 'A strange experience befell Dick Ayres, who had to dodge a light aircraft preparing to land on the eighth fairway. The pilot asked to be shown the right direction for Lydd Airport, taxied away to the correct position and took off.'

But not all such stories have a happy landing (see page 154).

PLAYING TO THEIR OWN RULES

HOYLAKE, MARCH 1930

The forty-seventh golf match between Oxford University and Cambridge University, played at Hoylake after several days of heavy rain, created a furore when the two captains made up their own rules about water-filled bunkers.

Victor Longstaffe, of St John's Wood, London, was outraged enough to write to *The Times*:

> Sir – If these young golfers from Oxford and Cambridge cannot play to the rules of golf, the sooner they learn to do so or give up the game the better.

The Oxford University captain was Bob Baugh, one of three Americans in the team. Cambridge, captained by Eric Prain, were the underdogs, even though they had not lost a Varsity golf match since 1925. The 1930 format was five 36-hole foursomes on the first day, and 10 36-hole singles on the second. There was a lot of confusion.

Problems came from a rule, mutually agreed by Baugh and Prain, that players may pick and drop when trapped in some of the waterlogged bunkers. Spectators and journalists found it difficult to understand the matches, and one reporter said it was 'a travesty of the R and A game'.

As far as could be judged by observers appraising the various definitions of the new laws, some of the waterlogged bunkers were treated as out of bounds, some as casual water whereby players could pick and drop without penalty, while others were playing under rules of golf whereby players picked and dropped in or out with the penalty of one shot. The top foursomes match became 'a joke'. Cambridge were frequently in bunkers and seemed to get the worst of the rules. Prain and Longhurst – that's Henry Longhurst of Charterhouse and Clare – were five down after six holes. Only the two captains seemed to know why the sixth hole had gone to Baugh and Sweeny; both sides had been in a waterlogged bunker but whereas Oxford must have picked up without penalty, Cambridge had to play out, taking two strokes to do so. The players were so often in bunkers that one correspondent reckoned their figures would have passed 50 for the first nine holes had they played normal golf rules. As *The Times* neatly put it, 'Hoylake, with a strong, cold, south-west wind blowing, is a course over which it is much easier to argue than to play.' The writer had to be Bernard Darwin.

Prain and Longhurst eventually went down ten and eight after trailing by eight holes on the morning round. Oxford won the foursomes four to one.

In spite of strong criticism, the two captains continued with their special rules the following day, when bunkers still contained pools of water even though the sun was out, the sky was blue and the wind had dropped. The top match – Prain against Baugh – attracted interest when holes were exchanged early on, even if the second hole, won by Prain, followed a shot into a watery bunker that he treated as out of bounds 'under the singular rules governing this contest'. The sixteenth produced a more glaring example of 'university rules', described by the *Oxford Mail* with an unfortunate typographical error: 'Prain was bunkered, but played a fine shot, while Baugh in the waterlogged hazard 80 yards from the green had a "free pick", and then his next shot finished only inches from the flog (*sic*) so that he won the hole for the lead.'

A similar problem arose at the seventeenth hole of the second game, frustrating Longhurst, who had courageously fought back from six down (at the eighth) against Marples and was now within range: 'Marples' first shot was out of bounds, his next travelled into a water-filled bunker, from which he had a "free pick", then he holed a niblick to actually get a half in five, which was to say the least ridiculous.'

Oxford won the singles comfortably (eight to two), and the overall score was twelve to three.

MOE AGAINST STOUT

ROYAL ST GEORGE'S, SANDWICH, MAY 1930

The youngest member of the 1930 United States Walker Cup team was 20-year-old Don Moe from Portland, Oregon. One correspondent was not too impressed with him during the practice rounds: 'Moe, who is tall and slim and quite young, was clearly out of practice and was not to be judged by his results. He is a long driver and shows in almost all his shots a great deal of body work, an almost artifically pronounced turn of the left shoulder and a slight "duck", two features which remind one a little of Von Elm. He was hitting his iron shots very high, and will, I imagine, have to modify his methods a little in order to combat a seaside wind.'

Moe, playing with Mackenzie, won his foursome against Sir Ernest Holderness and J. A. Stout, but his real impact on golfing history came in his 36-hole singles match against Stout. Bobby Jones, the American captain, might have been at his peak in his last Walker Cup, but his victory over his British counterpart, Roger Wethered, by nine and eight, was nothing like as dramatic as the match between Moe and Stout.

Stout started in devastating form. Hitting the ball with an open stance, he was one of the longest-ever hitters of a golf ball, and on this occasion he hit the ball vast distances. His five at the first was followed by four successive threes, a four at the Maiden and a tremendous three at the long seventh. He lost the eighth, when his ball was stuck in a hole and he had to pick up, but another three, at the ninth, completed a very successful first nine holes. Yet the British amateur was almost matched by his young American opponent. Moe reached the turn only one down.

Stout continued his amazing round, which was worth a 65 or 66 (one source says 68). Not only was his driving so powerful, but he clawed his way out of trouble well. At the fourteenth, for instance, Stout was in a bed of nettles after two shots. 'From here he played a "dunch" shot that shook Prince's clubhouse,' said one report, 'put the ball some six feet from the pin, holed his putt, and, with Mr Moe taking three more, won the hole.' At lunchtime, after 18 holes, Moe was four down. He had done well to keep it to that.

In the afternoon, Stout began with a three at the first and won the hole. Five up. He also won the second with a three. Six up. And a third successive three won him the third hole too. Seven up with 15 to play.

The destiny of the Walker Cup was settled by now – the United States went on to win by ten matches to Britain's two – but the thrills of the Stout-Moe match were just beginning. Stout, the bulky Briton from Bridlington, soon found himself in a different game.

First, seven up with 15 to play ...

... and then, seven holes later, one up with eight to play.

He had lost five successive holes and six out of seven.

Or, more fairly, Moe had won six out of seven.

Astonishingly, Moe squared the match at the twelfth and went into the lead at the fourteenth. Stout came back and squared it again at the fifteenth by holing a great putt. At the sixteenth, Stout nearly had a two, but, instead, a fine long putt from Moe halved the hole in three. The seventeenth was halved in four. All-square with one hole to play, and 7,000 people lined the fairways in anticipation. Everyone on the course had heard about what had happened. They wanted to be there.

Two good drives left the eighteenth tee. Then Moe chose a number-two iron and put his second shot five feet from the flag. It was an approach shot golfers dream of, on a hole 460 yards long. It was a killing blow. A successful putt gave the young American a birdie three and the match. From seven down, he had won one up, and Stout was left wondering what he had done wrong. In the afternoon, Stout had gone round in 72 and was five down on the round. There was only one explanation. While both had played brilliant golf over the day, Moe had been slightly more brilliant. His afternoon round of 67 came after a moderate start.

Out	544	343	433	—	33
Home	443	445	343	—	34 (67)

No wonder *Golf Illustrated* eulogized ecstatically about the 20-year-old: 'Polite, courteous, unassuming, modest almost to a fault, Mr Don Moe is a credit to his country and a type for whom this great game has always a warm welcome.'

In the changing-room, after the Walker Cup match was over, Stout walked across to Moe and congratulated him. 'Donald,' he said. 'That was not golf, that was a visitation from God.'

ROUND AFTER ROUND AFTER ROUND

DETROIT, MICHIGAN, AUGUST 1930

One night Edward Ferguson was reading his newspaper.

'Have you read about all these different marathons?' he asked his wife.

'Yes, everything from cross-country runs to dancing.'

'And tree-sitting. Don't forget tree-sitting.'

'Oh, yes, tree-sitting. The only thing they've missed is golf.'

'Golf?' mused Mr Ferguson. 'That's an idea.'

Edward Ferguson, of the American School of Theater Arts, was undeterred by his relative lack of golfing experience. He would play a golf marathon – 24 hours' continuous golf.

In fact, he played for far longer than 24 hours. He played for a week. He claimed to have walked over 327 miles while taking 3,999 strokes for 828 holes.

The venue was a nine-hole golf course at Ridgemont in Detroit. He started at 6 pm on 25 August, planning to rest for 10 minutes between each nine-hole round. But, as the week progressed, and news went round, a crowd of people interfered with his idea of rest. Rather than stop to autograph golf balls, pose for pictures or answer telephone calls from the press, he just kept on going. Round and round and round he went, until he had completed 92 nine-hole rounds of golf.

On the first night he was spurred by a hole in one at his eleventh hole, an achievement he failed to repeat in the next 817 holes, perhaps not surprisingly. He managed an eagle, and his overall figures were impressive. On a par 72 course, he claimed his 'ringer score' – his 'best at each hole' or 'eclectic' score – was only 55, but we can assume that he benefited from knowing the course pretty well by the end of the week. He averaged 86 for each 18 holes.

At night he was helped by a barn lantern and pocket flashlight. His caddie held the lantern on the green as he drove toward short holes, or between the tee and green on longer holes. The ball was covered with luminous paint, which made it easier to find in the dark.

Later, Ferguson described his band of followers: 'The "gallery" ran from about 25 in the wee small hours to mobs of I cannot say how many in the daytime and at night. In the early morning hours I would have a lot of golf professionals and newspaper men in the "gallery" – waiting to see me go to sleep, but they were disappointed.'

Ferguson claimed to have suffered no ill-effects from his endurance feat, although his hands were covered with soft calluses and blisters, and at the end he could not control the club. He somehow gained 5 lbs in weight during the week, despite walking at least 327 miles, and probably far more if you allow for hooks and slices.

He had played non-stop for 158 hours.

A HUMAN TEE

ESHER, NOVEMBER 1931

Ena Shaw, a young North London nurse, lay down on her back on part of the teeing-ground. A large rubber tee was strapped to her forehead, and a golf-ball placed on the tee. She lay very still, and George Ashdown studied the distance.

Wood or iron?

He chose the appropriate club and, with a smooth swing, struck the ball sweetly from the tee on Ena Shaw's forehead.

Ashdown did this at the first 13 holes of the 18-hole Thames Ditton and Esher Golf Club in Surrey. Ashdown, a young professional, was competing against Mr C. Mansell, a club player who played off a normal tee. The match received a lot of publicity, and even a slot in the cinema news.

This is how the *Daily Mail* described the event: 'At every hole Miss Shaw, who had a tee-peg fastened to her forehead by an elastic band, reclined on the ground and did not appear to be in the least nervous when Mr Ashdown played the stroke. The professional, who conceded one stroke at each hole to Mr Mansell, hit some splendid shots from his unusual tee and won the match in comfortable style by seven up with five to play.'

The editor of *Golf Illustrated*, however, held strong opinions on what he saw as a publicity stunt: 'All this freak golf is to be deprecated,' he said. 'It serves no purpose and proves nothing. On the other hand, there exists all the time a considerable possibility of its bringing the game of golf into disrepute. Driving a ball from a human head may sound terribly thrilling to the uninitiated, but it should never be forgotten that the gentleman

94

who is executing the shot is all the time gambling with a charge of manslaughter. There is nothing outstandingly difficult in the playing of a shot teed up on another's face, and for that very reason familiarity is apt to breed contempt, and, sooner or later, that familiarity will cause the player to lift his head or to duck his shoulder, and then, as we have said, he will find himself in the dock.'

Other golfers have engaged in stunts like this, most notably Joe Kirkwood who travelled the world with trick-shots, and was a good enough professional to win the Open Championships of Canada, New Zealand and his native Australia. Kirkwood had introduced himself to trick-shots when showing amputee victims of World War I how to play shots with one leg or one arm. Kirkwood could play a shot from the heel of a girl's shoe ... while the girl was still wearing the shoe. She would lie on the floor, face down, then raise her foot to create a 90-degree angle at the knee. The tee went on the long heel, and Kirkwood played the shot from beyond her head.

BEFORE THE THUNDER

MAIDENHEAD, MARCH 1932

Golfers were active on Maidenhead Golf Course. When the rain started, George Chaffe of Cliveden Mead was playing with Herbert Packer, the assistant professional. They decided to stop.

'Shall we head for the clubhouse?'

It was 400 yards away.

'No, there's a hut we can shelter in.'

As the storm broke with great force over the links, Packer and Chaffe ran towards a groundsman's hut, 100 yards from the seventeenth green. On their way, they noticed two men and a caddie sheltering under a large coloured umbrella on the seventeenth green.

Thunder exploded over Maidenhead. Then lightning returned, forked lightning which created a road atlas in the sky and lit up the links for a second. Darkness and gloom swiftly returned, and thunder was instantaneous.

From the shelter of their hut, Packer and Chaffe thought they heard someone shouting for help. They ran toward the seventeenth tee. They ran through heavy rain.

The voice belonged to a man called Edwards. He was found wandering on the course by a groundsman, who helped him into the clubhouse. His face and hands were severely burned, and his clothing damaged down his right side. He was too shocked, too injured, to tell anyone what had happened.

The other members knew something was seriously wrong.

★

Peter Kelly, a Booth Distilleries' director of retirement age, and his teenage caddie, James Miles, were killed instantly on Maidenhead golf course. Packer and Chaffe discovered their bodies, side by side on the ground. Both bodies were severely burned, the clothing badly torn, Kelly still grasping the handle of the umbrella. The head of the umbrella was burned, twisted and torn into ribbons.

Kelly's steel-shafted clubs were undamaged, but the bottom of the caddie's bag was completely torn out. People later theorized that the lightning found its way to earth partly through the medium of steel.

An ambulance arrived as soon as possible, driven through torrential rain over the links. Artificial respiration was applied for a long time, but the 72-year-old man and the 15-year-old boy were both dead.

TEMPER

GRANTHAM, JUNE 1932

Golf is usually thought of as a gentle game, but frustration has been known to result in golfers losing their temper and throwing an erring golf-club into a pond ... or, if that doesn't work, the whole bag of clubs ... or maybe the caddie ... or perhaps even themselves. Golfers have thrown their bag in a pond and then waded in to retrieve car keys before tossing the bag back in.

Perhaps the earliest frustration story is that in Andrew Lang's book *A Monk of Fife*. On 14 October 1428, Norman Leslie was playing golf at St Andrews with Richard 'Dicken' Melville. Although Melville was the bigger and stronger of the two, they were evenly matched at golf and a close contest ensued, accompanied by heavy wagers from two sets of followers. First one player led by a hole, then the other, until the fateful confrontation which sparked Leslie's hasty departure from St Andrews by boat. Melville, left to negotiate a stymie, lost his temper and said Leslie had stymied him on purpose. Leslie denied it, said it was just the luck of the game. Melville called him a liar.

'It was ever my father's counsel that I must take the lie from none,' thought Norman Leslie. 'Therefore, as his steel was out, and I carried none, I made no more ado, and the word of shame had scarcely left his lips when I felled him with the iron club that we use in sand.'

Melville was dead, and Leslie was on the run to France. Later, the 'Monk of Fife' fought for Joan of Arc.

★

Similar incidents have occurred more recently. On Australia's Sydney East Hills golf course in May 1966, John Gordon kicked Allen Goddard's ball off the seventh green, and Goddard retaliated by hitting Gordon over the head with an eight-iron. The wound needed 16 stitches, and 19-year-old Goddard was found guilty of malicious injury. He was bound over for two years and told by the judge to keep his temper.

An incident at the ninth green at Inglewood in October 1977 provoked a reaction from Jim Brown, the former professional American football player turned actor. Brown and Frank Snow argued about the way Snow had placed his ball on the green. Brown punched Snow and tried to choke him. He was found guilty of misdemeanour battery after a two-day trial.

In April 1982, a Sunday afternoon pitch-and-putt game at Folkestone's East Cliffe course was disturbed by an unsavoury incident. Barry Block, a 44-year-old Ashford man, had an argument with a group of five men about priority at the second tee. One of the men attacked him with a putter, and Block was left with a fractured skull.

Another incident occurred when a man threw his five-iron into the woods in disgust with its behaviour. The club somehow found a way through the trees and hit a man on the next fairway in the face. The injured man sued for a vast amount of money after he came out of hospital.

One incident at Grantham is of a different kind. It is a story of two caddies during an economic depression.

At the time, an unemployed labourer called Richard Smith was one of many youths in Grantham, Lincolnshire, who regularly walked to Belton Park to earn a little money from caddying at the golf course. One Sunday afternoon, 21-year-old Smith was waiting at the rear of the clubhouse with a dozen other caddies. They argued about the way one of the players held his clubs. Words were exchanged between Smith and another boy, 23-year-old Edward Herrick.

Smith said something to Herrick.

The two boys swore at each other.

Herrick, angry, threw his right fist and hit Smith at the side of the neck below the left ear. Smith went down on his knees, fell over on his side, and then got up. He started to walk, but fell down again. He rolled on to his back, changed colour, began to foam at the mouth and died.

A few days later Herrick was arrested on a manslaughter charge.

NINE DOWN WITH THIRTEEN TO PLAY

ST PAUL, MINNESOTA, AUGUST 1932

Al Watrous was so far ahead of Bobby Cruickshank in their first-round US PGA match that he felt sorry for his rival and conceded a six-foot, downhill putt for a half at the twenty-second hole. Had Cruickshank missed the putt, which was more than likely, he would have gone 10 down to Watrous with only 14 holes of their 36-hole match to play. Instead it set up an incredible finish.

Somehow the gesture sparked Cruickshank's fighting spirit and ignited his pride. The tiny Scot was by then in his late 30s, a veteran of World War I who had emigrated to America to play professionally. He had not won a major tournament, but had twice finished second in the US Open, losing a play-off to Bobby Jones in 1923 and finishing second to Gene Sarazen nine years later.

Watrous, in his mid-30s, had won the Canadian Open in 1922, and had finished runner-up in the 1926 British Open, losing only to a miraculous shot by Bobby Jones. He could be forgiven for thinking he was a cert for the second round of the US PGA in 1932. Nine up with thirteen holes to play.

Bobby Cruickshank won nine holes of the next eleven, forcing Watrous to hole long putts to escape with his two halves. They went to the last all-square and halved it. The match went to 'sudden-death'.

There were some odd results all round that day. The margin of victory was either easy (like nine and eight) or eked out in overtime holes. Of the 16 first-round matches, only one was won one-up over 36 holes, and none finished two-up, two and one, or even three and one. The margins were more like nine and eight, eight and seven (two matches), seven and six (two matches) and six and five (two matches). Among the 'orgy of overtime matches', as one newspaper called it, was Johnny Golden's shock defeat of Walter Hagen at the forty-third hole, two that went to the thirty-seventh, a 38-hole win for Vincent Eldred over Paul Runyan, and, of course, the amazing Cruick-shank-Watrous match.

Cruickshank and Watrous halved the thirty-seventh ... and the thirty-eighth ... and the thirty-ninth ... and the fortieth.

Watrous must have wondered why he couldn't have halved four of the last 12 holes of the 36-hole match.

At the forty-first, Watrous was nicely on the green in two. Then Cruickshank's recovery shot from the rough put his ball within five feet of the pin. Watrous's first putt left him three feet from the hole. No chance of Cruickshank returning the favour and conceding this one at this stage of the match. And, indeed, Watrous missed it.

There must be a lesson in there somewhere.

The next day a tired Cruickshank beat Vincent Eldred three and one in a second-round match that had eight stymies. In the quarter-final, however, Cruickshank was below his best, going down eight and seven to Frank Walsh.

The tournament was won by Olin Dutra, who beat Walsh four and three for his first major tournament victory.

SHUTE'S STRANGE SUMMER

SOUTHPORT AND ST ANDREWS, JULY 1933

There was a series of strange incidents in the summer of 1933, beginning with a couple at the British Amateur Championship at Hoylake. One involved Cyril Tolley, who had to play his ball from somewhere hidden under a lady's mackintosh raincoat which had been left lying on the ground. And at the twelfth hole a woman was emptying water and sand from her shoe when a ball landed in the shoe. Not knowing what to do, she waited until the players arrived, occasionally hopping on one foot. The players 'decided that equity would be served by the woman dropping the ball and the owner playing it where it fell. This was done.'

Golf interest moved on to the Ryder Cup at Southport, where the strange matches included a 36-hole singles between Olin Dutra (United States) and Abe Mitchell (Great Britain and Ireland). Dutra was three up after 10 holes, but somehow contrived to lose the match by nine and eight. The 1933 Ryder Cup, however, is best remembered for its ending – one of golf's most dramatic moments.

The last match was between Syd Easterbrook (Great Britain and Ireland) and Densmore 'Denny' Shute (United States). The overall score was five matches all, and one halved, and the United States would retain the Ryder Cup if the Easterbrook-Shute match was halved. The two protagonists did not know this. All they knew was that their match was all-square going to the last hole.

Syd Easterbrook, a black-haired sturdy man from Devon,

was first to the eighteenth tee. He hooked his shot into a left-hand bunker, and the match looked over. Next to the tee was Denny Shute, the 28-year-old from Pennsylvania whose father had been born in England at Westward Ho!. Amazingly, Shute put his shot into a bunker too.

Shute, playing first, courageously aimed for the green with his second shot, but found another bunker. Both players reached the green in three and were left with putts of five or six yards. Some 25,000 spectators scampered for a sight of the climax. Walter Hagen, the American captain, was watching from the clubhouse with the Prince of Wales. Hagen considered leaving the clubhouse to explain the match position to Denny Shute, but courtesy prevailed and he continued to watch with Prince Edward.

Easterbrook putted first and missed. The match, and the Ryder Cup, was left in Shute's hands. If he made the putt in one, the United States won the match and the Cup. Two putts would halve the match and enable the United States to retain the Ryder Cup. Three putts would return the trophy to Britain.

The Americans probably wouldn't have traded anyone for Shute, who was a tough match player and one of the most reliable with a decisive putt. Shute went for the hole rather than lay it up, and the ball hurried across the slippery green and went five or six feet past. 'Never has golf produced a more dramatic moment than that witnessed at the last hole in the last match in the Ryder Cup contest at Southport,' wrote the *Illustrated Sporting and Dramatic News*, 'or a more tense moment than that experienced when Densmore Shute was attempting to hole a putt of five feet to save the United States from defeat.'

Quiet descended. Shute tapped the ball with his putter.

'Good heavens,' shrieked one American voice. 'He's missed it.'

The frame froze for a moment as spectators tried to fathom the consequences. Shute had a six, Easterbrook, after tapping the ball in from less than a yard, a five. Easterbrook had won by one hole, and Great Britain and Ireland had won back the

Ryder Cup. It would be another 58 years before sport's patient quest for historical justice would inflict a similar miss on Bernhard Langer.

Two weeks after his tense missed putt, Denny Shute tied a strange British Open with Craig Wood. It was strange for Easterbrook's seven at the fatal fourteenth in the final round, when he needed only 23 from five holes to win. It was strange for the sight of Leo Diegel, elbows out, forearms parallel to the ground in his idiosyncratic putting style, playing 'an air shot' when a successful short putt on the eighteenth would have given him a place in the play-off too. It was strange for Craig Wood's drive of 430 yards into a bunker at the fifth. It was strange for an incident where a steward erroneously suggested that Gene Sarazen had taken seven at a crucial hole, mistakenly counting a shot when Sarazen was merely brandishing his club. And it was strange for Shute's amazingly consistent scoring over four rounds – 73, 73, 73, 73.

Shute won the two-round play-off with a score of 149 against Wood's 154, and perhaps the strangest thing that summer was that he three-putted at the final hole of the Ryder Cup match.

THE FIRST HOLE-IN-ONE
COMPETITION

LONG ISLAND, NEW YORK, AUGUST 1933

The first World-Telegram hole-in-one competition took place at the 148-yard third hole at the Salisbury Club's number-two course in Garden City. Its opening was unbelievable, almost stage-managed.

There are many assessments of the chances of a hole in one, and the only certainty is that the odds must vary on players' ability, their familiarity with a hole and the weather conditions. It is possible, of course, to assess the odds empirically, by dividing the number of 'aces' by the number of holes played – by player, by country, by course, whatever – but the value of this seems limited when we consider the evidence from the first World-Telegram competition.

The 340 competitors were invited on the basis of having previously recorded 'an ace'. Each competitor was allowed five shots at the target hole and the nearest to the pin would win a ring and a set of golf clubs. On the basis of one newspaper's assessment of the odds (20,000 to one), it seemed prudent to bet *against* a hole in one during the 1,700 shots of the competition itself.

First man on the tee was 53-year-old Jack Hagen, a Salisbury club instructor who was playing on his home course. In his long playing career, Hagen had achieved two aces. The first was at Bernardsville, New Jersey, in 1908, the next at the fifth hole of Salisbury's number-four course in 1930. He wasn't due another for a few years yet.

Hagen took a spade-mashie in his hand and prepared to play his five shots. The first landed on the green. Not bad. The second was also on the green. Good stuff. The third flew in a high arc and missed the green in unbelievable fashion. The ball dropped straight into the cup.

Hagen was stunned. Congratulations rained on him.

'Well,' he said. 'I won't shoot any more. I'll stand on that.'

He might not have been in any condition to play another shot.

The rest of his day was spent receiving congratulations and explaining how he did it. Reporters pumped him for information, photographers headed for the course, and one of Hagen's assistants hung up his spade-mashie with a pink ribbon in the professional's shop.

Hagen's three shots certainly started the tournament in sensational fashion. It was a tough target for the other 339 competitors, who, over the next two days, arrived at regular intervals for their five attempts. The last player on the first day, Harvey Hopkins, put one two feet from the pin, and the next day 46-year-old Charles Newman earned second place with a shot one foot from the pin.

A breakdown of the 1,698 shots played in the tournament shows that 743 landed on the green but only 61 were within a ten-foot radius of the pin, and only nine within four feet. More important for the organizers, Hagen's wonder shot ensured the competition a regular place in a hole-in-one golfer's diary.

In 1938 Jack Hagen won the World-Telegram competition again, only this time his best shot landed five inches from the pin. In the first six years, however, there were two further holes in one, which seems remarkable, even taking into account an expansion of entries (742 in 1938) and the choice of three short holes on different courses.

'THE WOMAN WHO PLAYED IN TROUSERS'

WESTWARD HO!, OCTOBER 1933

'Something of a sensation was occasioned on the course on Tuesday,' documented the *Bideford and North Devon Weekly Gazette*, 'when Miss G. D. Miniprio played wearing black trousers, black knitted pullover, a red leather jacket, and black woollen hat.'

Spectators at the Ladies' Close Championship were agog, reporters unusually active, and the chair of the Ladies' Golf Union reacted with indignation. 'I much regret there should be this departure from the usual golfing costume at the Championship,' she said.

Everyone was surprised when Gloria Miniprio arrived on the first tee at Westward Ho! for her match with Nancy Halstead. Reporters had gathered in numbers, expecting a mild sensation of a different kind, for it had been rumoured that Miss Miniprio, a four-handicap player from Littlestone, would play with only one club. Indeed she did. Her one club was a cleek. Her caddie carried the cleek, a spare cleek, a bag of balls, and held her red jacket when she played her shots. The caddie looked embarrassed at carrying so little.

It was a second-round match, as Miss Miniprio had had a first-round bye. Extra suspense was created with her late arrival on the tee. At five minutes past midday reporters were ready to chart her progress with one club, poised to nickname her 'One-club Gloria'. Then the gallery gasped at her appearance. Her trousers were beautifully tailored and fitted tightly, hugging her lower body. Two straps stretched under the insteps of her suede shoes to keep the trousers in place. She was described in one account as wearing 'the clothes of a cat-burglar in Paris'.

She wore trousers not for publicity, but because they were warm and comfortable for playing golf: far more sensible than voluminous skirts and petticoats which fluttered in the wind; and far more practical than weird blouses and pill-box hats that restricted swings.

'The sensation' of One-Club Gloria's dress has to be understood in the context of newspaper reporting of the time. Henry Longhurst pinpointed this in an account of the incident: 'This is a time when, if an errand boy falls from his bicycle, it is labelled by our lords and masters in Fleet Street as a "sensation" or "bombshell", but neither of these hackneyed and hard-worked words could do adequate justice to the pandemonium that was caused on the first day by the appearance of Miss Gloria Miniprio, who will go down in posterity with an immortality that is denied to kings and bishops, generals and statesmen, as "the lady who played in trousers".'

As for her play with one club, she hit the ball straight, her technique was sound, but she couldn't loft the ball except in a full shot and she certainly couldn't chip. She lost five and three to Nancy Halstead, a strong competitor. After the match she slipped away quietly, not one to relish the publicity caused by her dress. No one really knew much about her. It was said she had studied yoga in India, or was a talented conjuror, but those were only rumours.

Longhurst wrote appreciatively of the incident and hoped she would be at the next Ladies' Close Championship, 'for it is such little excitements as this that make the life of the golfing journalist worth while'.

Longhurst had his wish, but Gloria Miniprio, still using only one club, was beaten comfortably by Mary Johnson at Skegness. Miss Johnson was a much better player, disappointing those onlookers who were interested in how a one-club player would fare against a bag-of-clubs golfer of equal ability.

The *Daily Mail* covered Gloria Miniprio's appearance at

Skegness: 'A young woman golfer caused a sensation at Seacroft, Skegness, today when she went round in tight-fitting, beautifully creased dark blue trousers, strapped under suede shoes to match; a white pullover; a close-fitting blue hat; and white gloves.'

She was known as Dorothy Miniprio to her family, and was a member at Littlestone from 1931 to 1939. Her last appearance in the Ladies' Close Championship was in 1939, when she lost seven and five to Peggy Edwards. Soon afterwards, she married, became Gloria Godlewski and emigrated to Canada.

A ONE-CLUB MATCH

SUNNINGDALE AND WORPLESDON, FEBRUARY 1935

It was a match between two two-handicap players. They played 18 holes at Sunningdale and 18 at Worplesdon. One player used only a two-iron, the other a three-iron. One eye-witness was J. S. F. Morrison, who wrote his account in his regular golf column in the *Bystander*.

At Sunningdale the golfers went round in an approximate 77, only one stroke more than the standard scratch score. 'There were many interesting and valuable lessons to be learnt from this match,' wrote Morrison. 'First of all, the players took only one hour 35 minutes to play round the Old Course at Sunningdale, without hurrying in the slightest degree, and in spite of the fact that they had to look for lost balls on two occasions, and that the match was very evenly contested. The two-iron finished one hole up.'

One hour 35 minutes for a round of golf? Without hurrying?

Hmmm.

One-club players obviously save time in a number of ways. They have no need to ponder which club to use. They don't have to wait for caddies to catch them up or come over with a bag. And they don't have to go through the process of taking clubs from a bag. There is a pitch-and-putt freedom that comes with one-club play, although there needs to be some understanding about who does other duties of the missing caddie, like taking the pin out of the hole.

The other major advantage, according to Morrison, was that players become much more familiar with their sole club, and their play with that iron improves immensely. 'Once the players had got the feel of their club, every shot was a good or nearly good shot,' wrote Morrison. 'The chip shots were played extraordinary well, better than either player usually plays them with a full bag at his disposal.'

Morrison was in no doubt that players carried too many clubs, although he thought that restricting them to only one iron was maybe too much.

Is it best as a learning tool, or would it work at higher levels?

In recent years, a regular United States one-club tournament has shown that players can score consistently in the 70s. Before organizing your own club competition, however, here's a reminder of a thorny ethical issue that arose in 1907. At the eighth hole of a nine-hole one-club competition, a competitor accidentally broke his club in a bunker. He finished his round by borrowing his partner's club, and tied for first place. Should he have been disqualified for using a second club? That particular golf club had no rule for such a contingency, but contemporary rules would suggest that a player can replace a broken club, as long as it isn't one borrowed from another player on the course.

GENE SARAZEN'S FAMOUS ALBATROSS

AUGUSTA, GEORGIA, APRIL 1935

Craig Wood's total of 282 looked good enough to win the 1935 US Masters by a few strokes ... until one of golf's most spectacular single blows sent a gasp of surprise echoing through the countryside.

A messenger ran across the course to spread the news to the eighteenth green, where Wood was receiving congratulations from reporters and supporters.

'Mistuh Sarazen had a two at fifteen,' said the messenger.

They all knew it couldn't be true. The fifteenth hole was a 465-yard par five. Even Sarazen could not make an albatross there.

'A two!' one sportswriter snapped at the messenger. 'Go back out there and get the score right.'

The boy went back to the fifteenth hole.

Then he returned to the eighteenth.

'Yes, Sir. Mistuh Sarazen had a two at fifteen.'

Gene Sarazen had been the pre-tournament favourite, especially after playing four practice rounds in 271 (17 under par). Bobby Jones, in his second career, had also created pre-tournament interest, but was to finish only twenty-fourth, despite going out in 33 in his second round.

After three rounds, Sarazen was three strokes behind leader Craig Wood, who seemed to face a stronger challenge from Olin Dutra. Sarazen was known for spectacular finishes, and people were looking for signs in his first three rounds. Some people marvelled at what Sarazen's first-round score of 68 might have been had he not missed four putts of less than six feet. Others were concerned about his second-round 71, when 'Sarazen failed to score as well as yesterday because his short game lacked consistent control'.

In the final round, Dutra blew up with 42 strokes on the first nine, and Henry Picard, the early pacesetter with 67 and 68, dropped right out of it. The way was clear for Craig Wood, until Sarazen attacked the fifteenth hole. The tournament was in only its second year, and now Gene Sarazen made sure the public knew about it.

On that famous hole, then 465 yards, Sarazen stood 220 yards from the pin and contemplated his second shot. He decided to gamble on clearing the pond which guarded the green, and took out his 'spoon', a number-four wood, for a risky long shot. He knew he was two strokes behind Wood's score to that point of the course, and Wood had birdied this one.

Sarazen hit his shot and watched the ball head into the mist toward the 40-foot pond that acted like a moat to the green. What happened next is recorded by Tom Flaherty in *The Masters*: 'It dropped on the apron, popped up twice on the turf, and rolled steadily toward the cup as though homing on a magnet. A thousand voices in the gallery screamed as the ball disappeared into the cup for a double eagle two.'

If reporters found it scarcely credible, how did Craig Wood react? It was certainly a shock to his nerves. This new tournament – the US Masters was still known as the Augusta National Invitation Tournament – was tantalizing him. The first year Wood had been runner-up to Horton Smith by one stroke.

After his amazing two at the fifteenth, Gene Sarazen was one of the calmest people on the course. He didn't get lost in the euphoria of the moment. He wasn't swept away with the excitement that cascaded through the gallery. And he didn't decide to stop and celebrate his first-ever albatross. Instead he was busy calculating what it meant to the tournament's outcome.

The answer was three pars for a play-off.

Sarazen made his three pars. On the Monday he returned to the course for a 36-hole play-off with Craig Wood. Wood twice lost one-stroke leads early on, but the play-off was all-square after the first nine. The outcome was virtually sealed over the next four holes, Sarazen accumulating a four-stroke lead. Playing remarkably consistent golf – 24 successive pars from the eleventh to the thirty-fourth – Sarazen went on to win by five strokes. (Craig Wood finally won the US Masters in 1941.) Naturally Sarazen didn't attempt any risky shots at the fifteenth hole in the play-off, making his par five on both occasions.

His famous albatross – known as a double-eagle or golden eagle in the United States – is commemorated by a plaque at Augusta's fifteenth hole. Sarazen reckoned that only about 50 people saw the famous shot, but he also reckoned that it seemed as if at least 20,000 told him later that they had.

SUDDEN DEATH AT THE
INTERNATIONAL

TURNBERRY, JUNE 1937

Bridget Newell was 26 years old, and one of England's best golfers. The previous week she had played for Great Britain against France at Pulborough, and now she was in the England team for the four-way international tournament at Turnberry. The international series would take place over two days – Friday and Saturday – and the following week would see the British Ladies' Championship at the same venue.

Miss Newell had won the Derbyshire County Championship in 1935 and was Midland Ladies Champion the next year. In 1936, she lost five and three to Pam Barton in the final of the British Ladies' Championship. She was one of the favourites for the 1937 event, even though Pam Barton, then only 20, had also added the American title in the previous year.

Bridget Newell was a distinguished scholar who was called to the Bar when 21. She became the youngest magistrate in England and often presided on the same Matlock magistrates' bench as her father, a retired County Court judge for the Derby circuit.

On the Thursday morning she practised at Turnberry, but she had been suffering from tonsillitis for a few days. After lunch she withdrew from the England international team and retired to her hotel bedroom.

The next day the international tournament started without her. Doris Park, daughter of a former British Open Champion, surprisingly beat Pam Barton five and four, but England

116

beat Scotland six-three. Wales were trounced by both Scotland (nine-nil) and Ireland (eight-one), and England beat Ireland seven-two. England, with only Wales to beat, looked certain of victory the following day.

Bridget Newell died that evening. They said it was diphtheria.

The internationals were abandoned out of respect for her death, and a dozen players withdrew from the forthcoming British Ladies' Championship. They included Gwen Cradock-Hartopp, Bridget Newell's close friend, frequent playing partner and fellow member at Derby's Cavendish club. When the Ladies' Championship tournament started, Mrs J.B. Watson received a bye to the second round. She had been drawn against Bridget Newell, before her opponent's sudden death.

Six years later, Pam Barton, Bridget Newell's opponent in the 1936 British Ladies' Championship Final, was killed when a light aircraft crashed on take-off in Kent. She was a Flight-Officer in the Women's Auxiliary Air Force (WAAF) at the time, and, like Bridget Newell, was 26 years old when she died.

MYSTERIOUS MONTAGUE – 'THE BEST GOLFER IN THE WORLD'

HOLLYWOOD, CALIFORNIA, JUNE 1937

They said he could outdrive Bobby Jones by 50 yards and play an approach shot to within 10 feet of the pin from anywhere up to 200 yards. He had lowered the Palm Springs course record on four successive days, and had averaged 68 over a two-year period at Hollywood's par-72 Lakeside course. He was the only man to have ever driven the 550-yard eighteenth at Lakeside in two. And what about the time he won a bet by driving the 245-yard ninth hole with a putter?

George Von Elm said John Montague was 'the best golfer in the world', and George Von Elm was a good judge – he had won the US Amateur and US Open Championships. Grantland Rice wrote that the winner of the 1936 US Amateur Championship would not be 'amateur champion' because Montague had not entered, and Grantland Rice was another good judge – one of the best sportswriters in the business.

So why didn't John Montague enter tournaments?

What made him so secretive?

Why did he refuse to be photographed?

Was it true that he had once grabbed a photographer's camera and destroyed the film before offering $100 (£20) to take care of the damage?

On the West Coast John Montague was presumed to be a remittance-man, relying on periodic cheques sent by a rich Eastern family. His friends included famous entertainers like Oliver Hardy, Guy Kibbee and Bing Crosby, men who

118

marvelled at Montague's golfing ability, enjoyed his company and offered him guest rooms.

It was a strange match against Bing Crosby that finally brought Montague into the limelight and led to the revelation of his astonishing story. Montague wagered $5 (£1) a hole that he could beat Crosby using only a baseball bat, a shovel and a rake. The match started from the tenth tee, where Montague hit the ball 300 yards with the baseball bat, but straight into a bunker to the left of the green. Crosby's second shot, a six-iron, put his ball about 30 feet from the hole. He thought they would probably halve the hole in four. Then Montague used his shovel to play an amazing sand-shot from the bunker, and his ball was nearer the pin than Crosby's. Crosby putted for a birdie – he was about a three handicap at the time but Montague usually gave him five or six shots – but sent the ball three feet past.

'That's good, pal,' said Montague, knocking Crosby's ball away.

Then Montague used his rake to sink his ball and win the hole with a birdie three. One report says Montague used the rake like a billiard-cue, another says he held it upside-down and hit the ball with the handle.

Bing Crosby walked to the clubhouse conceding defeat. He had seen Montague do everything now.

On 11 June 1937, in New York State, two police officers studied a newspaper account of John Montague's freak match with Bing Crosby. For seven years they had been searching for Laverne Moore, an exceptional golfer and hard-hitting baseball player, to answer criminal charges.

Sheriff Percy Egglefield of Essex County sent a photograph and samples of Laverne Moore's fingerprints and handwriting to West Coast police. A few days later the link was confirmed.

Sheriff Egglefield and two husky State troopers set off for Los Angeles. When they met Laverne Moore (alias John Montague), the mystery golfer was friendly enough. He shook Egglefield's hand ... so hard that the Sheriff had some insight into why 'Hollywood's golfing genius' could drive a golf ball so far.

The Governor's office in Sacramento received 66 appeals to refuse extradition, most of them from screen actors and writers. Guy Kibbee, a bald-headed character comedian, then in his late 50s, wrote as follows: 'If my very good friend, John Montague, went astray as a mere youth, it is my opinion he has done everything in his power during the time I have known him to rise above the occasion, and has convinced me he has done a great deal to live down the little incident which happened to him in the East as a boy.'

On 20 August the 'wizard of the golf links' waived extradition and agreed to leave voluntarily for New York State to face charges.

Montague offered his hand once more to Sheriff Egglefield.

'Let's waive that too,' Egglefield replied, genially refusing to shake hands. He remembered the golfer's iron grip.

It was a five-day train trip across the United States, and Montague entertained his captors. In Chicago, crowds greeted the golfer as a hero. They were drawn to this mysterious star athlete, a handsome, smiling man of 31 who walked, acted and dressed like a film star. He was chubby-faced and cheerful, about five feet nine inches and 15 stones, a muscular, broad-shouldered man who seemed to make friends easily.

Montague was taken to Elizabethtown, New York, a small town of fewer than a thousand people. He admitted that his real name was Laverne Moore, but did not admit the charges. His new lawyer, whose fees were paid by Hollywood stars, sought bail. Montague spent two days in jail while Judge Byron Brewster deliberated whether bail was appropriate. The judge faced a difficult decision. On the West Coast Montague was respected as a gentleman, and his appearance at a trial seemed guaranteed. On the East Coast he faced a serious crime and could not be treated differently from other men arrested for the same crime. The judge's legacy was something like this:

Early on the morning of 5 August 1930, a gang of four armed robbers raided a roadhouse at Jay, a tiny place 10 miles from

Lake Champlain and less than an hour from the Canadian border. The robbers, masked and armed with a gun, bound and gagged the owner (a Japanese-American called Kin Hana), his wife and their four children. Kin Hana's father-in-law, Matt Cobb, then 67, heard the commotion and intervened. One of the robbers – Laverne Moore, according to the prosecution – used a revolver butt and blackjack to beat the old man senseless. Cobb was left on the bank of the Ausable River with bleeding ears, loose teeth and a badly bruised head. Seven years later, at the age of 74, Matt Cobb was still deaf as a result of the attack.

The four men ran out of the roadhouse with $800 (£165) and separated into two cars. One car, chased by the police, crashed and overturned. The dead body of John Sherry was found beside the wreck. The other occupant of the car, William Martin, alias William Carleton, a gunman who illegally shipped rum from Canada during the prohibition, was found walking dazed by the car. He was arrested and later served almost six years in prison for his crime. Inside the crashed car, police found various items belonging to Laverne Moore – a driving licence, a Gladstone bag, some letters addressed to him, clippings of his exploits with a Buffalo baseball team and a set of 17 golf clubs.

The police put out an alert for a green car with two men inside. One such car was stopped by a State Trooper at Schroon Lake. The men talked their way through, but one of them, Roger Norton, was later arrested. Norton, a distant relative of Kin Hana's wife, turned State's evidence. He served two years.

Certain facts about the life of Laverne Moore were clear. He was born in Syracuse in August 1905 and was a 'tramp caddie' in his youth, working at Glen Falls Country Club. He was a brilliant all-round athlete, a talented golfer and good enough at baseball to sign for the Boston Braves. At the age of 22 he was convicted on a petty larceny charge. Three years later, on the morning of 6 August 1930, he said goodbye to his mother and sisters and went off into the unknown, leaving behind the impression that he was seeking a career as a golfer or baseball-player. It was the day after the roadhouse robbery.

Mystery shrouded the last seven years of Moore's life, the seven years when he had called himself John Montague. The police thought they had some idea. They reckoned he had fled to Florida, drifted into Mexico, and then worked his way out to the Nevada gold fields to try prospecting. He stayed there for two years, made only small finds and then gave up. He had a job with a construction firm and usually referred to himself as a 'mining engineer'. At some point he had made contact with Hollywood. His accomplishments on municipal golf courses won him an invitation to the exclusive Lakeside Country Club, where, according to one report, he became 'a hero to the golf duffers of the motion-picture colony in Hollywood'.

'The Mysterious Montague' now had plenty of nicknames. He was 'the Garbo of Golf' and 'the Paul Bunyan of the links', while Judge Brewster called him 'a modern Jean Valjean'.

Released on bail of $25,000 (£5,140), Montague played golf. At the North Hempstead Golf Club, Port Washington, he went round in 65 with five birdies and 13 pars. He was never in trouble, a staggering performance for someone who had played only five rounds of golf in the previous year.

The trial began on 19 October. The prosecution submitted two automatic pistols and a blackjack as evidence, and Roger Norton told how Moore and Matt Cobb had struggled at the back of the roadhouse, Moore striking Cobb several times with a blackjack. Norton explained how their getaway car was stopped by the State Trooper at Schroon Lake – 'Moore said his name was Lawrence Ryan' – and then he dropped Moore off at a station in Schenectady (where Wright once invented the controversial putter).

Two of the Hana family testified that gang members called for 'Verne' at the scene of the crime, although it was not possible to identify masked men seven years after the event. Matt Cobb was also uncertain about identification, although he said Moore 'looks the same across the eyes'. Questions had to be shouted at Cobb from a foot away, one of the many bizarre scenes that dogged the trial. Another was when a two-minute preliminary hearing was delayed for a half-hour while everyone in court searched for a gavel. And yet another touch of farce concerned the 12-man jury. Closeted in their tavern over the week-end, bored with dominoes and tiddly-winks, the jurors sent out for fiddles·and organized an all-male square dance. In court, autograph hunters added to the farce. They hoped for Bing Crosby and Clark Gable to attend, but had to be content with stars like Pauline Lord and Otto Kruger.

The defence called two witnesses to show that Roger Norton had a reputation for not telling the truth. A parade of Hollywood and Syracuse citizens vouched for Moore's good character. Bing Crosby had known Montague in 'social friendship' for five years and confirmed him to be a gentleman, and Montague's handling of Olly Hardy's money proved to the burly comedian that he was 'absolutely above reproach'. There were depositions from Andy Devine, Richard Arlen, Guy Kibbee and many more.

The defence worked hard to establish an alibi on the fatal night. Moore's mother and his two sisters said he was at home asleep, 300 miles away from the Jay roadhouse. Francis McLaughlin confirmed this by saying he picked up Moore from a driving-range and drove him home to Syracuse just before midnight. William Martin, one of the convicted men, claimed that the fourth man was not 'Verne' but 'Burns', though he couldn't say what 'Burns' looked like. The prosecution did their best to smear the characters of Martin and McLaughlin, both of whom were known to the police.

On the last day Laverne Moore, alias John Montague, took the stand himself. He proved a good witness under direct examination, denying that he was ever at the roadhouse, denying he was ever called 'Verne', affirming that he was home in bed asleep that night, though admitting that at one time he had taken part in bootleg deals with Norton, Sherry and Martin (alias Carleton). Under cross-examination, Moore's personality changed. He was ill-tempered, argumentative, and visibly angry.

The trial ended after eight days, and the jurors considered their verdict for nearly five hours. They had two ballots.

The first vote was seven to five.

The next was ten to two.

They came back in and publicized the vote: Not Guilty.

Spectators cheered, Moore/Montague grinned, and Judge Owen made it clear to the jury that he thought they had made a mistake. 'I am sorry to say that your verdict is not in accord with the one I think you should have rendered,' the judge told the jury. 'But that's up to you, and not to me.'

The following November, John Montague made his public golf debut, at Fresh Meadow Country Club, Flushing, Long Island. Over 2,500 tickets were sold in advance – proceeds to be used for the care of underprivileged children – and it was another strange match. On one side were two of the most famous Babes in the history of American sport – baseball player Babe Ruth and athlete Babe Didrikson, who, later, as Babe Zaharias, became British Ladies' Champion and US Open Women's Champion. Montague was partnered by Mrs Sylva Annenberg.

On the day of the match, thousands of automobiles arrived in time for the 10 o'clock start, and an estimated 12,000 people flooded the course to watch the foursome. The spectators were out of control, thousand upon thousand, the course so overcrowded that the players could hardly play. There was little room for backswings, and lanes of only 10-15 feet through which to place their drives. The golfers took over an hour to play the first three holes. John Montague's drive at the sixth knocked off a spectator's cap and narrowly avoided doing him a serious injury. Montague picked up his ball.

The crowd was so unruly that the match had to be abandoned after nine holes, by when the two Babes were two up. In one of the most unusual public debuts ever, John Montague had shown enough to suggest that he might be able to compete at the highest level.

John Montague never succeeded as a professional golfer.

Some people doubted the veracity of the earlier stories, while others believed he was not suited to courses crowded with spectators. In the *New Yorker*, Robert Lewis Taylor wrote that 'he is better fitted for an easy-going country-club life, in which he can impress a small circle of friends with his special talent for trick shots, than for tournament play'.

John Montague died in Studio City on 29 May 1972, and left a brother and two sisters in Syracuse. His body rested at Utter-McKinley's Valley Mortuary for a week, until it was claimed by Arthur Adams, a Los Angeles photographer and former business associate.

HOW TO WIN WITH THE WRAPPING
STILL ON THE BALL

WIMBLEDON PARK, NOVEMBER 1937

The Colas Products Golfing Society annual 18-hole tournament was held at the Wimbledon Park Golf Club. John Weaver of Worcester Golf and Country Club went very well for the first six holes.

The seventh was a short hole of 140 yards. The carry was over a pond with other hazards nearer the hole. John Weaver put his ball in a ditch three times. Having already taken eight for the hole, he had to drop yet another ball. He thought his chance for the tournament had probably gone, and his mind was elsewhere. He took a new ball out of his bag and dropped it over his shoulder. He turned round, and looked at the ball. The wrapping was still on.

Weaver played his approach shot with the paper covering still sealed on the ball. To his great surprise, he holed out.

He took the wrapping off the ball before the next hole, and his game was back to its best. He went round in 82, an excellent score for a 12-handicap player. In fact, it was the best score of the day, but the officials didn't know what to do about the packaged ball. They presented John Weaver with the Cup, but it was conditional on a later decision. The secretary of the Wimbledon Park Club wrote to the Rules of Golf Committee of the Royal and Ancient Club of St Andrews and asked for a ruling.

The next day, Roland Allen investigated the possible outcomes in an article in the *Evening Standard*. A golf ball had to be *not wider* than 1.62 in and *no heavier* than 1.62 oz. Well, the width of an unwrapped ball was sure to be within the rules, but what about the weight? A leading manufacturer of the day claimed that every ball that left his company would be over 1.61 oz and under 1.62 oz. Otherwise it would be rejected by quality control. According to Allen, who spent time testing the various weights, the paper cover and seal of a wrapped ball almost certainly weighed more than 0.01 oz, assuming it to be a first-class two-shilling ball.

Other students of a ball's weight asked delicate questions. What happens if a ball collects mud on the way round? Does the ball have to be the right weight before every shot?

The Rules of Golf Committee replied the following January. It was clear that if the ball was overweight when it was struck, the player was liable to disqualification, but if the ball was not overweight the player could not be disqualified.

The secretary of the Colas Products Golf Society consulted his committee. Together they decided that John Weaver should retain the Cup. It was argued that there was no evidence concerning the weight of the ball when it was struck, and it would be impossible to find out with any degree of certainty seven weeks after the event.

So John Weaver won a tournament after holing out at the seventh with a ball that was still in its paper cover.

A GALE AT THE BRITISH OPEN

SANDWICH, JULY 1938

There was a lot of weather at Sandwich that week. For the first qualifying round it was mild and stuffy with a little drizzle but no wind. During the second qualifying round it rained 'cats and dogs' for most of the morning, feigned to clear up and then rained again with thunder and lightning.

The weather was still unsettled for the first round of the tournament proper. There were occasional short sharp showers, and the wind was now stiff, but the scores were low. Three Whitcombe brothers were in the top thirteen. A 70 by Ernest Whitcombe of Meyrick Park put him with the six leaders, while Charles Whitcombe (Crews Hill) and Reginald (Parkstone) had rounds of 71 to put them in the following pack.

On the second day, the wind changed direction and blew from the south-east. 'It was a wind that helped rather than hindered,' commented *The Times*, and scores were again reasonable. Clive Tolley had a 68 to total 145, but Jack Busson, Bill Cox and Richard Burton led on 140. Thirty-seven players qualified for the final day, when two rounds would be played, and only eight strokes divided them all. The competition was beautifully poised, and the three Whitcombes all made the cut. Reggie's 142 placed him sixth, while Charles (146) and Ernest (147) were further down the field.

But the weather was only practising for the final day.

Competitors and journalists didn't sleep too well that night.

Curtains billowed, windows rattled, branches creaked and crashed down, and the wind yelled at them as it came in from the coast and wreaked havoc. During the night a huge marquee on the course was ripped to shreds, and competitors were soon wanting to do the same to their scorecards.

It was an astonishing day's golf, a mixture of freak incidents and brilliant play. Only nine golfers broke 80 in the morning and seven in the afternoon, and it is easy to understand why. At the first hole, for instance, the 50-mile-an-hour gale drove across the course from right to left with such strength that players had difficulty walking against it. Putting was exceptionally problematic. Would the golfer retain his balance? Would the wind blow the ball off course? Many putts crept toward the hole, looked like stopping and then suddenly sprinted several feet past. Players sometimes missed a short putt and then failed to hole the long one coming back. Nothing was ever 'dead', but sometimes the wind blew the ball into the hole without a shot being played.

Henry Longhurst later painted an eerie picture of the conditions: 'Steel-shafted clubs were twisted grotesquely into figures-of-eight, assorted haberdashery soared away into space to be salvaged later as far away as Prince's, while frenzied traders battled to pin down the remainder of their wares.'

At the twelfth in the morning, one competitor hit three drives out of bounds in his third round. His 14 at that hole was the third highest score ever recorded for a British Open hole. Pemberton and French both took 91 for that round, and there were numerous double-figure scores for individual holes. Conversely, Alf Padgham drove the 384-yard eleventh hole in the morning and holed a short putt for an eagle two. Needless to say, the eleventh was downwind.

'It was a day on which nobody would dream of playing golf,' wrote the *Daily Mail*'s Fred Pignon, 'but some of the greatest golf I have ever seen was played by the three leaders.'

Reg Whitcombe (217) and James Adams (219) went out together for the final round. In accordance with the custom of the day, they set off first. When Whitcombe four-putted for six on

129

the first hole of the final round, Adams levelled the scores with a four.

The conditions suited big, strong men with short, compact swings, but even powerful golfers like Richard Burton were blown off their feet. Reggie Whitcombe pulled his flat cap down hard over his forehead and got on with the job. The lead switched hands, but the eleventh was a crucial hole. Although 384 yards, it was still downwind, and the two leaders knew it was within range. Astonishingly, Adams drove his shot on to the green and the ball ran on into the rough *beyond* the hole. He three-putted, and Whitcombe's birdie three put him three strokes ahead.

Whitcombe went four strokes up at the fourteenth but that didn't mean much in these conditions. Adams holed a pitch and run for a three at the fifteenth, and got his three at the sixteenth while Whitcombe took five. With two to play the margin was one shot, but Adams was bunkered at the seventeenth and that was it. Whitcombe finished two strokes ahead.

Further down the course came an unexpected challenger. Unexpected, that is, considering Henry Cotton's total after three rounds. The previous year Cotton had just pipped Reg Whitcombe in the final round. This time Cotton needed a 71 to win, and was out in 35. It was still possible when he reached the seventeenth and needed a three-four finish. But the wind finally did for him, and he took six at the seventeenth. It was not so much blowing up, as being blown about.

Reg Whitcombe proved a popular winner. When it was over, Whitcombe said the final day's play was like being on a high sea, and for some time afterwards he was swaying. As J.S.F. Morrison put it in the *Bystander*: 'We certainly do enjoy (if this is the right word) a most extraordinary climate in this country.'

A PLANTATION AT STAKE

CHICAGO, AUGUST 1938

Smitty Ferebee and Fred Tuerk jointly owned a 2,400-acre plantation in Princess Anne County near Norfolk, Virginia. They disagreed about how the land should be managed, but agreed that their dispute should be settled by a strange golf match. If Ferebee could play eight rounds of golf between dawn and dusk in one day, completing each round in no more than 95 strokes, he would win Tuerk's half of the plantation. If he failed, the plantation would revert to Tuerk.

J. Smith Ferebee was confident about the task ahead. A 31-year-old Chicago investment broker, he played golf virtually every afternoon and usually averaged in the mid-80s. Also, he had played 90 holes in a day about a month previously, and the professional at his home course, Olympia Fields, said that he was in excellent shape.

Fred Tuerk was confident too. He didn't think Ferebee had a chance of completing eight rounds. It meant walking more than 29 miles around the same golf course. Far more than 29 miles, if Ferebee couldn't hit the ball straight.

Tuerk had obviously not kept up with all the stories of golfing marathons. Captain George Morris had played 10 rounds in 889 at Walmer and Kingsdown Golf Club, but Bruce Sutherland's record 252 holes in a day seriously affected his health, and Stanley Gard had to retire with heart trouble after 220 holes of an attempt on Sutherland's record. Robert Coy had played 459 holes in 39 hours at Potrero Golf Links before being taken to hospital with badly swollen ankles.

131

All Ferebee proposed was a mere 144 holes. Admittedly, there was the extra tension of staking his share of the plantation - valued at around $10,000 (£2,050) – plus side-bets of $2,500.

The weather favoured Tuerk.

'It looks like rain, Smitty,' we can imagine someone saying when Ferebee arrived at Olympia Fields and briefed his dozen caddies. At 5.05, as dawn broke, he prepared to tee off for his first round.

There were four courses at Olympia Fields, all heavily wooded, all perhaps longer than those tackled by previous marathon golfers. If Ferebee was going to complete eight rounds – two on each course – he would have to play 51,568 yards, an average of 6,446 yards per round. And, of course, he had to complete each round in a score of under 95.

He managed 90 for the first round. It was cause for concern. Then he put together three successive rounds of 82 strokes, and they didn't take him very long. It took only six hours to complete these first 72 holes. One round – the third – had been breezed in one hour 16 minutes. He was halfway towards winning his bet without any real problem.

Then it started to rain.

Smitty Ferebee stopped playing for about 15 minutes. The course was already drenched. He restarted, but the wind blew strong and it rained again before he had completed his fifth round, a terrific downpour that flooded the fairways. Ferebee stopped for more than an hour. He used the time to change his clothes and organize coffee for his caddies. Ferebee himself drank a glass of orange-juice after 36 holes and a small beer after each nine holes thereafter. Following each round an attendant powdered his feet.

Back on the course, he completed the fifth round in 87 strokes. That still left him about seven hours of daylight for the last three rounds. After the next round – another 87 – Fred Tuerk conceded that Ferebee looked like winning the plantation. Tuerk followed Ferebee round the last 36 holes, and sportingly applauded many shots. Some 600 persons were on the course towards the end of his final round. It was now around 8 o'clock, and Ferebee looked pale and drawn, but he couldn't keep a grin from his face. At the sixteenth he took a six. Had he blown up after 142 holes? He had already taken 80 for the first 16 of this final round, and had to do the last two in less than sixteen. But he finished well – four, five – and a round of 89 sealed the bet in his favour. His eight rounds were remarkably consistent – 90, 82, 82, 82, 87, 87, 88 and 89. He was only 119 over par for the day.

It took him 15 hours seven minutes to earn half a plantation and $2,500, and he ate only three sandwiches and a chocolate-bar during that time. He took a shower and felt fine. That night he slept for more than eight hours. He got up, ate a hearty breakfast, did a day's work in his La Salle Street office and then played his usual round of golf in the afternoon.

The publicity from the event stimulated plenty of other 24-hour marathons – 171 holes from Bill Coleman, 196 holes from Carlton Brown, and 231 holes from Jim Caruso, just to mention three.

Smitty Ferebee was not one to be overtaken by events. His next marathon gave Tuerk a chance to win back the plantation and encouraged side-bets of $100,000 (£20,500). Ferebee said he could tackle 144 holes on four successive days, playing four rounds in each of eight different cities spread across the United States. On 25 September he began at Lakeside, Los Angeles, then after four rounds there, flew to the Encanta course in Phoenix, Arizona. A plane had been put at his disposal by Reuben Trane, a Wisconsin sportsman who took to the idea.

And so it continued ... four rounds at the Blue Hills course at Kansas City in the morning of the second day ... four at Norwood Hills in St Louis, Missouri in the afternoon ... Tuck-a-Way in Milwaukee in the morning ... his home course of Olympia Field in Chicago in the afternoon ... North Hills in Philadephia ... and finally Salisbury in New York.

Drawn and haggard, lame and sore, he putted out on the eighteenth green in his final round at 10.30 pm on the fourth day, helped by flares and floodlights from a borrowed firetruck. Bandaged from ankle to knee, his feet a mass of blisters, he hobbled from the final green into a waiting car. He had played 576 holes with the same poor ball.

One can sympathize with the sports editor of the *New York Times* in August 1939 who, when asked for information on the record number of holes and courses played in one day, ducked the question: 'The marathon golfers move at so fast a pace that the less hardy statisticians have been left far behind, exhausted.'

SIX DISQUALIFIED FROM THE US OPEN

CANTERBURY, OHIO, JUNE 1940

It was a strange tournament for starting-times from the moment Walter Hagen arrived slightly late on the first tee, banged off a quick drive and ran down the fairway to catch up with two playing partners who had set off on time. A mix-up over starting-times finally decided the outcome of the tournament.

Sam Snead's first-round score of 67 was a record for the US Open, but the Open had slipped away from Snead before (and would do so again and again). On the second day Snead's play was perhaps affected by the worst of a storm. Lawson Little, playing early in the day and avoiding the squall, joined Snead and Horton Smith on 141 at the halfway point.

Controversy came on the Saturday, when the final two rounds were played. While Sam Snead was almost predictably falling away with a last-round 81 and final score of 295, 23-year-old Ed Oliver came through the pack to finish on 287 and tie with Lawson Little and Gene Sarazen. There was only one problem: Oliver was disqualified.

What brought Ed Oliver into the reckoning was a third-round 70, when he came home in 33. A big man from Hornell, New York, Oliver weighed in at over 16 stones and attracted nicknames like 'Porky' and 'Tom Thumb' from reporters. This was his first big impact on such a prestigious tournament, but the impact took a perverse course.

Over lunch, between third and final rounds, the big topic of conversation was the weather. Electrical thunderstorms threatened, and players discussed ways of minimizing strokes lost to the conditions. A group of six players discovered an obvious way to avoid the worst of weather. They could start early if the first tee was free. They finished their food quickly, and drifted out to the tee for the first hole.

The official starter, USGA executive secretary Joe Dey, was still at lunch. He wasn't expecting any play for 30 minutes or so. The only people at the first tee were a marshal, the unofficial lady scorer, and a few reporters who advised the over-eager players to wait. The players didn't want to wait. They would take their chance with the tournament committee.

Six players were later disqualified by the USGA. The 'starting on time' rule was to prevent *early* starts as well as late ones. Besides Oliver, the players disqualified were E.J. 'Dutch' Harrison, John Bulla, Ky Laffoon, Claude Harmon and Leland Gibson, an unknown who had gone round in 71 in the first round. Harrison had been only five strokes behind third-round leader Frank Walsh.

After his excellent final round of 71, Oliver came off the eighteenth green to find the word 'disqualified' posted against his name on the scoreboard. When the consequences sank in, he was angry and tearful. He pleaded that he had made an honest mistake, but the USGA understandably stuck to their decision.

Two players equalled Oliver's total score. The first was Lawson Little, who for a long time looked an outright winner. However, 38-year-old Gene Sarazen, presented with a known target for the last six or seven holes, staged a remarkable finish. Sarazen needed three difficult pars to tie with Little. He holed a seven-foot putt for a par five at the sixteenth and a difficult 30-footer for a par three at the seventeenth. Watched by a gallery of 7,000, Sarazen needed a long putt for a birdie, and victory, at the last. His putt shaved the hole, he tapped in, and looked forward to the play-off. Both Little and Sarazen indicated that they felt Oliver should be included in a play-off. The USGA did not agree.

In the 18-hole play-off, Lawson Little won the first hole and led thereafter. A sub-par 70 brought him the title by three strokes. Meanwhile, Ed Oliver was left to rue his hasty decision to start before his time. He never did win the US Open, although he was runner-up to Julius Boros in 1952.

AN ODD ENDING

DENVER, COLORADO, JULY 1941

Until 1958 the US PGA Championship was decided by match-play, several gruelling days of 36-hole matches which called for stamina as well as skill. The 1941 final was decided by 'one of the most bizarre finishes in the history of the tournament'.

The finalists were Byron Nelson, the defending champion, who beat Gene Sarazen in his semi-final, and Vic Ghezzi, who accounted for Lloyd Mangrum in the other.

In the morning round of the 36-hole final, Nelson won the first hole and Ghezzi the second. Thereafter Ghezzi held the upper hand – one up after three, two up after five, one up after nine, two up after 10 and one up after 11 – until Nelson squared it on the fifteenth. Nelson won the last hole to take a one-hole lead into lunch. His round of 70 was one stroke better than Ghezzi's.

In the afternoon, Nelson extended his lead to three holes by the turn. Things looked bad for Ghezzi. Nelson was a very experienced competitor who had already won the US Masters, US Open and US PGA and was not yet 30 years old. Ghezzi was also 29 but had yet to win one of these three major tournaments.

The final nine holes kept the crowd on tenterhooks. Ghezzi birdied the eleventh, Nelson three-putted the twelfth and was then bunkered on the fourteenth. They came to the eighteenth all-square.

The eighteenth hole at Cherry Hills was an uphill 465 yards toward a lake. Nelson's second shot was very short. The ball stopped on the road below the green, but Ghezzi had hooked his second, so he wasn't on the green either. Nelson pitched on in three, but Ghezzi swung it his way with a superb chip-and-run shot which stopped only four feet from the cup. Nelson's difficult 15-foot putt went wide, and Ghezzi had a four-footer for the tournament. He tapped it three feet past the cup and almost missed coming back.

'Sudden-death' next.

At the thirty-seventh Ghezzi was once more in a controlling position. He had an 11-foot putt for a birdie three and victory. He missed it.

And on they went to the thirty-eighth, the scene of the bizarre finish.

Both players were tired. They missed the green with their second shots, but both chipped to within three feet of the pin with their third shots. The balls were so close together that it was impossible to decide whose shot it was. They flipped a coin, and it was Nelson who settled into his putting stance.

There are two accounts of what happened next. Newspaper accounts say that Nelson's short putt slid past the cup by a hair's breath, Nelson perhaps put off by the presence of Ghezzi's ball or by sheer exhaustion. The other story, Ghezzi's memory of the incident, suggests that Nelson clipped Ghezzi's ball on the follow through to incur a one-stroke penalty.

Either way, Ghezzi was the winner.

NO TRACE OF A BULLET

CROHAM HURST, NEAR CROYDON, SEPTEMBER 1941

Eric Humphries and Norman Radmall were playing golf near a wood at Croham Hurst on a Saturday. At the eleventh hole they saw three young girls come out of the wood. The girls ran along the fairway and threw themselves to the ground behind a bunker in the manner of soldiers taking cover. The war was affecting everyone.

The two men moved on to the twelfth hole. They reached the green and Radmall was putting. He played his shot and then heard a loud crack, rather like a rifle being fired. He looked up, and saw his playing partner on the floor.

'I'm shot,' Humphries shouted. 'Shot in the stomach.'

Radmall ran to him, opened his golfing jacket and saw a patch of blood on his shirt near the pit of his stomach. Radmall looked around for help.

'Mr Roper,' he called to another golfer playing nearby. Mr Roper came over, accompanied by two ladies.

Radmall ran off to the clubhouse, calling to players for an ambulance and a doctor. The message was passed on in relays. When he arrived at the clubhouse, he learned that an ambulance was on its way. When he returned to the twelfth green, he found the ambulance had arrived.

Eric Norman Humphries, a 35-year-old paper buyer of Sanderstead, was taken to hospital. He was conscious and severely shocked. He gave a statement to the police: 'I do not know who shot me. It came from the woods. My friend did not shoot me.

I do not know anyone who would do this. I have no bad friends. I did not see anyone in the woods.'

Within 15 minutes of his arrival at hospital, he was given a blood transfusion. He was X-rayed but no fragments of metal were visible. The bullet had entered his body and left it again, travelling on a slightly downward course. His condition held, but an operation was necessary.

He recovered consciousness two hours after the operation and seemed to be improving. The next morning his condition was fair, but he died at 1.25 pm that day. He was married with two children.

Police traced the schoolgirls who had appeared on the eleventh fairway but they were no extra help. The military helped the police search the golf course thoroughly but no bullet or weapon was found. The best guess was that the bullet was fired from a .303 Service rifle, one of the few weapons that could make a hole as large as that in the dead man's jacket. Or it could be a .300 rifle, used in some parts by the Home Guard. A .25 automatic pistol might make a hole that size but wouldn't penetrate the abdomen at a range of over 30 yards. This shot had been fired from over 50 yards.

The coroner passed an open verdict, death probably caused by a rifle bullet.

TWO TRIPLE TIES AND A CADDIE WHO KICKED A BALL

CANTERBURY, OHIO, JUNE 1946

Less than a year after the capitulation of Japanese forces, the 1946 US Open heralded a semblance of normality ... except that this Open tournament was not a normal one. It was one of the closest, zaniest and most remarkable. The only predictable thing was that Sam Snead led the field after the first round but didn't win.

It was the first US Open since 1941, the annual event having been halted after the attack on Pearl Harbor. Craig Wood not only retained the title for five years yet, at 44, was one of the oldest players ever to defend an Open title. But Wood failed to beat the second-round cut.

After four rounds, there was a three-way tie between Lloyd Mangrum, Vic Ghezzi and Byron Nelson. Each, in his own way, had put together a four-under-par score of 284, but Nelson's was agreed to be the oddest of the three because it included a shot he never played.

More than a dozen players must have thought they were only a shot or two away from winning the tournament outright. Big Vic Ghezzi had cause to regret sixes at the first and ninth holes in his final round. He took 39 on the first nine, then came home in 33. Ghezzi, joint leader with Ben Hogan after 36 holes, was the topic of much spectator talk, and one such interchange was captured by a contemporary reporter.

'Ghezzi works for a mayonnaise company.'

'That's what makes him good on the greens.'

There were many more 'might-have-beens'. Ben Hogan stayed in the running despite a seven at the eighth hole in the final round, and, needing to hole an 18-foot putt at the last hole to win the tournament outright, he three-putted and missed the play-off. Herman Barron needed pars on the last two holes to win the tournament outright, but got two bogeys instead and, like Hogan, missed the play-off by a stroke. Jimmy Demaret put together a superb run of birdies, and even one eagle, but missed the play-off by two strokes, as did Ed Oliver.

The biggest 'might-have-been' was Byron Nelson, the 'Lord Byron' of American golf, for Nelson lost a stroke without using a club at the thirteenth hole of his third round. His ball was just off the green, somewhere amidst a huge gallery that had gathered around the favourite. It wasn't easy moving among the crowd, estimated at 12,000, but Nelson's caddie, Eddie Martin, set off toward them. Martin, a young soldier who had caddied for Nelson on previous occasions, had obtained special leave of absence for this big tournament. Wearing his General Issue (GI) uniform, carrying Nelson's clubs, Martin approached the rope that marshals held just behind the ball. The crowd was pressed against the rope, and, as the caddie ducked under it, he didn't see the ball at his feet. Martin kicked the ball, and Nelson had to call a penalty-stroke on himself. His caddie was nearly in tears. The only comparable incident in a major tournament was at the 1921 British Open, when Roger Wethered stepped on his own ball at the fourteenth hole in the third round and yet recovered several strokes in the final round to force a play-off with Jock Hutchison. Hutchison won the play-off comfortably.

Some people argued later that this incident cost Nelson the title. It might have done, but the tournament still had a long way to run and Nelson had opportunities to win it. He needed only pars on the last two holes for 282 and a probable two-stroke victory. The odds swung his way when he was left with a 20-foot putt for a birdie two at the seventeenth hole. Somehow he turned it into a bogey four by missing a return putt from three feet. Nelson also bogeyed the last, so Lloyd

Mangrum, who managed pars on the last two, recovered two strokes.

There had been three previous triple ties in the US Open, the most recent being in 1939, when Nelson himself won the tournament in a play-off with Craig Wood and Denny Shute. But this one produced something extraordinary in the play-off – another three-way tie.

The play-off scores are worth recording:

Par	443 445 345	– 36	434 544 534	– 36 (72)
Nelson	433 446 345	– 36	534 444 534	– 36 (72)
Mangrum	442 535 245	– 34	433 654 544	– 38 (72)
Ghezzi	442 435 444	– 34	435 445 634	– 38 (72)

The lead was changing after virtually every hole, and all three players were in the lead at some point. The second play-off, in the afternoon of the same day, was just as exciting. They reached the last hole at dusk, occasional sparks of light coming from flashes of lightning which signalled the coming of a storm. On the eighteenth tee, Mangrum (67) led Ghezzi (68) and Nelson (69), but everyone knew that this US Open had been wide-Open, the lead continually changing hands, and when Mangrum put his second shot in a bunker, there was more excitement. Ghezzi was left with an eight-foot putt to tie with Mangrum. He missed it, Mangrum sank one from two feet for his five, and Nelson's four wasn't quite good enough to force another play-off.

Again the play-off scores were dramatic:

Nelson	443 444 245	– 34	444 644 544	– 39 (73)
Mangrum	353 435 346	– 36	435 443 445	– 36 (72)
Ghezzi	443 444 344	– 34	434 555 535	– 39 (73)

Byron Nelson retired from regular competition soon after the 1946 US Open. He was still at his peak. Exempted from military service – he was a haemophiliac – Nelson had won 11 consecutive victories in 1945, but he was tired of the pressures of competitive golf. He competed occasionally in the 1950s, and added the 1951 Crosby and 1955 French Open to his astonishing record of success.

SCRAMBLING AMONG THE MOSS AND THE LEAVES

JACKSONVILLE, FLORIDA, MARCH 1947

Before describing the bizarre ending of the 1947 Jacksonville Open, let me begin with Ben Hogan's 11 at the par-three sixth in the third round.

Hogan had reached the tournament's halfway point with scores of 69 and 71, so his double-quadruple bogey was hardly in keeping with the form of one of the greatest players ever. Hogan, winner of the 1946 US PGA (and soon another eight majors), was experiencing a one-off hiccup at such a short hole. His tee-shot went in the water (one), he tried to blast it out (two), tried again (three) ... and again (four) ... and yet again (five) before lifting to the back of the pond (six). Then he flubbed a chip shot to send the ball back in the water (seven), lifted to the back of the pond again (eight), chipped on to the green (nine), laid up a putt (ten) and finally ended his work at the hole (eleven).

After that, anything could happen.

Clayton Heafner was the third-round leader with scores of 69, 68 and 70. The big, sandy-haired, ex-Army Sergeant from North Carolina was 33 then, an unpredictable golfer who wasn't beyond the occasional outrageous act. He had been a war hero with Patton's Third Army and would become the hero, or anti-hero, of many golfing stories.

By March 1947, Heafner had yet to win an important tournament, and he looked to be faltering once more when he ran into problems on the fifth and eighth holes in the final round of the Jacksonville Open. He scrambled a score of 74, but it didn't look good enough, especially with Lew Worsham, the US Open Champion, making a late surge. Worsham birdied the fifteenth, sixteenth and seventeenth, and needed only a par four at the last to win the Jacksonville Open by one stroke.

Now, here's where golf is sometimes a difficult game to watch. Imagine you are in the gallery at the eighteenth green, and, some way in the distance, just off the fairway, Lew Worsham is scrambling among the moss and the leaves preparing to play his second shot. Then he stops, walks around, talks to one or two people, and finally resumes his position in the rough.

What's taking him so long?

Worsham plays his approach shot and the ball lands on the green, although some distance from the hole. You wait for him to walk on to the green. Here he comes now. He's the winner if he can get down in two. Applause, applause, applause.

Worsham putts but the ball stops several feet away from the pin. He needs this one for the tournament, you think, and it's a tricky one. You watch him study the green, you feel the tension mount, and you see him sink the putt. He's won. Or has he? The reactions don't look right.

Something else had happened in the rough before Worsham played his second shot. While he was brushing away moss and leaves, he accidentally touched his ball and moved it a fraction of an inch. Without hesitation he called a penalty stroke on himself. His approach to the green, therefore, was really his third shot, and he made a five on the hole. Instead of winning by one stroke, Worsham had tied Heafner on 281 and would have to return for an 18-hole play-off. (Hogan, incidentally, finished on 290 after rounds of 69, 71, 82 and 68. After his 11 at the sixth in the third round, he birdied the next in three.)

The Heafner-Worsham play-off was not straightforward. After 18 holes they had tied again, each scoring 71, and they went into a 'sudden-death' play-off. They halved the nineteenth with par fours, and also halved the twentieth with par fours. At the twenty-first Worsham's play went out of control. His drive went through the woods and into a bunker on another fairway. It took him seven to get down, and Heafner, with a par four, had the unusual honour of winning a 'sudden-death' play-off by three strokes.

'SUDDEN-DEATH' NOT SO SUDDEN

DETROIT, MICHIGAN, JUNE 1949

At the time of the Motor City Open, the big money earners for the year were Sam Snead, Cary Middlecoff and Lloyd Mangrum. Snead did not compete at Detroit, where Mangrum and Middlecoff both finished the four-round tournament with scores of 273. The top six places were as follows:

Lloyd Mangrum	67	69	68	69	—	273
Cary Middlecoff	66	67	71	69	—	273
Jim Ferrier	69	70	66	70	—	275
Henry Ransom	66	69	72	69	—	276
Jim Turness	70	68	68	70	—	276
E.J. 'Dutch' Harrison	69	71	69	67	—	276

Earlier that year, Cary Middlecoff had won his first US Open Championship, only three years after turning professional. Prior to that he had served as a Captain in the US Army Dental Corps during World War II, and played golf as an amateur. Mangrum, at 35 several years the elder of the two, was a war hero, wounded in France. Credited with the comment that 'it is not "how" but "how many" that counts,' Mangrum won the US Open in 1946 after a play-off with Byron Nelson and Vic Ghezzi. So both Middlecoff and Mangrum were experienced professionals, but their experience of 'sudden-death' in the Motor City Open was unique.

They set out after a brief rest. As it turned out, they might have needed more. They played nine holes with copy-cat scores, both completing them with par scores of 35. When one made a birdie so did the other. When one bogeyed a hole, so did the other. If one made his par, the other was sure to. They birdied the second, bogeyed the eighth and parred the rest.

Par	454	443	434	—	35
Mangrum	444	443	444	—	35
Middlecoff	444	443	444	—	35

At this point, after nine holes of 'sudden-death', Middlecoff and Mangrum entered discussions with the tournament's organizers. They decided to play two more holes. If the tournament wasn't settled, they would share the top two prizes, which were worth $2,600 (£930) and $1,900 (£680).

The tenth hole of the 'sudden-death' play-off was halved with par fours.

The next was a 210-yard par three, and Middlecoff was soon in trouble. His drive curved to the right of the green and left him 40 feet from the pin but in the rough. Mangrum was well-positioned for a birdie – only 10 feet to the left of the pin.

Middlecoff played a beautiful shot from his difficult position. His ball came to rest a foot from the hole to ensure his par three.

Mangrum putted for the birdie that would give him the tournament. The ball stopped three inches from the hole. Another par. Another hole halved.

The gallery of more than 8,500 spectators applauded loudly. After 11 holes of 'sudden-death', Mangrum and Middlecoff became joint winners of the 1949 Motor City Open, taking $2,250 each in prize money.

It is probably the only 83-hole tournament not to be won outright.

THE BRADSHAW BOTTLE INCIDENT

ROYAL ST GEORGE'S, SANDWICH, JULY 1949

Most of the drama of the 1949 British Open focused on two men, genial Irishman Harry Bradshaw and stocky South African 'Bobby' Locke, but for much of the week the Championship could have been won by any of a number of players.

From the qualifying rounds, Bradshaw and Locke were in concert with their scores. They led the qualifiers with scores of 139 (Bradshaw) and 140 (Locke) after rounds at Sandwich and Deal, but Locke was probably the favourite. Remembering events in the 1938 Sandwich Open, people eyed the weather curiously, especially when the wind played a few tricks during the second qualifying round. When the tournament proper started, however, the weather was sound and the scores were good.

After the first round, James Adams led with 67, followed by Bradshaw and Roberto de Vicenzo of Argentina, who were both on 68. Locke's 69 included a seven at the fourteenth.

The Bradshaw beer-bottle incident occurred at the fifth hole of the second round. Bradshaw started very well that day, mowing the ball down the fairways with his no-nonsense, scythe-like swing. He made fours at the first four holes, and then came to the 451-yard fifth hole, a straightforward par four. He cut his drive slightly and walked forward to discover a strange outcome. A broken beer bottle, lying in the rough looking for more trouble, was nestling against his ball.

Bradshaw was faced with an unsettling decision. He had been disqualified from his last tournament for playing his fellow-competitor's ball, so he didn't want a similar mistake when so well-placed in the British Open. He could have decreed his ball unplayable and either gone back to the tee and driven again (penalty loss of distance only) or played his next stroke at a spot not more than two club lengths from where the ball lay unplayable, but not nearer the hole (for a one-stroke penalty).

Instead, rather than risk a possible disqualification or a delay awaiting a ruling, Bradshaw opted to try to dislodge his ball from the bottle. Using a sand-iron, he smashed at the ball and bottle. He saw the former bobble 15 or 20 yards toward more difficulty, and felt small pieces of the latter hit him in the face. He missed the green with his next shot, and took six for the hole – two over par.

Bradshaw, obviously unnerved by the experience, struggled through the round for a 77. Locke also had a poorer second round. The South African's 76 put him level with Bradshaw on 145, but there were 11 players ahead of them. The halfway leader was Sam King with 140.

In addition to the bottle incident, other strange offerings were provided by Charles Rotar, who was disqualified for using a Schenectady putter, and Francis Francis of Sunningdale, whose opening rounds of 72 and 74 contained a seven and an eight respectively.

On the Friday, the day of the final two rounds, Bradshaw and Locke continued their progress in sweet tandem. They had identical scores and tied for the Championship.

| Bobby Locke | 69 | 76 | 68 | 70 | – | 283 |
| Harry Bradshaw | 68 | 77 | 68 | 70 | – | 283 |

Later, people were to reflect on what might have happened had Bradshaw's ball not skirmished with a broken beer bottle at the fifth hole or had the Irishman saved a stroke by interpreting the rules correctly and opting for an alternative action. But golf is rife with hindsight. The reality of the 1949 British Open was a 36-hole play-off.

Locke and Bradshaw halved the first four holes of the Saturday play-off. Then they came once more to the fatal fifth hole, the hole of broken bottles, broken parity and broken hearts. Bradshaw missed a short putt, and the South African took a lead that he never lost. Locke gained further strokes at the ninth and twelfth, and his three at the 520-yard fourteenth put him six ahead as Bradshaw had a six there.

Bobby Locke went on to win the 36-hole play-off by 12 strokes and became the first Commonwealth Champion of the British Open. He won the Championship three more times in the 1950s.

TWO WOMEN AND A PILOT

JACKSONVILLE, FLORIDA, MARCH 1952

At 10 o'clock in the morning, two women reached the 405-yard seventh hole at the Timuquana Country Club. They were good golfers. One of them, Bertha Johnson, had been city champion in 1938 and, now in her early 50s, was still good enough to compete in tournaments. She had been president of the Jacksonville Women's Golf Association for the two years after the war.

Bertha Johnson and Mary Dempsey, a 38-year-old mother, drove off from the seventh tee and started walking toward their balls. They were oblivious of any danger. It was just another golf round to be enjoyed.

The pilot was on a routine practice flight from the US Navy air-base that bordered the Timuquana Country Club. He was worried. The oil-pressure gauge of his Corsair fighter plane was registering a low reading and his engine power was below normal. He called for an emergency landing. The duty runway was cleared and prepared.

He made his approach to the runway, but all was not right. The engine of the single-seater plane was behaving erratically. The pilot didn't have enough control for a landing. He flew the plane on, turned right and hoped to reach the airfield again. Then the Corsair's engines died completely. The Corsair was now a glider. No power, no noise, and no chance of returning to the runway. The pilot looked at what was available below. Was there anywhere to land?

He saw a strip of grass on the golf-course of Timuquana

Country Club. It was the seventh fairway.

A man driving a van was making a delivery from his fruit-and-vegetable stall on Roosevelt Boulevard to the Air Station. He saw the plane come in low over the buildings with smoke pouring out.

'It's going to crash,' he said to his wife.

The plane pulled back into the air a little, but no higher than the tree-tops. The man and his wife watched it disappear behind the trees.

The two women played their second shots about 220 yards from the seventh tee. Then they strolled in a leisurely way down the centre of the fairway toward the green. Their caddie, 19-year-old Theodore Rutledge, walked about 35 yards behind them, along the eastern edge of the fairway. The caddie looked up. He saw the plane. It was coming in silently against the wind, strangely unobtrusive, its long nose and black engine smoke obscuring the pilot's forward vision.

The caddie yelled a warning to the women, who didn't hear, and then ducked and ran.

The plane landed on the seventh fairway and hit the women from behind with a propeller. One body was thrown 35 feet, the other 65 feet. The women were killed instantly.

The plane continued down the fairway for another 155 yards, veering towards a clump of pine trees in the rough, near the western edge. It crashed into the trees and the impact broke off the engine and nacelle. The pilot scrambled out of the wreckage and then watched it burst into flames. He was standing by the side of the plane when the golf-course grounds superintendent arrived.

'Are you hurt?' asked the grounds superintendent.

'No, thank God,' said the pilot. 'I got out before the fire started.'

The caddie rushed up and blurted out the news that two golfers had been killed.

The pilot went to pieces.

WHEN BEN HOGAN WASN'T IN THE FIRST SEVEN THOUSAND

ALL ACROSS NORTH AMERICA, MAY 1952

Ben Hogan was probably the best golfer in the world in the early 1950s – inside four years he won the US Open three times, the US Masters twice and the 1953 British Open – but on one day in 1952 he did well to finish in seven thousand and twelfth place in a national competition against amateurs.

A film on Ben Hogan's life, *Follow the Sun*, released in 1951, tells of how Hogan (played by Glenn Ford) rose from a poor Texas family to establish himself as golf professional. Hogan won a caddies' tournament, married his childhood sweetheart and achieved huge success immediately after the war, including victories in two major tournaments, the US Open and the US PGA, in 1948. Then, in February 1949, driving home to Texas, Hogan was seriously injured when a bus collided with his car. They thought he might not walk again. Yet, within a year, he was competing again, and he won the 1950 US Open after an exhausting play-off. It is one of golf's most dramatic stories, and made Ben Hogan into a household name. By 1952, any golfer, amateur or professional, knew that Hogan was the player to beat.

On the first National Golf Day, 31 May 1952, Hogan took on golfers throughout the United States and Canada. Hogan played a round over the Northwood course, scene of the forthcoming US Open, and thousands of golfers played on their home courses in an attempt to beat Hogan's score. It was a handicap competition sponsored by *Life* magazine and the

156

Professional Golfers' Association, and each entrant paid $1 for the privilege of competing against the world's best golfer. Proceeds went to the United Services Organization (USO) and the National Golf Fund.

Hogan knew he had a tough task, as he was playing his round on a demanding course of 6,811 yards, some 47 yards longer than it would be for the US Open a fortnight later, whereas the amateurs would be playing on their home courses. The handicap system also made it difficult for him. He needed to play exceptionally well if he was to set a really tough target.

Watched by 1,500 spectators at the Northwood course, Hogan made a 10-foot putt for a birdie at the second, and an 18-footer for a birdie at the fourth. He was out in 34 (two under) but bogeyed the eleventh by missing from a foot before his 30-foot birdie putt at the twelfth. Hogan fell away slightly with two more bogeys – at the thirteenth and sixteenth – and his final total of 71 was par for the course. It took him three hours to play the round.

The 55,015 entrants took on Hogan on courses all over the continent, and the handicapping led to some unusually low scores. One Washington housewife, Marian Bradley, picked up 106 strokes under the Calloway Handicap System and an extra five because she was a woman. She went round in 178 (net 67) and beat Hogan by four strokes.

Eight-year-old Diane Wilson, daughter of the professional at Kansas City's Quivera Country Club, put together a round of 69, helped by a 48 handicap. The oldest player to beat Ben Hogan was probably 79-year-old John Haine, a 14-handicap player who shot five strokes under his age and therefore netted a 60 at Tres Pinos, California.

The most sensational round was probably that by Andy Sword, a Dallas policeman. At the Tenison Park course in Texas, not too far from Hogan's home course, Sword, a scratch golfer, went round in 64 to beat Hogan by seven strokes. It was a proud day for him, as it was for 15-year-old Lloyd Syron, who turned in a scratch score of 69 at Pontiac, Michigan.

Among the personalities who beat Ben Hogan were Bing

Crosby (gross 74 and net 69) and New York Yankee pitcher Allie Reynolds (gross 78 and net 67). Among the dignitaries who didn't were Chief of Staff General Omar Bradley (gross 85 and net 74) at the Army-Navy course in Washington and Senator Robert Taft (gross 94 and net 78), who played through heavy rain at Burning Tree.

By the end of the competition, 7,511 golfers had bettered Ben Hogan's score, and it must have been a sweet thought the following year, when Hogan won three of the four major tournaments. In future years, many amateur golfers had a story for their grandchildren: 'Did I ever tell you about the time I beat Ben Hogan?'

ON THE THIRTIETH HOLE

WALTON HEATH, SEPTEMBER 1952

In the third round of the 1952 British Professional Match Play, the match between Fred Daly and Alan 'Tiger' Poulton created a new record for number of play-off holes. The previous professional record had lasted since 1904, when Willie Fernie beat James Braid at the twenty-seventh on the Bogside course. In the British Amateur Championship, a 1908 match at Sandwich between L.O.M. Munn and C. A. Palmer had gone to the twenty-eighth before Palmer won.

Fred Daly was a cheerful, determined Irishman who had won popular acclaim in the immediate post-war period. British Open Champion in 1947, he won the first of two successive Match Play Championships that same year. When he took on Alan Poulton at Walton Heath in the 1952 Match Play, however, Daly was only a month short of his forty-first birthday. The match went to 30 holes and took over five hours to complete.

It was a third-round match, and Daly was twice two holes up, but each time Poulton fought back to level the match. Poulton even took the lead at the fifteenth, when he made a birdie three, but Daly was immediately back on terms with a birdie four at the sixteenth.

They halved the next 13 holes.

'At the extra holes Daly repeatedly saved himself by brilliant putting,' said one account. 'And at the thirtieth, the dog-legged twelfth, though there was some mud on his ball, the Irishman holed from 12 yards for a birdie "three", which gave him success after more than five hours' play.'

Some golfers might have been exhausted by this struggle, especially when told that they had another match immediately. Daly, however, seemed to go out again with only one thought in mind – to win his fourth-round match as quickly as possible. His opponent was Peter Alliss, who had been waiting patiently for two hours. Daly eagled the first hole in two, turned in 31 and beat the promising young Alliss by six and five.

Daly beat Eric Brown (three and two) in the fifth round, George Johnson (two and one) in the semi-final and the Belgian Flory van Donck, another 40-year-old, in the final. The final, played over 36 holes, was won four and three after Daly had led convincingly for most of the match. Curiously, the same two players – Daly and van Donck – had met in the 1947 Match Play final, when Daly had won the tournament for the first time.

It was Daly's third Professional Match Play victory in six years. On this occasion, however, Alan Poulton could legitimately say that he had run Daly very, very close in the third round.

A BIG SHOT FOR BIG MONEY

CHICAGO, AUGUST 1953

Tam o' Shanter's eighteenth hole was the scene of many amazing incidents that week, but the most dramatic came in the final round with one of the greatest finishes any tournament has produced.

The 'world' professional tournament at Tam o' Shanter offered the richest prizes in golf at the time – $25,000 (£8,920) for the winner, and $75,000 in total. The lead changed frequently as players put together runs of success and failure, and even the more experienced players had to adjust to the pressures of so much money at stake.

One of the first to show was Lew Worsham, who was to play a major part in the final drama. In the first round, he came home in 31 for a 65 which gave him a three-stroke lead. Worsham was then 36 years old, a Virginian who had won the US Open in 1947.

After 36 holes, however, Worsham had slipped to joint second, two strokes behind Ed 'Porky' Oliver, the bulky veteran from Delaware with a history of runner-up positions in the big tournaments. Oliver had finished runner-up to Ben Hogan in the recent 1953 US Masters. With scores of 68 and 67 at Tam o' Shanter, Oliver was playing consistently well.

Worsham, meanwhile, gave some hint of his penchant for drama at the eighteenth hole. In the second round, he looked to be faltering when he used his putter from well off the final green and then missed a six-foot putt for a bogey five. Folk recalled how Worsham had let a lead slip in the last round in the previous year's Tam o' Shanter world tournament.

If Worsham had trouble at the eighteenth in the second round, though, it was nothing compared with Oliver's escapades there in the third. On his second shot the ball scuttled past a permanent grandstand and lodged against an outdoor bar on a concrete patio. Oliver reckoned that he should be permitted to drop on to the grass from behind such a 'temporary obstacle'. He could foresee a way of chipping over the permanent stand from the grass to make a five and stay in contention with the leaders. Instead, tournament officials ruled that he had to play the ball two club-lengths from the bar. Oliver's obscene language to an official cost him two penalty shots, his chip on to a temporary grandstand won him a drop on the edge of the green, another chip fell short and he three-putted for what in effect was a nine (including the two penalty shots). It completed a round of 81 and left him framing an apology to the official.

Suddenly, a whole bunch of golfers were in contention. Four were tied on 209 – Dave Douglas, Doug Ford, Al Besselink and Chandler Harper. By the sixty-third hole, however, there was yet another leader, Freddie Haas, who was one stroke up on Al Besselink and Chandler Harper with nine to play. Haas faded over the last five, ruining his chances with three bogeys.

The tournament began to swing the way of Chandler Harper, who, like his friend Lew Worsham, was a Virginian. The slim, balding Harper had won the US PGA in 1950 and now, at 39, he was no stranger to tight finishes.

Harper saw off the other third-round leaders, but Worsham was making a challenge from further down the field. Worsham managed birdies at the tenth, thirteenth and fifteenth, before sending his next tee-shot over the sixteenth green. The bogey four was a major setback, and Worsham's challenge now looked over.

At the final hole, a 410-yard par four, Harper played his second shot to within two feet from the pin. It set up an easy birdie three on a difficult hole and secured a certain win. The 10,000 spectators certainly thought so.

The only mathematical threat came from Worsham, who needed birdie threes at the seventeenth and eighteenth to force a play-off. At the penultimate hole, the 375-yard seventeenth, a par four, he played an approach shot to seven feet from the flag and sank the putt for his birdie.

Worsham moved on to the difficult eighteenth, where he had made a bogey five in the second round and where Oliver had blown up in various ways in the third. A birdie three looked unlikely, but a tremendous drive left Worsham not much more than 100 yards from the flag. There was just a chance that he could drop the ball on the green and sink a putt to square the tournament and take it to a play-off. Some spectators swarmed around him, but most congratulated Harper on the eighteenth green, leaving Worsham to play in semi-privacy. However, once Worsham's ball reached the eighteenth green, it would be in range of national television cameras. Chandler Harper had already thrilled the viewers by putting his second shot so close to the pin for his birdie. Surely Worsham could not match that.

Worsham took out a wedge, looked at the hole, and gave the ball what he could. Eyes followed the course of the ball as it sailed to the front of the long green, bounced about 30 feet short of the pin, bounced again, and curved smoothly over a small ridge into the hole. An eagle two for the tournament. Pandemonium broke out.

No one could remember anything quite so dramatic. There had been shots as spectacular – Gene Sarazen's albatross spoon shot in the 1935 US Masters for instance – but never the final one of such an important tournament in order to elicit an unlikely victory.

Recent years have brought other stunning finales, like Isao Aoki's 128-yard pitch for an eagle three at the final hole of the 1983 Hawaiian Open and the legerdemain shots that discomfited Greg Norman in the late 1980s and early 1990s, but Lew Worsham's wedge shot was a benchmark. It took tournament finishes into a new domain, linking the spectacular to a huge television audience.

Worsham ended 1953 as the leading US money-winner, helped by the difference between the winning prize of $25,000 and the runner-up's $10,000 that was effected by the luckiest shot of his life.

Initial estimates put the length of Worsham's shot at 140 yards, but Worsham later watched film of the shot, estimated where it was played from and had the distance measured. He reckoned it was more like 104 yards.

Lew Worsham	65	72	73	68	—	278
Chandler Harper	69	69	71	70	—	279
Al Besselink	69	70	70	72	—	281
Cary Middlecoff	70	70	73	69	—	282
Jim Ferrier	72	70	70	70	—	282
Freddie Haas	68	71	72	71	—	282
Lloyd Mangrum	72	71	70	70	—	283
Dave Douglas	72	65	72	74	—	283

'BRITANNIA WAIVES THE RULES'

MARION, MASSACHUSETTS, SEPTEMBER 1953

The 1953 Walker Cup match was expected to be won by the United States. They had lost only one of the first 13 of the Walker Cup series – the British had won at St Andrews in 1938 – and now had home advantage for the fourteenth. In the circumstances, a sporting gesture by the British was particularly honourable.

The venue was the Kittansett Golf Club, exposed to a wind that blew across Buzzards Bay. The American team included 48-year-old Republican Congressman Jack Westland, who had won the US Amateur Championship the previous year, singer Don Cherry, and a young Ken Venturi, who later won the 1964 US Open in emotional circumstances. The British team relied heavily on the influence of Gerald Micklem and a fine performance by Ronnie White.

On the first day, the third foursome matched James Wilson and R. C. MacGregor (Great Britain) with James Jackson and Gene Littler (United States). Littler, the 1953 US Amateur Champion, was then a 23-year-old serviceman in the US Naval Air Army. Like Venturi, he later turned professional, played in the Ryder Cup, won the US Open and earned the Ben Hogan award for courageously overcoming physical difficulties. His text-book style was to be a major factor in the strange foursome match of 1953, but the early drama surrounded his partner.

Wilson holed a brilliant long putt to win the first hole for Great Britain, but a far greater problem faced the Americans at

165

the next hole. Jackson was walking along the second fairway when he realized that he was carrying 16 clubs, two above the maximum number. He had brought an extra brassie and a spare wedge from Missouri but had forgotten to take them out of his bag on the morning of the match. Disconsolate, he reported his discovery to the referee of his match, expecting the inevitable punishment – disqualification.

There were precedents. Other players had infringed the 14-club rule introduced in 1938. Frank Stranahan was probably the first, in March 1938, when he figured in a bizarre incident in the Dixie Amateur Tournament. After 18 holes, Stranahan appeared all-square with Bob Odom, but there was a debate about whether Odom should be penalized one stroke under local rules or two under USGA rules for an out-of-bounds shot. In the midst of discussions, Stranahan's caddie tossed in some news about 16 clubs, and Stranahan was disqualified. Likewise Ray Ottman of Louisville, who was disqualified from a 1939 US PGA Tournament qualifying trial for carrying 17 clubs.

The 1953 Walker Cup incident, however, had a stranger outcome. The referee of Jackson's match, Charles Pierson, called for a USGA ruling. The USGA official, Isaac Grainger, said that Rule 3 called for disqualification. And that appeared to be that.

Then enter the formidable figure of Lieutenant-Colonel Tony Duncan, non-playing captain of the British team. Duncan overtook Jackson to explain that there might be a way out of the disqualification. Duncan mustered the support of the two British golfers involved, Wilson and MacGregor, and made a stirring plea to Isaac Grainger that Jackson and Littler need not be disqualified. The British wanted to win by being better players, Duncan argued. He was familiar with Rule 36 section 5: 'The committee has no power to waive a Rule of Golf. A penalty of disqualification, however, may, in exceptional individual cases, be waived or be modified if the committee consider such action unwarranted.'

The executive committee was brought together from different parts of the course. The members met, discussed and decided. It had to be quick. Matches were going on all around them.

Duncan's plea was accepted, and the British captain summed up the situation neatly: 'Britannia waives the rules'. The committee ruled that Jackson and Littler should forfeit two holes rather than the match. The British pair, therefore, won the second and third holes by default, and went to the fourth hole three up. The match resumed, and Jackson's caddie carried a lighter bag.

The British won the seventh hole to go four up.

But there were still 29 holes to play.

Littler and Jackson, both playing in their first Walker Cup match, pulled one back by the turn and then played brilliantly on the homeward nine in the morning round. They came back in 33 to finish two up. Some of Gene Littler's recoveries were magnificent, and the Americans were helped by the British dropping shots on the seventeenth and eighteenth.

Jackson and Littler won the first four of the afternoon round to make it six in a row. After having lost the match through a disqualification, they were now six up with 14 to play. The British won four holes, including three in succession from the tenth, but when they lost the thirteenth the match was virtually over. Jackson and Littler won three and two. Instead of the Walker Cup match being poised at 2-2 after the foursomes, it was 3-1 to the Americans, thanks to a sporting gesture.

The next day the Americans dominated the singles, and won the overall match 9-3.

The rule was later changed. In 1973, the maximum penalty for exceeding the club limit was two holes, something Brian Huggett discovered in that year's Double Diamond International Team Tournament. Huggett was all-square with Manuel Ballesteros on the third hole when he discovered he had 15 clubs in his bag.

LONDON TO OXFORD

THE A40, JUNE 1956

There was only one hole. It began at Marble Arch, London, and ended 55 miles away in Oxford. And the first hazard was particularly unusual. At the appointed starting time – 9 pm on 26 June – a large crowd of people blocked his fairway. They weren't waiting to see him tee off. They were waiting for Gina Lollobrigida. The voluptuous Italian actress was attending the premiere of *Trapeze*, a film in which she starred.

Humphrey Crum-Ewing waited patiently for 15 minutes while the crowd disappeared into the Odeon Cinema. The 22-year-old Oxford University student could then begin his 55-mile golfing journey to the Canterbury Gate of Christ Church College. He stood to win over £135 if he could complete the journey inside 20 hours, which meant maintaining an average speed of 2.75 miles per hour. It was a tall order.

The Gina Lollobrigida interruption wasn't the first thing to go wrong. Crum-Ewing had originally intended to attempt the journey some three weeks earlier, but the Censors of Christ Church College had refused permission for him to be absent from college for a night. The Dean of the College, Dr John Lowe, felt that members of the college had received undue publicity that term. He might have been referring to an incident over the purchase of two pictures for the Christ Church Junior Common Room. One committee member had resigned over the way the pictures had been bought. Or he might have been referring to publicity given to another student, who,

168

earlier that year, had attempted to beat the record time for an Oxford-to-London walk.

Crum-Ewing was reconciled to attempting the 'hole' in the privacy of his vacation. At Marble Arch he was accompanied by his caddie, 18-year-old Kamilla Jessel of Banbury, who planned to stay with him until he had reached the outskirts of London. Another Christ Church undergraduate, Viscount Furneaux, the Honourable John Dawnay, planned to keep pace with Crum-Ewing in a car during the earlier stages of the adventure.

By agreement with those placing the bets, who included the president of the University Dramatic Society, a University Divots' golfer and a golf blue, Humphrey Crum-Ewing was allowed 36 balls. In fact he carried only a dozen. He relied on his putter, sending the ball 20 or 30 yards along the A40 with each stroke. The major problem was the light, or, rather, lack of it. He tried tying pieces of cloth on the ball so he could see the ball on its journey, but the cloth came off. He ran after the ball to keep it in sight, but he lost one after another. He was tempted to hit them before they stopped to keep them in range but, of course, such a dribbling stroke was outside the rules.

When he reached Beaconsfield, at 5 am, he had covered about 25 miles of the 55-mile 'hole' in eight hours. He was slightly ahead of schedule but his hands were sore and in Beaconsfield he lost his last golf ball. He gave up and lost the bets. Because of his failure he was obliged to pay a penny to an Oxford bookmaker. No doubt there were further penalties – fatigue and plenty of teasing.

ALMOST A GREAT VICTORY

MAMARONECK, NEW YORK STATE, JUNE 1957

Jackie Pung listened to her caddie and decided to play the last five holes sensibly. Something approaching pars would win her the American Women's Open Championship and its $1,800 (£645) first prize. Her major rival, Betsy Rawls, was near the end of her round, but Mrs Pung had a two-stroke lead.

Or so it seemed.

Jackie Pung made pars at the fourteenth, fifteenth and sixteenth, and she held her two-stroke lead over Betsy Rawls, who finished with a four-round total of 299. At the seventeenth, Jackie Pung dropped a stroke, but she had no reason to panic; a par four at the eighteenth would give her the Championship.

Wouldn't it?

She was on the green in two and putted close to the hole. She had a four-foot putt for the tournament. Down it went, and she was the new Champion.

Wasn't she?

Jackie Pung, a 35-year-old Hawaiian-born matron from San Francisco, looked a popular winner in those next few minutes. Her 15-year-old daughter Barnett applauded her success, and the press clamoured round her, enjoying her jovial personality and somehow discovering that she weighed 16 stone 11 pounds. She was interviewed for several minutes as the new Champion. Unlike Betsy Rawls, Mrs Pung had not won the tournament previously, though she had come very close in 1953 when she lost a play-off to Rawls.

Jackie Pung referred to that near-miss when the Press questioned her. She explained that she had been keen to avoid a repeat of a play-off with her old adversary. She was photographed with the $1,800 cheque and briefed for the presentation ceremony.

Jackie Pung enjoyed her success for about 40 minutes. Then a voice over the loudspeaker system officially announced that she hadn't won. She had been disqualified for signing a scorecard with an incorrect score for the fourth hole. Her six had appeared as a five. Had she signed for a higher score than the actual, the score would have stood, but a score too low on the card provoked the more severe penalty. The previous year, in the US Open at Rochester, Jack Burke had escaped with a two-stroke penalty for recording a lower score but the rule had been changed since then.

At the par-five fourth, Jackie Pung had driven into the rough, was short of the green in three and finished with a six. Betty Jameson had also taken six, yet both had entered five on their scorecards. Their final-round totals were correct on the scorecards – 72 for Mrs Pung and 85 for Miss Jameson – but that didn't matter. Rule 38 stated that golfers were responsible for the correctness of the score for each hole. Both had the scorecard error for that fourth hole. Both were disqualified. Both cried.

Betty Jameson's 85 had effectively put her out of the running anyway. Before the final round she had trailed Jackie Pung by only three strokes, and was six behind Betsy Rawls. However, that was no consolation for the errors. Both golfers knew they had taken six at the crucial hole, but they hadn't repeated it to each other when marking the cards. Betty Jameson was experienced enough. She had been Champion herself in 1947 and was now greatly disturbed by the error, drawing people's attention to the pressure of the tournament. Journalists also blamed themselves, for being in a hurry to interview Mrs Pung before their deadlines.

Reporters and Winged Foot members quickly organized a collection to compensate for the financial loss of the heartbroken 'winner'. Later that day Mrs Pung was presented with $2,367 (£850) by Mrs Ellis Baum of Winged Foot. The sum was more than the $1,800 prize money, although Mrs Pung would also have received a bonus from the manufacturing company she represented.

Meanwhile, the 1957 American Women's Open Champion was once again Betsy Rawls from Spartanburg, South Carolina. It was her third success, and she had been runner-up to Babe Zaharias in 1950. She was still only 29 years old.

Mrs Pung regained her composure about an hour after the decision was made. She referred to her achievement as 'a great victory – almost'. When she reflected further she made constructive suggestions. She believed the USGA should appoint an official scorer or put the scorer's tent in a quiet spot where golfers could check their cards in a more peaceful setting.

Had the warnings been heeded throughout golf, another strange story of disappointment might have been averted (see page 201).

SLAMMIN' SAMMY BREAKS SIXTY

WHITE SULPHUR SPRINGS, WEST VIRGINIA, MAY 1959

It was 'one of the greatest competitive rounds in golf history', and, fittingly, it was by one of golf's greatest-ever competitors – Sam Snead.

Born in 1912, Snead won 135 tournaments during his career, including 84 on the US Tour. He won seven 'majors' – US Masters (1949, 1952 and 1954), US PGA Championship (1942, 1949 and 1951) and British Open (1946) – and came close to winning the US Open on countless occasions. His first disappointment was in 1937, when Ralph Guldahl swung the tournament on the last nine and Snead was runner-up. In 1939, a five at the last hole would have won it, but Snead, thinking he needed a birdie, took eight and finished fifth. In 1940, his final round was 81, after a first-round lead, and he lost a two-stroke lead over the last three holes of the 1947 play-off. He was second in 1949, second in 1953 and third in 1955. Golf has not known as many near misses as Sam Snead in the US Open. He even finished twenty-fourth when he was 53 years old, and was still trying 12 years later.

Some of his best performances were saved for his home course at White Sulphur Springs, where he won the Greenbrier Open on eight occasions. In fact, the tournament was so dominated by Snead that it was renamed the Sam Snead Festival Invitational in 1955. Snead won the event as late as 1965, when he was nearly 53 years old, but his fifth win, in 1959, was his most sensational.

His 11-under-par third-round score of 59 was the best for a
tournament on a private course. One delving historian
managed to unearth a tournament round of 59 by Earl Fry of
Alameda, California, but that was on a public course,
the Northern Californian Municipal Course. No one would
begrudge Snead a place in records, and he had previously
recorded a 60 in the 1957 Dallas Open.

There was a wind on the Greenbrier course that day, and the
determined Snead mastered it with 11 birdies and an eagle. The
birdies began at the first (from ten feet), and continued at the
third (eight feet), fourth (five feet) and sixth (five feet). He went
for the pin at the ninth, and his ball might have been near the
hole but for hitting a woman who stood too close to the green.
She was unhurt.

Three successive birdies – at the twelfth (from five feet), thirteenth (five feet) and fourteenth (20 feet) – put him in with a
chance of a record. 'It was on the twelfth that I began to realize something wonderful,' he wrote in *Slammin' Sammy* (with
George Mendoza). 'I could feel in my gut that the yips had, for
once, decided to leave me be ... I then began making what I
considered the best run of putting in my career, finishing seven
under par on the last seven holes.'

He eagled the fifteenth with a 35-foot putt and then sank a
seven-foot putt for a birdie at the sixteenth. He had the chance
of another birdie at the seventeenth, where he hit one of the best
iron shots of his life, but his seven-foot putt lipped the hole. On
the eighteenth he took a number-five iron to play his second
shot, knowing that it was a 59, 60 or 61 shot. A birdie three
would seal a sub-60 round. The ball jumped forward a couple of
feet on landing, and came to rest two feet from the pin.

How the crowd cheered.

Snead's card looked like this:

| Par | 434 444 444 | — 35 | 344 435 534 | — 35 (70) |
| Snead | 333 343 444 | — 31 | 343 323 433 | — 28 (59) |

His total of 122 for the last 36 holes bettered the previous record for two consecutive rounds by four strokes. His four-round aggregate of 259 – 68, 69, 59, 63 – was only two off the PGA record achieved by Mike Souchak at the 1955 Texas Open. Snead also came close to Souchak's nine-hole record of 27, and, curiously, it was Souchak who finished second, 11 strokes behind Snead, in the 1959 Greenbrier event. As a contest it was over well before the end. As a third round, though, it was one of highlights of Snead's career, as he had always wanted to break 60. It also ensured that Snead would not hang up his sticks for a long time yet. Indeed, he was still performing well in the 'majors' at an age when most professional golfers would be happy with the Seniors or happy to be playing at all. In 1988, aged 75, he competed in the Senior Skins game and the Legends of Golf Tournament.

THE RIVER CROSSING

THE RIVER THAMES, NEAR CHISWICK, AUGUST 1959

It was a match between two pubs, the City Barge and the Bull's Head. The challenge was to hit balls across the River Thames near the pubs. The carry was 175 yards, and, if nothing else, it would be good practice in case any of the players ever graduated to the sixteenth tee at Cypress Point.

The match was nine-a-side, and each player was allowed to hit two balls. A perfect shot that cleared the river would be awarded 10 points. Other points were awarded, but few of the onlookers and none of the reporters had any great idea what they were awarded for. The consensus was that clearance shots would win the match for one pub or the other.

The captain of the Bull's Head won the toss and went to the tee first. He struck the ball well and, as the ball soared, the spectators had every confidence. Then the ball curved in an all-too-familiar downward arc and fell into the water with a plop. The sight of ball hitting water was soon repeated.

To be fair, it wasn't easy. Playing from the Middlesex side, they were against the wind and were permitted to use only one club – a three-iron. The City Barge captain failed with his two shots, and four balls had now been fed to the fish.

The second Bull's Head player put one in the river and then removed his shoes. No, he didn't intend to wade after the ball, he was just getting comfortable for his second shot. He hit it well and it cleared the river, greeted with a tremendous cheer from the spectators. Ten points to the Bull's Head.

The competitors showed a great variety in style and content. One old-timer put his two shots slap in the middle of the Thames. But one City Barge player put both his balls over the other side of the river, earning his team an invaluable 20 points.

City Barge went on to win 50-35.

THE SPECTATOR WHO HOLED HIMSELF

BRISTOL, MAY 1960

Sidney Gray went to Long Ashton golf course to watch a *Western Daily Press* league match between Long Ashton and Filton. He was a well-known local golfer, a past president and former captain of Filton Golf Club. He hoped Filton would win.

He disappeared near the ninth green.

The Filton golfers were back in the clubhouse when they realized he was missing.

Where was he?

The golfers had no idea. They began to search the course.

He had fallen down one of the biggest holes ever found on a golf-course, a hole 120 feet deep, narrow at the top, wider at the bottom. He was lodged on a ledge down the hole. It was dark and depressing for the 62-year-old former civil servant, and he was in pain.

Eventually he was heard by the search party. His cries came from a thicket near the ninth green. When they investigated they found that the bushes concealed the entrance to a disused iron-ore mineshaft, fenced off with a warning notice posted at the top of its slope. Sidney Gray must have slipped and fallen into the shaft.

The golfers sent for help.

Police and ambulance arrived.

They needed 120 feet of rope to make the rescue. A police sergeant was the first to be lowered down the shaft. He descended into the darkness, securely fastened to the rope that

lowered him. He comforted Mr Gray, and examined his injuries – a head wound and abdominal injuries. Later, at Bristol
Royal Infirmary, a fractured pelvis and fractured rib would be
confirmed.

The policeman looked around the eerie mineshaft, and saw
an earlier victim – a dead fox.

An ambulance driver was lowered down next. It took nearly
two hours to complete the rescue. At 8.15pm, Mr Gray was
secured on to a stretcher and lifted to safety. He was greeted at
the entrance to the mineshaft by the concerned Filton captain.

'Did we win?' asked Sidney Gray.

BEATEN AT THE THIRTY-FIRST

WALTON HEATH, SEPTEMBER 1961

In successive years, a World Match Play Championship match went to 31 holes.

In 1960, at Turnberry, Sid Collins and Bill Branch eclipsed the 1952 Daly-Poulton record by playing 31 holes in the first round. Collins, the winner, was able to rest until the following day, when his second-round match, against E. R. Whitehead of Walton Heath, went to the twentieth hole. Collins won that one too, but lost a rare 18-hole match in the third round – by one hole to J. G. Hewitt.

The following year, at Walton Heath, Harold Henning (South Africa) and Peter Alliss (Parkstone) played 31 holes in the third round. Henning had reached that stage by beating E. G. Lester (Hazel Grove), two and one, and R. J. Foreman (Wentworth), five and three. Alliss had got there with wins over L. Thompson (Shirley), six and four, and Ray Brown (Minchinhampton), at the nineteenth.

Henning was two up on Alliss with five to play. Then Alliss birdied the fourteenth and Henning visited bracken on the sixteenth, so the match was suddenly all-square. Alliss was in a bunker at the seventeenth and Henning took a one-hole lead to the last, where a peculiar incident was recorded by the *Scotsman*: 'Henning mis-hit his drive to the eighteenth when a dog close by suddenly and noisily barked as he swung. So they entered their long safari in the heat ...'

It *was* a long safari. Peter Alliss and Harold Henning were almost subjects for a search party. They were on the course for just under five hours, and played excellent golf. For 12 extra holes – all halved – they were three strokes under fours. The match was finally settled at the thirty-first. Henning played two brilliant shots to finish 12 feet from the pin, whereas Alliss missed the green and took five.

In the fourth round, Henning lost three and two to Neil Coles. The tournament was eventually won by Peter Thomson, who beat Ralph Moffitt, three and one, in the final.

A HOLE HALVED IN ONE

TURNBERRY, AUGUST 1963

In 1991, two punters won hefty sums from small bookmakers in northern England by seducing them into offering generous odds on a hole-in-one at three important British tournaments. They were quoted odds ranging from 7-1 to 33-1, yet Jay Townsend (Benson and Hedges International), Wraith Grant (Volvo PGA) and Brian Marchbank (British Open) duly sank tee-shots in the three tournaments in question. Obviously the bookmakers were unaware that European professionals were averaging a hole-in-one per tournament. Indeed, any book-maker familiar with the detail of the 1989 US Open, when four players holed in one at the sixth hole in the second round, would shorten odds dramatically.

So what odds on a hole being halved in one?

It has happened plenty of times, though it doesn't always in-volve two players holing in one. There is a tale of James Braid, for instance, holing his tee-shot at Walton Heath's sixth hole only to halve the hole because his opponent received a stroke and did it in two.

The first time two golfers holed in one at the same hole was probably at Forest Hills Golf Club, New Jersey, in 1919, when Mr G. Stewart and Mr F. Spellmeyer did it at the eighteenth hole. An early reference book states that one of the players offered a bet of $10,000 (£2,055) to a dollar against it being repeated in his lifetime. It sounds a bit risky ... unless he meant at the same hole.

The first time in Britain was in May 1925, when Gwendoline Clutterbuck (St Augustine Ladies) and Mrs H. M. Robinson (Herne Bay Ladies) halved the 110-yard fifteenth hole, one of seven short holes on the St Augustine course at Ramsgate. Two quick mashie shots and history was made.

Later in 1925, two players at Claremont Golf Club, Swinton, Messrs Evans and Matthews, halved the fourteenth hole in one stroke. The hole was nearly 140 yards, and the players sensibly called up witnesses before going near the hole. Two years later, Colonel F. G. Crompton and E. Macey both holed in one at a much longer hole, one of 175 yards at Royal Eastbourne Golf Club.

In July 1936, there was a case in New Zealand. Two golfers halved a hole-in-one at the Shirley Links in Christchurch. Both balls landed in almost the same spot, slightly to the left of the flag, and then rolled gently into the hole. A true case of 'playing the like'.

Wales too. In 1948, two golfers holed in one at the sixteenth hole at Ashburnham. The beauty of this match was that it was all-square, and the golfer playing second had no choice but to go for the hole.

My personal favourite concerns a match at Turnberry on Sunday 4 August 1963, when a week-end four-ball reached the eleventh hole. Two men, George Gordon and Hugh Wilson, were playing against their wives, Margaret Gordon and Jean Wilson.

From the ladies' tee, Margaret Gordon sank her tee-shot from 137 yards.

The men must have been impressed.

From the men's tee, eight yards further back, Hugh Wilson put his tee-shot on the green. Not good enough.

Presumably Jean Wilson had no need to play.

Then came George Gordon. Yes, you've guessed. He emulated his wife by clipping a nine-iron shot into the air and watching the ball disappear into the hole.

Hole halved.

The men were fortunate that it wasn't one of the seven holes that they were conceding a stroke to the women. It must have been a demoralizing blow. The men won the match by one hole.

FINISHED TWO MONTHS LATER

RYE, JANUARY AND MARCH 1964

An inch of snow fell on Rye during Friday night and Saturday morning. An Arctic icy blast blew in from the coast. The damp, cold air cut through human flesh and searched for bones. The golf, of course, continued.

Every January since 1920, the Oxford and Cambridge Golfing Society has organized the President's Putter as a four-day match-play tournament at Rye Golf Club. The tournament is for Cambridge and Oxford University golf Blues, namely those who played in the annual Oxford-Cambridge Varsity match when they were students.

Played during the British winter, the President's Putter has a history of harsh weather, and golfers often prepare by packing at least three pairs of trousers (to wear at the same time), pyjamas (to wear under the trousers), balaclavas, the latest in hand-warming machines and as many sweaters as possible. Golfers at Rye compete against one another. They also compete against the weather.

Perhaps the Oxford-Cambridge foul-weather golfing heritage has its origins in the 1898 Varsity match, when an Arctic blizzard almost stopped play at Sandwich. Golfers were too cold to hold clubs properly, and balls were frequently lost in the snow. Four golfers, hardly a ball left between them, stumbled off the course in the hope of an abandonment, only to be sent out again later. 'Mr Ranson and Mr Horne had a good match, ending all even both rounds,' said one report of that 1898 Varsity match. 'In the second round, the former, whose hands were perfectly numb, missed his ball twice on the same tee, but won the hole because his partner could not find his ball.'

Despite inclement weather, the President's Putter tournament has always been completed in some form. In 1926 there were two winners, Roger Wethered and Eustace Storey, who halved and halved and halved. On one occasion, in the 1950s, golfers coped with fog so dense that, according to Alistair Cooke, 'It seeped into the hotels so you needed a link boy to light your way to your plate of bacon, baps and bangers'. In 1962 play was impossible at Rye, and the tournament was shifted to Littlestone, a few miles along the coast. In 1964 it took even more ingenuity to complete the President's Putter.

The first day's weather was placid enough. Talk was more about golf than wind, rain and cold. Players and officials discussed whether Francis Ricardo's two-faced club, a croquet-like putter on one side and a chipping iron on the other, was legal. David Physick's bag contained eight wooden clubs, and his irons started at number six. He hadn't hit many good iron shots for years and this seemed like the answer.

Friday was colder than Thursday but still manageable. The problems started on Saturday morning. An inch of snow covered the course. Sixteen players remained in the tournament, and the fourth-round matches went ahead. The rules were bent slightly. Players were allowed to chip on the greens, snow could be cleaned off balls on the fairways, and golfers were permitted to sweep a path from ball to flag on the greens. Most of them painted their balls red – women have been known to colour balls with lipstick for use in snow – and markers were sent down the course to spot where balls landed.

The sweeping, cleaning and marking all took up extra time. Most of the 18-hole matches took about four hours to complete, and the one between Gethyn Hewan, a Winchester schoolmaster, and Colonel Tony Duncan, an ex-Walker Cup captain and twice winner of the President's Putter, took nearly five hours. Duncan won at the twenty-first hole.

Snow continued to fall, and another round was impossible.

Eight players remained in the tournament, but conditions prevented any play on the Sunday. The solution was to complete the tournament on a day when all the eight players were again available. After consulting diaries, they settled on a day late in March, and the format was to be two 12-hole rounds (the fourth round and semi-finals) followed by an 18-hole final.

The tournament was therefore completed later. Donald Steel, a London golf writer who later wrote *The Guinness Book of Golf Facts and Feats*, beat Tony Duncan two and one in the fourth round, and took care of Pyett at the thirteenth hole in his semi-final. Steel then won the competition by beating Michael Attenborough by one hole in a more conventional 18-hole final.

THE MILWAUKEE MAIL-SORTER

ROYAL BIRKDALE, JULY 1965

Amateur or professional?

Walter Daniecki looked at the application form and thought about his answer. There was big money in golf and he didn't see why he shouldn't touch some of it. It wasn't only the title he wanted. He was chasing money too.

Professional, he wrote.

But he didn't give up his job as a mail-sorter in Milwaukee, Wisconsin.

The British Open at Royal Birkdale was his first tournament. He had been a professional for three years but was not attached to a club and he still queued for a game at his local municipal course. He had never had a lesson in his life. He saved money for a year so he could travel to England, and he kept it secret from his friends and colleagues at work. He didn't want them to know his ambition. He would sneak across to Britain, play in the Open Championship, win it and then reveal everything.

It was a beautiful fantasy.

His first task was to qualify for the Open. That meant playing two rounds in the Hillside section. He played with the small ball, rather than the larger American one he was more familiar with. He later doubted whether the change made too much difference.

Daniecki was then 44 years old, a tall, well-built, dark-haired bachelor who was living out his golfing dream. Sadly, for him, the dream went no further than qualifying rounds of 108 and 113, and he finished 81 over par. He missed the cut by 70 strokes and was 82 behind Fred Boobyer, the leading qualifier. But the public loved his pretension. Rabbits all over the world identified with Daniecki's dream and wished they had had the courage to emulate him. He was also respected for continuing to the end. Others might have been tempted to record 'no return' when they had so little chance in the final round – a substitute had been nominated to take his place – but Daniecki completed his round with the following scores:

778 557 955 – 58   96ten 465 546 – 55 (113)

In mitigation it should be said that he had a sore right hand. However, even at peak fitness, it is unlikely that he would have made too much impression on Peter Thomson, who won the British Open for the fifth time and whose score after the first three rounds (214) was better than Daniecki's for two.

Daniecki was not the last unlikely golfer to sneak into the qualifying rounds for the British Open. In 1976, Maurice Flitcroft, a Barrow-in-Furness crane-driver, slipped through the screening process as an unattached professional. He went round Formby in 121 – a mere 49 over par. As Pat Ward-Thomas wrote, Flitcroft's qualifying round was 'marred by only one par'. And Bo Brit, who entered in 1988 as the professional from New Mexico State University, was persuaded to hand in his card at the third hole after hacking his way through the rough at Fairhaven.

HELP FROM THE ARCHERS

CARLISLE TO NEWCASTLE, OCTOBER 1965

The Cumberland archery champion Ron Willis stood on the battlements of Carlisle Castle, pulled back his right arm to curve his bow, let go and released an arrow 300 yards to start a weird golf match.

Archers and golfers have met several times in the history of freak matches. This 1965 match, started by the archer and ended 60 miles away with two putts by the president of Newcastle United Golf Club, was a co-operative venture. Usually the archers were in direct competition with golfers, and sometimes with other sportsmen, such as fishermen or baseball players.

Golfer-archer matches go back at least to 1906, when Sir Ralph Payne-Gallwey, a well-known archer, played W. Hunter, the Richmond professional golfer, in a singles match. Payne-Gallwey used a Turkish bow and arrow from tee to green, and then putted the ball in the normal way. His 'drives' went nearly 400 yards, but Hunter, who received a third, defeated the archer by five and four. In December 1913 Harry Vardon was involved in a foursome, which saw two golfers take on two javelin-throwers. The javelins had to be thrown into a two-foot square around the hole. The golfers, conceding two-thirds in distance, won by five and four.

During the inter-war period, matches between golfers and archers were too common to merit the label 'strange'. At Royston Golf Club, in March 1926, a team of Cambridge Archers won four and halved one of their seven matches. Using bow and arrows, the archers aimed to transfix a ball of straw (diameter 4¼ inches) on the green, while the golfers aimed for the usual hole with customary ball and clubs. If an arrow fell into a bunker, the archer lost a stroke. The captain of the Cambridge archers went round in 70, two under par.

Several such matches were staged at Letchworth in the late 1920s and early 1930s. 'The archers had little difficulty shooting arrows and hitting the greens in regulation figures,' wrote Rodney Hawkins in *Golf at Letchworth* about the 1929 match, 'but could not master the putting.' The golfers won that one, as they did at Tyrrells Wood, Leatherhead, in 1926, but victory usually went to the archers.

The joint venture from Carlisle Castle to Newcastle United Golf Club, which began on 11 October 1965, owed a lot to the initiative of Charles Macey, assistant professional at the Crowborough Beacon Golf Club, near Tunbridge Wells, Sussex. The Crowborough Beacon club has an ever-continuing good record of strange matches, and Charles Macey is a candidate for a place in Golf's Hall of Strange Fame.

Macey first wrote himself into the *Golfer's Handbook* in June 1944, when, as a young man of 20, he played 12 rounds of Folkestone Golf Course in one day. He started at 7.30 am and finished at 10.50 pm, continuing through an air-raid warning and a German bombardment. He played with a borrowed set of clubs and had four different caddies, including a non-commissioned officer (NCO) and a policeman. He walked approximately 40 miles, played 949 shots and averaged 79 for his dozen 18-hole rounds.

While Charles Macey was around, the future of strange golf matches was in suitably 'unsafe' hands. In August 1959, for instance, Crowborough Beacon members claimed 'the longest hole in the world', playing just over 37 miles from the first tee at Crowborough Beacon to the eighteenth green at Downs Golf Club, Eastbourne. A team of four played 896 teed shots with Penfold Patented golf balls, and 65 Penfolds disappeared into various parts of the Sussex landscape. Equipped with bicycles, it took the golfers only 16 hours.

And so to Carlisle in 1965, for an even bigger venture. The 60-mile hole was along Hadrian's Wall. The terrain was so rugged that the team of four golfers expected to be stuck in impossible lies and faced with difficult obstacles. Hence the two archers. Their role was to fire an arrow if rough country made a golf shot impossible. Each arrow fired would naturally count as a shot. The target was to get from Carlisle to Newcastle in under 1,000 shots. It was a tough target but the archer could 'hit the ball' a long way.

After Ron Willis's first shot, he 'played' the second too – across the River Eden. Soon, the six players were trekking along Hadrian's Wall, searching for balls and arrows, and selecting the next shot. They made nine miles that day, and stayed the night at Newtown, near Irthington. It had taken 94 strokes, and they had lost 11 golf balls and broken two arrows. They had brought a white Alsatian called Penny with them to track down lost balls, but, in case Penny didn't always succeed, they had 250 balls tucked away in duffel-bags.

It took them five days to reach Newcastle. They negotiated hills and treacherous ravines, sometimes driving balls off 100-foot crags. Always there was the 60-mile wall of Emperor Hadrian to guide them. When they did get lost, it was not in the rugged Northumberland countryside but on a Newcastle housing estate a mile from their destination. They were guided to the wrong golf course and lost several important shots. Finally, at the Newcastle United Golf Club, they were met by Robert Clough, the club president, and he was allowed to putt out on the eighteenth green. It took 612 shots (388 under par), but they lost 110 golf balls and 19 broken arrows.

The four golfers were Charles Macey, Keith Ashdown, Miss P. Ward and K. Meaney, and the two archers were Bill Hulme and T. Scott. Their aim was to raise money for the Guide Dogs for the Blind and Friends of the Crowborough Hospital.

PLAYER AND LEMA

WENTWORTH, OCTOBER 1965

Gary Player and Tony Lema, both around 30 years old, were at their peak, confident and successful. That year Player had not only won his native South African Championship again but had added the coveted US Open Championship. The previous year Lema had won the British Open and done it in style. The American was known as Champagne Tony, after keeping his promise to reporters at one tournament that he would provide champagne if he won.

Player and Lema were drawn together for a semi-final of the 1965 Piccadilly World Match Play tournament. In the quarter-finals, Lema had beaten Peter Alliss five and four, and Player had brilliantly beaten Neil Coles by the same score. The matches were played over 36 holes. The Lema-Player semi-final was an astounding test of physical and emotional strength. More than one golf correspondent later considered it as perhaps the greatest of all golf victories ever recorded.

The previous year, Player had been thrashed by Arnold Palmer in a World Match Play semi-final. He was anxious to make amends, and his match with Lema was given added spice from another direction. Slazenger had dropped Player's club-endorsing contract and negotiated with Lema instead. Tony Lema was a real threat to the 'Big Three' of the 1960s – Palmer, Player and Jack Nicklaus.

In the morning, Gary Player went out in 34, including an eagle three at the fourth, and was one up at the turn. He was almost two up at the tenth, but Lema saved his half by holing a 15-foot putt. Then, as Player suddenly began to struggle with his game, Lema hit top form and strung together a run of success. Lema won the eleventh, twelfth, thirteenth, fourteenth, fifteenth, sixteenth and seventeenth. Seven successive holes. Lema's phenomenal run of seven holes included five birdies. He came back in 32 for a round of 67. After a half at the eighteenth, where Player holed a character-testing putt to save the hole, Lema went into lunch six up.

Player had already had a tiring year. Now, he was trying to adjust to match-play, a less familiar form of competition. Furthermore, he was six down and needed to correct his swing, which had developed a slight hook. Player spent lunchtime on the practice-tee.

When Lema won the first in the afternoon, to go seven up, surely most players would have given up and settled for an easy round.

Not Gary Player.

Seven down with 17 to play was just more of a challenge.

Player birdied the second and third, and his deficit was now five holes. At the sixth Player received an unexpected boost. It came from two spectators who were debating whether to watch the match behind instead. One of these spectators was adamant that Player's match would soon be over. Player suggested that the spectator should stick around – he might just see something that would surprise him.

At the tenth, Lema missed the green and his lead was cut to four. At the eleventh and thirteenth Player collected birdies. Now he was only two down with five to play.

They halved the fourteenth and fifteenth.

At the sixteenth Lema hooked a shot into the trees and conceded the hole. Now only one hole separated two golfers who were searching for last reserves. At the seventeenth, Player holed a difficult putt to keep the match alive, and the hole was halved. Player still needed to win the eighteenth to square the match. His second shot was a four-wood which somehow missed the trees and dodged the bunkers to finish pin high. Player took the hole.

Now for a 'sudden-death' play-off.

At the thirty-seventh hole of the match, Lema was short and bunkered, while Player was on the green. Player left himself a putt of a yard to win the match. It was almost more than he could manage. He was emotionally drained. He sized up the putt, tapped the ball with his putter – on the right jerk of his club, as he later explained – and the ball went into the hole.

Gary Player had beaten Tony Lema at the thirty-seventh. He had been living inside a peak experience on the homeward holes, spiritually and physically uplifted. Only when it was over did he succumb to trembling hands and exhaustion.

The South African had come home in 33 (if we assume he would have putted a short one at the sixteenth). Then, far from relaxing, he had had to start again at the thirty-seventh to take another hole. Lema, dazed and demoralized, showed no bitterness, but wished he hadn't been playing such a fighter as Player. Even the next day, at the airport, Lema was still trying to believe it had really happened. As Player pointed out, golf was a mean, mean game at the top.

Often, when players win a draining semi-final, they are too exhausted to raise their game again for the final. Not Player. His opponent in the final was Australian Peter Thomson, who led by one hole at lunch. In the afternoon, Player turned it on again. He won three and two, and took the tournament.

The following year Tony Lema and his wife were killed in a private aeroplane while travelling to a pro-am tournament.

DAVE HILL'S EXTRA STROKES

CLIFTON, NEW JERSEY, AUGUST 1966

After two rounds of the Thunderbird tournament at Upper Montclair Country Club, the bottom placings were more eye-catching than those at the top. Billy Casper (138) was in the lead after rounds of 70 and 68, closely followed by Milton 'Babe' Lichardus (71 + 68 = 139) and Mason Rudolph (69 + 70 = 139), while, at the bottom of the list, there was no doubt that Dave Hill had missed the cut:

Lou Barbaro	80	79	—	159
Dick Howell	81	78	—	159
Tom Nieporte	83	77	—	160
Dave Hill	79	178	—	257

Dave Hill's second-round score of 178 looks like a mistake. Indeed it was, but the mistake was on Dave Hill's card rather than in the actual scores. He had inadvertently recorded his score at one hole as 108 rather than 10. The official PGA statement explains what happened: 'It is now determined that the score came about in this manner: Hill's scorekeeper (Gardner Dickinson) recorded an '8' and Hill wrote a '10' beside it but failed to erase or cross out the '8'. When Hill turned in the signed card it read 108 and the score stands as recorded.'

Without the mistake, Hill would have recorded a round of 80, which would have lifted him only one place in the standings. He would have missed the cut anyway, so this was one occasion when a mistake on the card made very little difference, unlike the 1957 US Women's Open or the 1968 US Masters (see page 201).

The 1966 Thunderbird Classic tournament, continuing without Dave Hill, developed into a close contest with several changes of lead. Billy Martindale had a two-stroke advantage after 54 holes, but Jack Nicklaus, Tommy Aaron and Mason Rudolph were in the chasing pack. It was Rudolph who came through to win in a nail-biting finish. He was all-square with Nicklaus with four to play before a birdie at the fifteenth and Nicklaus's bogey at the seventeenth gave him a two-stroke lead. Rudolph had been the most consistent of the leaders over the four rounds.

Mason Rudolph	69	70	70	69	—	278
Jack Nicklaus	71	72	66	70	—	279
Billy Martindale	72	69	66	74	—	281
Tommy Aaron	74	68	67	73	—	282

THE LONG FINAL

SEWICKLEY, PENNSYLVANIA, AUGUST 1966

The finalists for the 1966 US Women's Amateur Championship were two of the best-ever women golfers – 27-year-old JoAnne Carner of the United States and 32-year-old Marlene Streit of Canada. They contested a gripping final that swung back and forth through 41 holes.

But first a flashback of 10 years ...

It is the 1956 US Women's Amateur Championship final and the same two finalists. JoAnne Gunderson is only 17, a precocious golfer who has already won the National Junior Championship. Marlene Stewart, a 22-year-old from Fonthill, Ontario, has already won the Canadian Closed Championship six times and the British Amateur Championship. This 1956 final is strange in its own way. At the Meridian Hills Country Club, Gunderson has a one-hole lead after 18 holes, extends it to two, then three, before holing a 38-foot chip to birdie the sixth and take a four-hole lead. Gunderson three-putts at the next and only halves the hole, but she is still four up with 11 to play. Suddenly the 17-year-old's game goes to pieces. She loses the eighth, ninth and eleventh, and fails with a two-foot putt at the twelfth to lose that too. Her lead has disappeared. Marlene Stewart's par five at the fourteenth wins her that hole, and a par four at the seventeenth wins her the match, two and one. Gunderson has lost six out of 10 holes. She has done the last 11 in seven over par.

In the intervening 10 years, between the 1956 and 1966 finals, JoAnne Gunderson established herself as one of the all-time American greats. 'The Great Gundy', as she was known before her marriage to Don Carner, won the US Amateur Championship in 1957, 1960 and 1962 (with more to come). Marlene Stewart-Streit had gone on to further success too. Three times Canadian athlete of the year in the 1950s, she was well on the way to her career total of 11 victories in the Canadian Open Amateur Championship.

So the 1966 finalists were the two biggest names of the era.

Would JoAnne Carner avenge her defeat of 1956?

On the Sewickley Heights golf course, Carner led by three holes after the first nine, but it was still early in the 36-hole final. After going out in 35, Carner returned in 43, and Marlene Stewart-Streit, with a more consistent round of 74, was one up after the day's first round.

The second round had a similar pattern to the first. Carner was ahead again at the third, and three up after the seventh. Then the fortunes swung dramatically. Does it remind you of the 1956 final?

Marlene Stewart-Streit won three successive holes on the way home, and she went to the seventeenth with a lead of one hole. It was all too familiar for those with 10-year memories, but JoAnne Carner's par five at the seventeenth was good enough to win the hole because the Canadian three-putted from 32 feet for a bogey six. All-square with one to play.

That last hole was an exciting one. It was a 354-yard dog-leg right, and JoAnne Carner's drive put her ball behind trees. She played it out and then hit her third into 'a thick fringe'. She was in trouble but got down in two for a five, putting out from 15 feet.

The Canadian hit a good drive but put her second into a bunker. She recovered well and had a comfortable putt for a birdie and victory. It looked in but rolled round the rim and out.

On they went. On and on and on.

In 'sudden-death' they halved the first four holes. It looked all over at the thirty-ninth when Stewart-Streit's ball went in a bunker but somehow she extricated herself for a half, helped by

Carner taking three putts. Another good putt by the Canadian rescued her half at the fortieth.

The match was decided at the fifth extra hole – their forty-first of the day. It was a par-four hole of 309 yards, and Marlene Stewart-Streit's drive struck a tree and bounced into the rough. Her second went into a bunker. She blasted out of sand and was left with a putt of 18 feet. She missed it, bogeyed the hole in five and JoAnne Carner had a two-foot putt for victory. Carner might have missed a similar one in the 1956 final, but she wasn't going to miss this one. Down it went to secure her fourth US Amateur Championship victory. She had done 41 holes in 174 (five over), one stroke less than the Canadian.

Two years later, JoAnne Carner won her fifth title, only one behind Glenna Collett's record. Having achieved so much in amateur golf, Carner turned professional in 1970 and went from strength to strength. The 'Big Moma' of the US Ladies tour, she won 42 professional tournaments, including the US Women's Open in 1971 and 1976, and she lost a play-off for the US Women's Open, to Laura Davies, as late as 1987. JoAnne Carner defied golf history by having such an impact on both amateur and professional golf, and she continued to hold people's respect by playing at the top in five different decades – the 1950s through to the 1990s.

DE VICENZO'S BIRTHDAY CARD

AUGUSTA, GEORGIA, APRIL 1968

The day of the final round of the US Masters was also Roberto de Vicenzo's forty-fifth birthday. He had achieved a lot during those 45 years, progressing from Buenos Aires caddie to British Open Champion, a title he had won the previous summer. He had also won a lot of friends.

In the major US tournaments, de Vicenzo's best finishing positions were eighth (US Open) and tenth (US Masters), but this particular Sunday he had a chance to win. After three rounds he was two strokes behind Gary Player, the formidable leader, and a stroke behind three other players. The list ran as follows:

Gary Player	72	67	71	—	210
Frank Beard	75	65	71	—	211
Bruce Devlin	69	73	69	—	211
Bob Goalby	70	70	71	—	211
Roberto de Vicenzo	69	73	70	—	212
Tommy Aaron	69	72	72	—	213

For the final round, de Vicenzo (fifth) partnered Aaron (sixth). It was a pairing that produced memorable golf and a sensational climax, albeit for the wrong reasons.

De Vicenzo began his final round by holing a nine-iron for an eagle two at the 400-yard first hole. He birdied the second and third to take a two-stroke lead, and reached the turn in 31. The crowd sang 'Happy Birthday' and de Vicenzo celebrated. In the

201

past he had had troubles with his putting. Not this year. Not on this occasion.

What made this a stunning day's play was that de Vicenzo wasn't alone in playing brilliantly. On any ordinary day the tournament might have been won by Yancey's 65 (for 279), Devlin's 69 (for 280), or Nicklaus's 67 (for 281). Frank Beard's 70 (for 281), Gary Player's 72 (for 282) and Tommy Aaron's 69 (for 282) could hardly be considered evidence of 'cracking up under pressure'. In the end, however, the contest was between de Vicenzo and Bob Goalby, a relatively little-considered 37-year-old American. Goalby was matching de Vicenzo's performance. When he putted in from off the fourteenth green and eagled the fifteenth with a 15-foot putt, Goalby went 12 under par, having gained five strokes on par in only eight holes.

De Vicenzo was playing the seventeenth while Goalby played the fifteenth. The seventeenth was to prove the crucial hole of the tournament, for bizarre reasons.

Watched by a huge television audience, the Argentinian reached the green in two shots, then holed a putt to go 12 under with Goalby. Most observers saw it as a birdie three, but Tommy Aaron marked de Vicenzo's card with a 'four' for the hole.

De Vicenzo's incredible golf was spoiled slightly by a bogey five on the final hole to give him a round of 65, but Goalby took three putts on his next hole – the seventeenth. With Goalby to play the 420-yard eighteenth, the two men were level.

Goalby's tee-shot on the par-four eighteenth struck trees on the right but bounced back into play. His second finished 60 feet from the hole, and a long putt left him with another stressful putt of four or five feet for par. He made it, and finished on 277, level with de Vicenzo.

The drama had begun. De Vicenzo, emotional at the end of the round, excited at such a birthday present, had one more task to perform. He had to sign his card. He looked it over three or four times. That 'five' at the last hole was what he saw, the bogey he thought had cost him an outright victory in the US Masters. He didn't notice too much else. He signed the card, handed it in and left the roped-off area around the last green. People wanted to talk to him. He had plenty to talk about, in his familiar charming manner.

The mistake on the card was noticed by officials. The rules were very clear. If a golfer signed for a score higher than that achieved, the score must stand. If a golfer signed for a lower score, the outcome must be disqualification. De Vicenzo's card showed a score too high – four rather than three – for the seventeenth hole. It had to be included in his total as a four, even if millions of television viewers had witnessed the birdie three. His 65 became a 66. He lost the Masters by one stroke, a stroke he had never played.

Bob Goalby	70	70	71	66	—	277
Roberto de Vicenzo	69	73	70	66	—	278
Bert Yancey	71	71	72	65	—	279
Bruce Devlin	69	73	69	69	—	280

When the mistake was discovered, everyone behaved with dignity. The officials checked whether there was any leeway. Had de Vicenzo really left the roped-off area? Yes, he had. The rule had to apply. The scorecard was part of the game, and the scorecard was de Vicenzo's responsibility.

De Vicenzo blamed only himself. 'What a stupid I am,' he said, endearingly, in his heavy English accent. He conceded that Goalby's final round had put him under pressure, and forced him to make two mistakes – a hooked drive at the last hole and signing for the wrong scorecard.

It was hard for Goalby, who would probably rather have played off and lost than won on such a technicality. He received little of the credit he deserved. Goalby had, after all, legitimately tied with de Vicenzo and was playing golf superb enough to win the play-off. He won 11 PGA events in his career, and no one could begrudge him the 1968 US Masters.

There were, of course, lessons to be learned. While playing partners were generally shown to be more expert markers than non-players, it was apparent that de Vicenzo might not have made his mistake if he had been taken somewhere quiet to check his card. The system was changed the next year, and officials went through the card hole-by-hole.

GOLF ON THE MOON

FRA MAURO DRIVING RANGE, FEBRUARY 1971

'Houston, you might recognize what I have in my hand is
the handle for the contingency sample return,' Captain Alan
Shepard reported to base while standing on the surface of the
moon. 'It just so happens to have a genuine six-iron on the
bottom of it. In my left hand I have a little white pellet that's
familiar to millions of Americans. I'll drop it down. Unfortunately, the suit is so stiff I can't do this with two hands but
I'm going to try a little sand-trap shot here.'

Captain Shepard, commander of the Apollo 14 spacecraft
and the fifth man on the moon, duly set up his lunar golfing
experiment. He had prior permission to take the golf club on
board, but some of his colleagues were surprised. The club
had been devised by Jack Harden, a golf professional at River
Oaks Country Club near Houston. The head was that of a normal six-iron, but the shaft was in three aluminium sections,
which fitted together with Teflon joints and inserted into the
30-inch handle used by astronauts for moonwalk tasks requir-
ing a shovel and an axe. The overall weight was 16½ ounces.

Millions of television viewers were captivated by the idea
of hitting a golf shot on the moon. It was one giant shot for
golfkind. If Shepard, a 15-handicap golfer, could hit a normal
six-iron shot about 140 yards, how far could he hit one on the
moon, where the gravity was one-sixth that of earth?

About 800 yards?

It wasn't going to be easy with the restrictions of his stiff
space-suit and his one-handed swing.

Indeed, when Shepard waggled his space-suit, kept his head down and brought back his strange club, he was restricted immensely by his suit material, and his back-pack shortened the swing. He found it difficult to hit the ball.

'You got more dirt than ball that time,' commented Commander Edgar Mitchell, Shepard's companion on the moon. The third man in the party, Major Stuart Roosa, stayed in orbit while the other two collected soil samples.

Undeterred, Shepard threw down his second golf ball – he had brought three – and swung his six-iron again. The ball sailed away. It went a long way. He later estimated a couple of hundred yards, although it wasn't possible to measure it. His third attempt was even better, and Shepard estimated about 400 yards. But there wasn't a green in sight. Not even green rocks.

After Apollo 14 returned to earth, the Royal and Ancient Golf Club of St Andrews acknowledged Captain Shepard's feat by sending him a telegram: 'Warmest congratulations to all of you on your great achievement and safe return. Please refer to Rules of Golf section on etiquette, paragraph 6, quote – before leaving a bunker a player should carefully fill up all holes made by him therein, unquote.'

Captain Shepard was later honoured by awards from the Metropolitan Golf Writers' Association and *Golf Magazine*. In 1974 he presented his custom-made six-iron club to the United States Golf Association Museum at Far Hills, New Jersey, where it can be seen today.

THE BLALOCK CASE

LOUISVILLE, KENTUCKY, MAY 1972

Jane Blalock could be easily distinguished from other golfers on the Ladies Tour in the 1970s because she played in shorts and wore her hair in pigtails. Then something else set her further apart from the other women.

It began at the Women's Bluegrass Invitational at Louisville's Hunting Creek Country Club. Blalock was the leading LPGA Tour money-winner at the time. After a first-round 75, and outward 40 in the second round, she hit top form – five successive birdies in an inward half of 32. But that evening the LPGA executive board disqualified her from the tournament. They said that she had been observed mismarking her ball on the greens, thereby moving it to her advantage. If true, it amounted to cheating.

At the next tournament, the Titleholders, she was again accused of moving her ball. The distances talked about were small – a few inches – but the LPGA thought that the principle was big. Jane Blalock apologized, in case she had inadvertently done something wrong, and thought that would be the end of the matter. Instead it was seen as an admission of guilt, and the incident escalated. At the end of the tournament – she finished seventh – she was suspended for a year. She protested her innocence.

Lawyers were soon involved. A temporary injunction allowed Jane Blalock to play in the next tournament, the LPGA Championship, where she finished second. Her lawyers filed a law suit for $5,000,000 (£2,065,000) against the LPGA and five

207

members of the executive board. They considered it a breach of the Sherman Anti-Trust Act, because, as the executive board included current golfers, the suspension was tantamount to a group boycott, denying Jane Blalock her right to earn a living. A further injunction allowed her to continue to compete until the case was settled, but any winnings would have to be held over by the courts.

Golfers on the Tour took sides, and the atmosphere was tense. 'It was like a hair-pulling contest,' said Jane Blalock in her autobiography. Sandra Palmer, a staunch ally of Blalock's, was sued for slander by another competitor and then placed on probation by the LPGA. More claims and counter-claims were set rolling.

The case lasted for two turbulent years. Jane Blalock won the 1972 Civitan Open at Dallas after a play-off with Kathy Whitworth, and she also won the last event of 1972, the Lady Errol Classic, when she beat Palmer and Whitworth in a three-way play-off. In 1973, however, her play showed signs of the strain, and she finished ninth on the list of money-winners.

In June 1973, over a year after the ordeal began, Judge Moye ruled in Blalock's favour. The decision was confirmed in August, when permission to appeal was denied. Judge Moye saw the LPGA action as an unlawful group boycott and restraint of trade.

Another year went by before the matter was closed. On 26 August 1974, Jane Blalock was awarded $98,000 (£42,000) as compensation for lost earnings. It was less than her lawyer's bill. She said later that there were no winners, financially or emotionally.

A TALE OF TWO PERMITS

BUFFALO, MAY, 1972

The tragic death of 41-year-old John Mosley, after an incident on the first tee at Delaware Park Golf Club, is a sobering, strange tale.

John Mosley played regularly at the Delaware Park course and had a permit to play. Unfortunately, on this particular morning, when he turned up shortly before 10 o'clock, he discovered that the permit was in his wife's car in Alabama. Perhaps another fee-collector might have recognized him. The one on duty wanted to see his permit.

The dispute between Mosley and the fee-collector attracted the attention of a special officer named Solomon Fletcher. It was the first year that the Parks Department had employed a 'security guard' on golf courses, and Solomon Fletcher's main task was to ensure that golfers didn't avoid payment by sneaking on to the course at a hole other than the first. Golfers worried about on-course muggings may even have been reassured at the sight of an armed guard, for Fletcher carried a gun. During the 1960s, while working for a number of security firms, he had held a pistol permit for four years. The permit had been reissued in December 1970 and renewed in April 1972 for this new job. Fletcher had twice been convicted of minor offences.

Solomon Fletcher and John Mosley began to argue. Fletcher arrested Mosley for disorderly conduct. The two men walked towards Fletcher's car, about 40 feet from the tee, and Fletcher started putting handcuffs on Mosley when a scuffle started.

'Officer Fletcher took a night-stick out of his cart and struck the victim with it', stated one report.

Another scuffle followed. The night-stick (truncheon) fell to the ground. Fletcher stepped back, drew his pistol from the holster, and shot Mosley once in the chest with no apparent warning. The wounded man was rushed to Sisters Hospital, where he died at about 10.07.

Over 20 golfers witnessed the shooting, and the police began to build up a strong case of first-degree manslaughter against the security guard. The Parks Department reassigned Solomon Fletcher to the Humboldt Park wading-pool as a timekeeper and clean-up man. Then, when they received complaints about the fatal shooting from the public, and realized that Fletcher was only a seasonal worker and had no permanent status, they struck him off the payroll. His pistol permit had been withdrawn after the shooting incident.

It was a tale of two permits.

How does a golfer confirm he has permission to play the course?

How does a man come to carry a gun?

Solomon Fletcher was later sentenced to seven and a half years in prison, and John Mosley's wife was awarded $131,250 (£55,400) in an action against the City of Buffalo and the guard.

'SARAZEN LICKS THE POSTAGE STAMP'

TROON, JULY 1973

He was 71 years old when he stood on the elevated eighth tee that Wednesday afternoon, playing in the British Open yet again. Troon was where the British Open had started for him, 50 years ago, so this was a sentimental journey. He had no need to do anything strange or sensational over the 126 yards of this eighth hole – his place in golfing history was already assured – but he did it all the same. Gene Sarazen's drive at 'the Postage Stamp' hole, the shortest hole on a championship course in Britain, was an abiding memory for those who saw it on television. Whatever the result of the 1973 British Open, part of the tournament belonged to Sarazen, and the newspaper headliners were in their element. 'Sarazen licks the postage stamp' was a favourite.

He was born as Eugene Saraceni in Harrison, New York, on 27 February 1902, and a quick glance at the record books would place him as a great *pre-war* golfer rather than in the same era as Lanny Wadkins, Sam Torrance and Graham Marsh, who were all at Troon in 1973. Sarazen won both the US Open and US PGA in 1922, and retained the US PGA the following year. In 1923, at Troon, he began his long connection with the British Open by failing to make the cut after inglorious rounds of 75 and 85. Fifty years later, the captain of the Royal and Ancient Golf Club presented Sarazen and Arthur Havers, winner in 1923, with inscribed silver cigarette boxes.

Sarazen didn't win the British Open until 1932, his victory

211

coming just a few weeks after he had won the US Open again. Bob Jones was the only man before Sarazen to win the US Open and British Open in the same year, and, by 1973, only Ben Hogan and Lee Trevino had repeated the achievement. During his career, Sarazen won all four majors, his most spectacular success coming when he turned the 1935 US Masters tournament with an albatross two at the par-five fifteenth in the final round. In the 1950s he won the US PGA Seniors twice, and in 1960 he competed in the British Open at St Andrews and went round in 69 on the Old Course.

A small, stocky man, even smaller than Trevino, Sarazen was usually dressed elegantly in plus-fours and flat cap. At 71, the arthritis in his shoulders had sapped some distance from his drives, but he wrapped up well to face the wind and rain of Troon, and matched his age when practising on the Monday of Open week.

Come the tournament proper, and Sarazen played with two other past Open Champions – Fred Daly (1947) and Max Faulkner (1951). It was a delightful threesome for a gallery to enjoy. If they found it a long way to the 577-yard sixth hole – the longest on a British Championship course – they made the eighth seem even shorter than 126 yards.

The eighth could be daunting. 'The narrowness of the target is unnerving from the elevated tee,' stated one summary. 'and many have come to grief in the five vast bunkers.' Sarazen took a five-iron and punched his shot into the wind, 'an old-fashioned half shot' which landed 20 feet from the pin, bounced once and trickled gently into the cup. A hole-in-one in the British Open ... at the age of 71. He had holed in one six times before, including the first shot of a nighttime game, but never in a Championship and never in an era that could be recorded by film.

Fred Daly's drive at the same hole finished five feet away from the pin, but it was rather overshadowed by Sarazen's. Another player Sarazen upstaged was David Russell, a Midlands amateur, who had holed the eighth in one a couple of hours before, his shot going in-off a greenside knoll.

If a hole in one wasn't enough, Sarazen grabbed attention at the eighth hole on the second day too. Although his first shot went into one of the 'vast bunkers', his second went into the hole on the fly. He had done the eighth in one and two, and hadn't used his putter on the hole. David Russell also added a second-day two to his first-day hole-in-one at the eighth but achieved his birdie by driving on to the green and holing his putt.

Not everyone could 'lick the Postage Stamp' like Sarazen and Russell. The bunkers lived up to their 'unnerving' reputation for some. Peter Oosterhuis failed to make his par on each of the first two days, and Arnold Palmer played three in the bunker before escaping for a seven in his second round.

The three golden oldies – Faulkner (153), Sarazen (160) and Daly (173) – all failed to make the qualifying score of 152, but somehow that wasn't the point. All had entertained and displayed inter-generational skills, and Gene Sarazen's 160 was exactly the same 36-hole score as for his first British Open in 1923, when his failure to qualify had been a surprise. This time he publicly presented his five-iron, used to hole the Postage Stamp in one, to the Royal and Ancient Golf Club, and he left as a hero.

For the realists, the tournament was dominated by big-hitting Americans – Tom Weiskopf (first), who led after every round, Johnny Miller (second) and Jack Nicklaus (fourth). For the romantics, the tournament belonged to Gene Sarazen.

ALONE WITH NATURE

TURNBERRY, SEPTEMBER 1973

'When playing golf you want to be alone with nature,' wrote Charles B Macdonald (1856-1932), a pioneer American golfer and golf-course architect. Macdonald was explaining why he felt golf courses should be built in remote land free from roads and railways. He had learned his golf in Scotland, where an affinity with nature is a prerequisite for most golfers. A reminder of this came with the 1973 John Player Classic Tournament.

The Player Classic was the most financially attractive tournament in Europe at the time, with £58,000 prize money, plus a special Grand Masters prize for the lowest 288-hole aggregate score for the US Masters, British Open, US Open and Player Classic. The bait was enough to attract British Open Champion Tom Weiskopf and US Open winner Johnny Miller, who were tied on 848 strokes for the Grand Masters, but many other Americans stayed home to compete in conflicting events on the US Tour. Perhaps they knew about how the September equinox affected Scottish weather. Maybe they remembered the weather during the recent British Open at Troon.

On the first day of the Player Classic the players found the weather tolerable and returned low scores, but nature's haunting presence was not missed by Raymond Jacobs of the *Glasgow Herald*: 'A choppy sea sparkled under the sun and Arran and Ailsa Craig were etched clearly against the blue sky. A freshening westerly wind brought out the finest qualities of a splendidly conditioned championship course.'

Sited on the west coast of Scotland, within view of rocky islands, Turnberry is one of the most beautiful settings in the world ... when the sun is out. That first day, Neil Coles celebrated his thirty-ninth birthday with a 66 and shared the first-round lead with Johnny Miller. Tony Jacklin and Charles Coody were two strokes behind.

Overnight the weather changed beyond recognition.

The wind became a gale-force south-westerly with gusts of up to 65 miles per hour, the rain was horizontal, and the damage phenomenal. A television-viewing marquee collapsed and two men were injured. Hoardings were torn down, exhibition tents flattened and most of the tented village destroyed, even though extra guy-ropes had been quickly fitted. Only two of the seven marquees in the complex were left standing, one being the press tent, where 'reporters felt like last survivors of an abandoned ship'. Many Ayrshire roads were blocked by fallen trees, and farmers throughout the county were busy trying to remove the debris.

Mark McCormack's annual, *The World of Professional Golf*, documents the extent of the damage on the course: 'The tented village, no rope and canvas affair but a solid encampment of metal-framed structures, could not have been more comprehensively ravished if it had been over-run by the marauding army of Oliver Cromwell. One tent was lifted bodily onto the tenth fairway. The rest resembled the wreck of an airship, a tangled skeleton of broken spars and tattered plastic. The cost of the damage dwarfed the £58,000 prize fund.'

Astonishingly, despite this ferocious weather, golf continued until 5 pm, when play was finally abandoned for the day. Twelve of the 36 players were left with incomplete rounds, including some with nine holes still to play. While wringing out wet clothes in the clubhouse, they told stories of trying to hold wet clubs with bitterly cold hands. 'Jacklin thought for a moment he remembered a worse day,' chronicled *The Times*, 'but then decided they had not played.'

The scores were surprisingly good on that second day. Gary Player made a miraculous 70, Coles kept his lead with a 75 for

141, although Weiskopf was also one under after 32 holes. Jacklin and Coody had 74s to stay one stroke behind the leaders. Only four players had over 80, but there were 34 sixes, a seven, an eight and a nine (by Maurice Bembridge at the ninth hole).

The third day was a mixture of teasing sunny spells and heavy squalls of rain and hail. In the middle of the day, play was suspended for 40 minutes to allow a particularly savage hailstorm to pass. The golf was again problematic, even though five tees had been moved forward and the flag-stick placings were deliberately favourable. Charles Coody took a four-stroke lead by the end of the third round, and his final round of 77 – three sixes in the first nine holes – earned him the £15,000 first prize with an aggregate of 289 (five over par). Jacklin (292) was second, and Weiskopf (294) third, despite an outward 44 in the final round. Weiskopf also won the Grand Masters prize.

It wasn't the first time nature had issued a stern reminder to professional golfers – the 1965 Dunlop Masters at Portmarnock and the 1938 Sandwich British Open are other examples – and it certainly wouldn't be the last.

ROUNDS OF 123 AND 114

TALLAHASSEE, FLORIDA, APRIL 1974

The 1974 Tallahassee Open coincided with the Tournament of Champions so none of the very big names in golf were competing, but it was a good opportunity for others to establish themselves on the circuit. Allen Miller won the tournament, playing great approach shots at the seventeenth and eighteenth when it looked as if his lead had slipped away, and the top four places looked like this:

Allen Miller	65	69	67	73	—	274
Eddie Pearce	68	68	70	69	—	275
Dan Sikes	67	69	67	72	—	275
Joe Inman	73	68	63	71	—	275

To students of strangeness, however, the bottom four places were more interesting. These four players made the cut but made no money.

John Quick	75	70	76	73	—	294
John Ruby	72	72	77	74	—	295
Steve Cain	73	72	75	76	—	296
Mike Reasor	73	71	123	114	—	381

You have to admit, something looks odd about Mike Reasor's scores. After two rounds he wasn't too far out of contention, only three strokes behind Joe Inman, who eventually finished joint second (though admittedly with the help of a superb third round).

So what had happened to Reasor?

The answer was that he had been horse-riding. While out on a horse, he had run into a tree, bruising his right knee and tearing muscles in his left shoulder and side. His left arm was out of action for the final two rounds.

Most golfers would withdraw with such injuries, but Reasor faced an interesting problem. In order to gain exemption from one week of the nerve-racking qualifying process, he had to play through *all 72 holes* of the Tallahassee Open. The automatic entry to the next tournament was for those who had *completed* the current tournament, regardless of score.

So Reasor played one-handed.

Spectators near the first tee laughed when they saw him, especially when his first attempt took the ball barely past the ladies' tee. Wearing check trousers, a white shirt and white shoes, he looked as good as usual, but his swing was not one for novices to study. His left arm hung limply at his side, his left hand rested on his left thigh, and he swung the club with his right arm, rather like someone chopping through long grass looking for a ball. He played his two Sunday rounds with only a five-iron and a putter. On the greens, he used his left hand to steady his putter. His scores of 123 and 114 showed a distinct improvement. On the first round, he was proud not to have strayed into double figures more than once – a 10 at the seventh.

He earned his exemption from the next tournament, the Byron Nelson Classic, and looked forward to three days of rest beforehand.

·AFTER HOURS

AKRON, OHIO, SEPTEMBER 1974

The World Series of Golf, an event staged primarily for television audiences, was designed to bring together the winners of the four major Championships – the US Masters, British Open, US PGA and US Open. Gary Player earned two invitations in 1974 – he won both the US Masters and the British Open – so Canadian Open Champion Bobby Nichols filled the gap. Nichols joined Player, Lee Trevino, the US PGA Champion, and Hale Irwin, winner of the US Open, for a 36-hole stroke-play tournament.

Hale Irwin had recently returned to golf after a six-week lay-off, deliberately taken shortly after the birth of his son. He had also been upset by the death of a playing partner during a Philadelphia professional-amateur tournament a couple of days before the World Series. His first-round 76 put him nine strokes off the lead, and Nichols, on his home course at Firestone, lay third with a 72.

The two leaders, Player (67) and Trevino (70), took up an exciting struggle towards the end of the final round. With 10 holes remaining, Player led Trevino by five strokes, but then Trevino discovered he could do little wrong with his putting. Player dropped shots at the ninth and tenth, and, as Trevino birdied the tenth with a 12-footer, the gap had suddenly dropped to two strokes.

At the thirteenth, Trevino sank an eight-foot putt for a birdie, and Player's bogey lost him the lead. Trevino completed the incredible turn-about by taking the lead with a birdie at the fourteenth. Then Trevino's bogey at the sixteenth enabled Player to draw level. Both birdied the seventeenth, and they completed the eighteenth in pars for a tournament tie.

Gary Player	67	72	—	139
Lee Trevino	70	69	—	139
Bobby Nichols	72	71	—	143
Hale Irwin	76	72	—	148

It was the third play-off in the 13-year history of the World Series and certainly the most unusual. Trevino and Player started at the fourteenth – a suitable hole for television coverage – and Trevino just missed a 10-foot putt that would have given him the tournament. At the fifteenth and seventeenth Trevino rescued his pars, and there was still no winner. Both parred the eighteenth, and, after five holes of 'sudden-death', the outcome was still undecided.

It was also dark. They adjourned till the next day.

They started again from the fourteenth hole – the fourth time they had played the hole in only 42 holes. They holed good putts for birdies; Trevino from 28 feet; Player from eight feet. And so to the par-three fifteenth, where Player caught a bunker to the left of the green. He blasted the ball out and left himself an 11-foot putt, which he missed. Trevino putted from a yard and won the tournament.

The Trevino-Player 'sudden-death' play-off bore some resemblance to a third-round match in the 1907 Irish Open Amateur Championship, when Pickeman and Jeffcott played seven extra holes on their home Portmarnock course. Likewise, five holes were played one day, darkness set in and they came back for two more the next day.

LIGHTNING SURVIVORS

CHICAGO, JUNE 1975

At 4.04 pm on 27 June, the atmosphere around the Butler National Golf Club looked outwardly calm. Then officials of the 1975 Western Open were informed of an approaching storm. They sounded the siren to warn the players. Golf courses are among the worst places to be during lightning storms.

Some of the world's greatest golfers and 16,000 spectators were on the course. Their reactions were different. Some, like Tom Watson, were cautious. A week before, during the US Open, Watson had invoked the lightning rule at Medinah Golf Club and left the course just in case.

Lee Trevino and Jerry Heard were relaxed. They expected the storm to pass in 10 minutes, so, rather than return to the clubhouse, they arranged a picnic on the thirteenth green. After a fine approach shot, Trevino had been contemplating a two-foot putt for a birdie when the siren interrupted.

Trevino and Heard sat down on the edge of the green and waited for a caddie to bring them soft drinks and hot dogs. Trevino leant against his golf bag. Heard held his umbrella between his legs.

They courted disaster in several ways. They were by a lake, they were at a high point of the course, and they were touching metal objects.

Lightning struck.

Trevino was lifted a foot and a half off the ground and thrown on the floor quivering like a vibrator. His life passed before him, and he thought of his wife and kids. He was scared and hurt, but forced himself to keep breathing and stay conscious as long as possible.

At first he thought he'd broken his shoulder. Later, a hospital examination would reveal four small spider-like burn marks on his left shoulder where the lightning had left his body, and a doctor would comment that she rarely saw such marks on a living person.

Jerry Heard, shaken, suffered burns on his groin, where his umbrella had been resting. Elsewhere on the course, Bobby Nichols was treated for head burns after he and his 14-year-old caddie, Peter Mortimer, were knocked to the ground; Tony Jacklin and Jim Ahern felt tingling in their arms and clubs flew out of their hands; Jim Colbert was knocked to the ground; and others fell to the ground intentionally – for safety reasons.

Trevino was taken to the intensive care unit of a Hinsdale hospital. Through the night he lay in his bed and watched the second-hand of a clock sweep from second to second, each sweep satisfying him that he had lived a second longer. His attempts at humour were never far away, and he was soon wondering aloud whether he might get a two-stroke penalty for slow play.

He stayed in intensive care for another night, and then returned to his home at El Paso, where medical tests showed a good recovery. Trevino was soon competing in the British Open, but both he and Heard would be affected by back problems the following year.

The impact of lightning at the Western Open is far from an isolated occurrence involving professionals. And major tournaments are not immune, as spectators at the 1991 US Open discovered on the first day. One of them, a 27-year-old man, was killed by a bolt of lightning.

There are other forms of storm tragedy. In 1923, a golfer was killed when an elm-tree branch fell on him on a Hertfordshire course. A similar incident caused a spectator's death during the opening round of the 1981 Byron Nelson Classic. The damage was done by a branch of a partly rotted oak tree, and three other spectators were injured.

A MEMORABLE INAUGURAL
MEMORIAL

DUBLIN, OHIO, MAY 1976

The Muirfield village course was difficult that first year, with severe bunkers, small greens and unwelcoming water hazards, but the inaugural Memorial Tournament should be remembered for a strange play-off and a fluke shot rather than the difficulties that led to many bogeys.

The Memorial Tournament was an event to honour an outstanding player, living or dead, and the inaugural tournament honoured Robert Tyre Jones, Jnr. Jack Nicklaus was the instigator of the tournament and course designer – the course was a few miles outside his home town of Columbus – but a few players objected to a current player being so involved. Nicklaus finished joint eighth, four strokes away from the play-off score of 288 which was achieved by Roger Maltbie and Hale Irwin.

| Roger Maltbie | 71 | 71 | 70 | 76 | – | 288 |
| Hale Irwin | 71 | 74 | 74 | 69 | – | 288 |

Don Bies (289) and Jerry McGee (290) might have made the play-off too, but they both bogeyed the sixteenth hole in the final round. Jerry Pate (290) was joint fourth with McGee, while Tom Kite and Lou Graham tied on 291.

The success story of the final round was Irwin's 69, which enabled him to pull back seven strokes on Maltbie. Irwin, out in 33, was actually two under before he double-bogeyed the fifteenth, and three successive pars completed an exceptional round in the conditions. At the final hole, Maltbie recovered from a stream and would have won the tournament had he holed an 11-foot putt.

The play-off, therefore, was Maltbie against Irwin. It was a novel three-hole stroke-play play-off, following a format pioneered in the Far East (and later used in other Western tournaments). If the scores were level after three holes, it reverted to the more customary 'sudden-death'. It was the first time the format had been tried in the United States.

Maltbie and Irwin began at the fifteenth. They both birdied the par-five fifteenth, and both parred the short sixteenth in three. In effect, it now reverted to the accustomed 'sudden-death' procedure, and the odds swung Irwin's way when he made the green with his second shot at the seventeenth.

Maltbie, faced with an approach shot of 176 yards, took a four-iron. His shot was too strong. The ball soared over the green and into the crowd on the left. Then, miraculously, it pinged against a metal stake and bounced back on to the green. The stake, about an inch in diameter, held the ropes that kept back the gallery.

To Maltbie, some distance away, it looked as if the ball had bounced off a spectator's head. Someone in the gallery plucked the stake out of the ground and kept it for the golfer as a souvenir. It was certainly a rare stake.

Both players two-putted on the seventeenth. Maltbie, with the help of his stake, stayed in the tournament.

On to the eighteenth, where Irwin erred with his drive. The ball landed behind a large tree guarding the green. It took him four shots to extract the ball from the rough, and the tournament was virtually over. Maltbie holed a 15-foot putt, not dissimilar to the one he had missed an hour earlier, and won on the fourth play-off hole.

It was Maltbie's third victory in 16 months. The 24-year-old Californian, PGA rookie of the year in 1975, gave a few interviews and then walked away clutching a cheque ... and his souvenir stake.

A HEAD FOR HEIGHTS

PARIS, OCTOBER 1976 AND OCTOBER 1977

Golf and mountaineering are related.

Yes, you might think, remembering that ball on the clubhouse roof. Yes, you may agree, recalling how Bernhard Langer scaled a tree to play a shot in the 1981 Benson and Hedges International. Indeed, some people argue that golfers and mountaineers have similar temperaments – persevering, intrepid, disciplined and forever seeking a course that beats the weather.

The relationship, though, is simpler than all that.

One of the most extreme examples of combining golf and mountaineering features two United States Army sergeants who, in 1956, played a course of 4,132 yards. Most golf courses of that length would be par 59 or 60. This one was par 1,275. Their course was not 4,132 yards long but 4,132 yards high. It was the 12,395-foot Mount Fuji, a sacred mountain of Japan.

Mount Fuji presents a rocky course, but the daring sergeants, carrying one club, chipped and shovelled their way to the top, taking only 10 hours 50 minutes. It was impossible to tee a ball on the mountain, and not always easy to reach the ball after hitting it. They went through 27 balls, and then lost the last one holing out into a two-mile wide crater at the top of the mountain. With a hole that size, at least the putting was easy.

Then they came down in one.

If you have a head for heights, you may be able to make money by betting that you can drive a golf ball a prodigious distance.

In 1925, for instance, Waldo Chamberlain of Washington University drove 650 yards off Pinnacle Peak, a 6,562-foot mountain in the Mount Rainier National Park, Washington. Nine years later, Gust Kupka whacked a ball from the top of the Washington Monument. *Warning: Those who suffer from vertigo may wish to skip to the next paragraph.* Kupka climbed out of a window at the end of the elevator-shaft and edged himself up a ladder. He stepped on to the top of scaffolding that was surrounding the top of the Monument while it was being cleaned. He was 555 feet above the ground and fighting a 60-mile-an-hour wind, but he managed a swing at the ball.

In October 1976, on the morning of the first round of the Lancôme Tournament, French police stopped traffic in the Champ de Mars while Arnold Palmer drove a succession of golf balls from the second stage of the Eiffel Tower, that huge upside-down tee-peg in the centre of Paris. It was wet and windy that morning, and conditions were not good for ground-floor golf, let alone driving from a height of 377 feet. Palmer's best shot went only 276 yards. The wind ravaged the Lancôme Tournament itself, and on the final day a young Severiano Ballesteros out-Palmered Palmer by bravely making five birdies in the last nine holes and winning the tournament.

A year later, immediately before the 1977 Lancôme, Palmer tried again from the second stage of the Eiffel Tower. 'Two monuments are going to find each other again after a year's separation,' the press handout said, 'the monument of golf, Mr Palmer, and the monument of Paris, the Eiffel Tower. Together they are going perhaps to establish a new world record.'

Pressmen ate croissants and drank coffee, photographers swung from the tower above Palmer's head and clicked shutters, and diehards talked about how the conditions were much better than the previous year. The sun shone, the air was still, and Arnold Palmer took out his number-one wood and considered his swing. The platform was cramped for space, handrails in front and a steel stanchion behind, and Palmer needed to position himself perfectly.

His first shot went 323 yards and landed in the pond halfway between the Tower and the Ecole Militaire. The second was a great bad shot. It was hooked towards the Invalides, but bounced off the roof of a passing bus. The distance was measured at 402 yards. Trust Palmer to find a daring shot.

The promotional stunt ended with a third shot of 363 yards. Palmer moved on to the Lancôme Tournament, where he scored a first-round 75 and was not really in contention.

MR 59

MEMPHIS, TENNESSEE, JUNE 1977

One of the most astonishing rounds in the history of golf was played on Friday 10 June 1977. Allen Geiberger's second round in the Danny Thomas golf tournament took place at Memphis in very hot weather on the 7,193-yard Colonial Country Club course. Conditions were not ideal, but Al Geiberger went round in 13 under par, still a record for a PGA tournament (although since equalled).

At the time, Geiberger was 39 years old, playing some of the best golf of his career. He had won the US PGA title in 1966, and, after a few quiet years, had won both the Tournament of Champions and Tournament Players Championship in 1975. His style was slow, Californian, seemingly casual, but it was well-suited to the hot, humid June weather of Memphis. If there was a breeze, it was only a slight one.

His first round was a par 72. Nothing sensational. Just enough to keep him in contention.

His second round was the one to remember. It started at the tenth hole, as Geiberger was asked to play the back nine first. He birdied the tenth from 40 feet, parred the eleventh and birdied the twelfth from 15 feet. Then two successive pars did nothing to draw attention to him. In fact, he two-putted from eight feet on the fourteenth.

Geiberger took off at the fifteenth and strung together four consecutive birdies to complete his first nine, the back nine of the course, in 30. None of his four successive birdie putts was longer than 15 feet, indicating some excellent approach shots.

228

Under a 'winter rule', golfers were allowed to lift, clean and place the ball on fairways as the course had been subjected to winter damage, but that was no explanation for Geiberger's scintillating run.

He eagled the first hole, which he was playing tenth, by pitching in with a wedge from 30 feet, then birdied the next two with putts of 18 feet and 20 feet. He had now played seven holes in eight under par, and was aware that he had a real chance of beating the PGA record of eight successive birdies. A share in the record looked likely when Geiberger was left with a putt of 12 feet for another birdie at the fourth. He missed it, and missed that record, but something bigger was to come. Birdies at the sixth and seventh left him 12 under par for the course. He needed one more birdie to break sixty.

At the eighth, his seventeenth, Geiberger putted from 20 feet for a birdie but the ball didn't drop. At the ninth his excellent nine-iron shot left him with a putt from eight feet for his birdie. He studied the putt carefully, aware that this was a once-in-a-lifetime opportunity to break sixty. 'I mustn't leave it short,' he said to himself, memorizing the uphill slope and break to the right. He putted for the twenty-third time in the round ... and down it went.

Al Geiberger was the original 'Mr 59'.

Never before had sixty been broken on a full-length course during a fully recognized PGA Tour tournament. Sam Snead had managed a 59 in a professional tournament and Gary Player a 59 in the 1959 Brazilian Open, while half a dozen golfers had managed 60s in a PGA tournament – Al Brosch, Bill Nary, Wally Ulrich, Tommy Bolt, Mike Souchak and Sam Snead – but their rounds were on shorter courses than that at the Colonial Country Club which Geiberger blew apart. His card looked like this:

	Holes 10 to 18	Holes 1 to 9
Par	443 443 545 – 36	543 434 544 – 36 (72)
Geiberger	342 442 434 – 30	332 433 443 – 29 (59)

Geiberger won the tournament … but only just. His 59 gave him a two-round aggregate of 131 and a six-stroke lead over Keith Fergus. A 72 in the third round kept him three strokes ahead of Steve Taylor (206), but the real danger was to come from Gary Player (207), Tom Weiskopf (208) and Jerry McGee (209).

After his record round, Geiberger continued almost in a daze, but he had to snap out of it after nine holes of the final round because his lead had disappeared, his confidence not helped by going out of bounds at the fourth for a two-over-par six. Gary Player had drawn level, then gone two ahead, so Geiberger needed to scrap hard if he wanted to win. His record round was now a thing of the past, almost as though it was part of another tournament.

Geiberger birdied the tenth to Player's bogey and was back on terms. Another two-stroke swing occurred at the fourteenth, and this time Geiberger hung on to the lead. His final round of 70 gave him an aggregate score of 273 and left him three strokes ahead of Player and McGee.

Strangely, when Geiberger made his debut on the Senior Tour, in 1988, he had an outside chance to break 60 again. On the Hillcrest course, in the Arizona Classic, he was eight under with seven to play and 10 under with three to go. Three birdies on the last three holes would do it, but he scrambled pars at the sixteenth and seventeenth, then three-putted for a bogey at the eighteenth. His 63 – out in 30, home in 33 – was still a new course record.

THE FAST TEAM

ROCHESTER, NEW YORK, AUGUST 1979

The Guinness Book of Records suggests caution when comparing fast times for a round of golf. The length of the course needs to be taken into account, and conditions may vary. Some golfers attempt speed records by playing a moving ball; others wait until the ball comes to rest before playing their next shot. Some golfers use golf carts; others run around. Some play on their own; others have help.

The fastest rounds involve more than one golfer, each player stationed at a strategic point on the course. These record attempts also come in different forms. Some have been played with one ball; others with a different ball ready on the next tee.

One early attempt at a world speed record, at Chicago's Westward Ho course in 1935, relied on 24 golfers and only one ball: 'Spread over each hole were a driver, two second-shot artists and a pair of combination approach-shot and putting specialists. As the team covered only the first five holes, automobiles were used to hustle the players to their next assignments.'

That team managed a round of 78 in only 14 minutes 56 seconds, but one reporter noted that there was room for improvement: 'The time might have been better had not a caddie, in tossing the ball from the eleventh green to the twelfth tee, cut loose with a wild pitch into the bushes. Almost a minute was lost in the search for the ball. Another loss was suffered on the twelfth hole when a 240 lb [17-stone] member of the squad fell while pursuing the ball.'

On 25 August 1979, 42 members of the Ridgemont Country Club – 41 men and one woman – spread themselves across the golf course ready for an attempt on the world record. The time they had to beat was 10 minutes 11.4 seconds, achieved by 43 high-school golfers on a 6,109-yard course at Huber, Texas, three years earlier. The Ridgemont attempt was over a 6,161-yard course, with four holes played from men's tees and 14 from women's tees.

The 42-strong Ridgemont team aimed to break the nine-minute barrier. They practised for four months, with long-ball hitters on the tees, accurate iron players on the fairways, and specialist putters on the greens. Admittedly, practice sessions didn't take up too much time. You can imagine a few smug parting words from people leaving homes near the Ridgemont course: 'Just going out for a round of golf. Back in 10 minutes or so.'

On the day of the record attempt, the golfers were joined by 12 official judges – local politicians, policemen, radio and television personalities and a sports administrator – and official timekeepers. *The Guinness Book of Records* has a code of practice for record attempts.

The round went well. The team received a terrific boost on the fourth hole – a par three of 120 yards – when Lyle Klier nearly holed in one. His putting specialist was left a mere tap-in, and the hole took only six seconds (according to one estimate).

The team took eight minutes 53.8 seconds for their round-on-the-run. They were all delighted. They had broken the old record – over a longer course and with 42 golfers rather than 43 – and had cracked the nine-minute barrier.

THE GOOSE INCIDENT

BETHESDA, MARYLAND, MAY 1979

On 3 May 1979, a Canada goose was killed on the seventeenth green of an exclusive country club. The mysterious circumstances of the goose's death provoked debate throughout the United States, especially when a golfer was charged with illegally killing the bird and possessing its dead body.

The man at the centre of 'the goose incident' was Dr Sherman Thomas, a 66-year-old family physician who had been a member of the Bethesda Congressional Club for 30 years. He was subjected to two competing theories about what had actually happened. The 'mercy-killing' theorists suggested that Thomas's ball had hit the goose when the golfer was playing an approach shot to the seventeenth green, and the bird was so maimed that the doctor, in his medical opinion, decided that it should be put out of its misery as humanely as possible. In contrast, the 'fit-of-rage' theorists argued that the bird's honking had so disrupted the golfer's putting concentration at the seventeenth that he had clubbed the bird to death with his putter.

When the authorities received several letters of complaint, they investigated possible violations of the Migratory Bird Treaty Act. By law, a Canada goose could be killed only during the hunting season (October to January) and only by an appropriate method. It was legal to use shotgun, bow and arrow, falcon or goshawk ... but not a golf club. It didn't matter why the bird was killed, only when it was killed, how it was killed and how the body was disposed of. The District Attorney's office decided to prosecute, and Dr Sherman Thomas faced two charges: unlawfully killing a migratory bird; and unlawfully 'possessing the goose', i.e. carrying the dead bird away in his golf-cart. If found guilty, each charge carried a maximum penalty of six months' imprisonment and $500 fine (£230).

The case against Thomas was prepared. An expert would testify that the goose's mate and goslings had been found near to the seventeenth green. Witnesses would be called, perhaps some members of Dr Thomas's foursome. But the prosecution had one problem – the body had not yet been found.

Across the nation, newspapers ran the story with headlines like *Golfer Gets His Birdie* and *A Birdie at the Seventeenth*. The *Detroit News* ran a sardonic editorial, suggesting that any goose that honked to unnerve a golfer when he was putting would not be looked upon favourably by courts: 'And surely if the goose had unwisely flown into the path of a golf ball, sustaining serious injury thereby, the doctor did the only humane thing by ending its suffering. And considering that the shot might have been heading directly for the pin and was maintaining a lovely backspin that might very likely have put it in the cup, or at least in the immediate vicinity, Dr Thomas should be commended for his extraordinary good will. Case dismissed, we'd say.'

John Gonella, in a letter to the *Washington Post*, suggested that the dead goose should be commemorated in golfing terminology. He recommended extending the use of ornithological names for shots under par – birdie, eagle, albatross – so that the name 'goose' would be given to a hole-in-one where a golfer has a handicap stroke (i.e. net zero). So far as I'm aware, this hasn't happened, and, anyway, if it were the case, 'goose' wouldn't be a word golfers use a lot.

Art Buchwald, a distinguished columnist, raised a more technical question. What would the Royal and Ancient Golf Club Rules Committee say if a golfer did use his putter to club a goose to death on a green? Did it count as a stroke every time he hit the bird? Did it make a difference if the bird was on or off the green? Others pointed out that surely the driver was a more appropriate club for taking a shot at a goose (and let's hope they were talking about John Gonella's innovative use of the term).

Despite many light-hearted comments, it was a serious predicament for Dr Thomas. His lawyer quickly succeeded in winning a court order to prevent Bethesda Congressional Country Club's board of governors from voting on 'the goose incident'. The officials planned to make a decision on whether to suspend Thomas, expel him from the club or take no action. Now they would have to await the outcome of the court case.

It was a worrying time for the doctor, who had to wait five months before the court case was settled and his fate at the country club known. Charged at the end of May, he pleaded innocent in a District Court hearing on 22 June, and his jury trial was fixed for the end of August. In the end it was settled by plea bargaining. The two sides agreed on a reduced charge – a hunting citation that did not carry a prison sentence – and the doctor was fined $500.

The two competing explanations of the incident – the 'mercy-killing' and 'fit-of-rage' theories – were probably both incorrect. The true story was probably somewhere in between. Although witnesses had seen Thomas wielding his putter, it seemed more likely that he had quickly wrung the goose's neck to kill it after first encountering the bird on his approach shot. In late September he was suspended from the club.

FALDO AND LYLE

WENTWORTH, OCTOBER 1982

When Nick Faldo of England met Sandy Lyle of Scotland in the first round of the Suntory Match Play Championship, the outcome was a match which rivalled the 1965 Player-Lema epic for dramatic transformation.

Faldo, then 25, was slightly older than Lyle, but both players were still hopes for the future rather than the world champions they later became. Their 36-hole match looked all over after the first round, when Lyle trailed by six holes. Over lunch he must have thought his main aim was avoiding a double-figure defeat. It had been a soul-destroying morning for him. Even when he birdied the eighteenth, he lost to Faldo's eagle.

In the afternoon, the match took a different shape.

They halved the first, but Lyle won the second with a birdie two, won the third too, and took the fourth when Faldo three-putted. At the sixth, Lyle holed a putt of over 40 feet, and suddenly Faldo's lead was down to two. It reminded some people of 1980, when Faldo had led Greg Norman by four holes at lunch before losing the match.

At the eleventh hole, Lyle played a wonderful eight-iron shot to within a few feet of the pin. It was a crushing birdie. Faldo was only one hole ahead.

Lyle birdied the twelfth too.

All-square. Six to play.

At the thirteenth, Lyle played another supreme approach shot. He won the hole with a birdie, and went two up at the fifteenth when Faldo was bunkered.

236

Lyle's run ended at the sixteenth, when Faldo holed out from a bunker. But Lyle was still one up with two to play.

At the seventeenth, Faldo faced a 15-foot putt, and Lyle one from twice that distance. Lyle holed the longer putt, and won by two and one after being six down.

Sandy Lyle worked his way through to the final, where he lost to Severiano Ballesteros at a rainswept thirty-seventh hole.

SPORTSMANSHIP AT RISK

WENTWORTH, OCTOBER 1983

The lineage of 'fair play' is uncertain. The English often claim its birthright in their public-school system, and a Frenchman familiar with that system, Baron Pierre de Coubertin, adopted sportsmanship as an underlying theme for the modern Olympic movement. Olympic effort was not only to better performances, but also to improve character and display chivalry. The honour was not only in winning; it was also to be in taking part. And 'fair play' meant not only respecting a game's written rules but also abiding to the spirit of the sport.

In this century, there has been a complex shift towards an emphasis on winning rather than taking part. The classic dictum from American football coach Vince Lombardi – 'winning is not everything, it is the only thing' – captures this. Stephen Potter's *Gamesmanship*, and his later *Complete Golf Gamesmanship*, set the tone for something different – all is fair if it gets the right result and doesn't quite break the rules.

In the 1980s, any English hold on sportsmanship seemed to disappear with a succession of incidents which cut across all sports. Surely golf was safe, people thought. Golf was a quiet, civilized sport whose professionals were good role models of modesty and dignity, if perhaps a bit intense and obsessive. And golf-course spectators were usually quiet when shots were played. Perhaps the worst that could happen was isolated heckling from spectators, fractiousness from professionals at key times, or over-ebullient cheering from supporters when a hero successfully played a daring Palmeresque shot.

238

Then, for a few days in October 1983, the golfing community was worried by an unusual incident in the World Match Play at Wentworth. There had been problems at Wentworth the previous year, when Sandy Lyle's ball had taken a couple of unusual deflections in a match against Raymond Floyd. Now came a bigger incident. It happened at the sixteenth hole, at a critical point in the match between Nick Faldo and Australian Graham Marsh.

Marsh and Faldo were all-square with three to play. Faldo's approach shot scuttled through the green and into a crowd of spectators. After a very short pause – three or four seconds according to one report – Faldo's ball reappeared, a few feet in the air, conveniently bouncing on to the green.

The two players, hidden from the action, had no clue what had transpired, but many nearby onlookers had no doubt that the ball had been thrown back by a patriotic spectator. John Hennessy of *The Times* referred to it as 'an appalling piece of dishonesty on the part of some baboon in the crowd'.

The referee had been unsighted. He conferred with a greenside official and concluded that the ball had not stopped moving, in which case Faldo was entitled to play it as it lay. It was 'a rub of the green', and Marsh sportingly accepted the ruling.

Faldo might have made a four anyway with a chip and putt. With his ball safely on the green, he made a safe four, and Marsh was left an awkward three-foot putt to halve the hole. He missed it, and some spectators confounded the existing 'unfair play' felony by cheering the miss.

Faldo was in an awkward position. He had come to the green ignorant of its events. He might have conceded Marsh's second putt, to ensure a half on the hole, but he did not feel that was the right course of action. He was criticized for it by journalists.

Faldo won the seventeenth hole with a birdie and beat Marsh two and one. He won his next two matches too, before losing to Greg Norman, Marsh's compatriot, in the final.

A PRESIDENT ON THE GOLF COURSE

AUGUSTA, GEORGIA, OCTOBER 1983

Ronald Reagan's press conference was steered towards the subject of golf by a question from the gallery of newspaper reporters.

'Can you explain to us why you've decided to spend the coming weekend in Augusta at a golf club that is very exclusive and that we understand has no black members?'

'I don't know anything about the membership,' began the President, 'but I know there is nothing in the bylaws of that club that advocates any discrimination of any kind. I saw in a recent tournament down there, a national tournament, I saw blacks playing in that tournament on that course. I've been invited as a guest to go down and play a round of golf on the Augusta golf course, and, as I say, I think I've covered all that I know about it.'

The racial-discrimination issue, denied by Augusta National Golf Club, was soon displaced by other news items. Ronald Reagan's quiet week-end of golf was disturbed by a golf-course kidnapping and a Beirut bombing. It is only one example of golf's part in political history.

In the United States and the United Kingdom, political leaders have usually had fond feelings for golf. Perhaps the most significant early example was Arthur Balfour, British Prime Minister (1902-5), who learned his golf in Scotland and helped to popularize the sport in England. On three occasions, Arthur Balfour won the British Parliamentary Golfing Society handicap, a tournament which started in 1891 and continues today.

Herbert Asquith (1908-16), David Lloyd George (1916-22) and Ramsay MacDonald (1924, 1929-35) were other British Prime Ministers very keen on golf. Lloyd George once holed in one at a course in the south of France, but *Golf Illustrated*'s reporter did not rate his style very highly when he watched him in Britain: 'Mr Lloyd George, who was one of the successful Parliamentary team at Bishop's Stortford on Saturday, is not a good model for the young idea. He is a typical example of the middle-aged player who, by perseverance and a rubber-cored ball, contrives occasionally to confound the critics by doing a four-hole in the par figure. The Chancellor does not waste time over preliminary waggles. He lays his club behind the teed ball, takes one glance in the direction of the flag, as though he was about to putt, and then stares fixedly at the ball. You might think he was trying to hypnotize a recalcitrant elector.'

American Presidents, from Taft onwards, have usually been hooked on the game, although Jimmy Carter is the post-war exception. A strange golf match has yet to decide the outcome of a war, but, in the 1980s, the Afghanistan war paused for an informal truce on Friday mornings to enable Western diplomats to play golf in the hills just beyond the Kabul city limits. In the spring of 1958 a match between General Dwight Eisenhower (United States) and Harold Macmillan (United Kingdom) looked possible, with much debate about who would win, but Macmillan was too busy. Or maybe he realized that Eisenhower did summit diplomacy on the golf course.

That same year, 1958, Eisenhower gave his name to the Eisenhower Trophy, which was inaugurated as a World Amateur Team Championship. In 1968, at the thirteenth hole of the Seven Lakes Country Club course, he became the first ex-President to hole in one, a feat emulated by Gerald Ford in 1977 at the 177-yard fifth hole of the Memphis Colonial golf course. Ford attracted media attention with many other shots. If only the spectators had seen them coming.

Ronald Reagan was simply following tradition when he accepted the invitation from the Augusta National Golf Club. He scheduled a round on the Saturday and another the next day. As it happened, both rounds suffered from outside interference.

While Reagan was on the course playing his Saturday round, a 44-year-old unemployed millwright called Charles Harris drove a pick-up truck through a side gate at the Augusta club. Brandishing a pistol, he took seven hostages, including two White House aides, and detained them in the golf professional's shop while he demanded to talk with the President.

The President was several hundred yards away on the course, playing golf with Secretary of State George Schultz, Treasury Secretary Donald Regan and former Senator Nicholas Brady of New Jersey. Ronald Reagan did not seem in any danger. When he heard news of the siege he left the course and attempted to speak with Harris by telephone. Harris hung up on him. Reagan tried again. This time Harris didn't reply, despite the President's attempts to engage him in conversation.

Harris released his hostages one by one. He was arrested two hours after the incident began, and no one was hurt. Later that evening Harris was taken to University Hospital. He was declared fit to face charges and transferred to Richmond County Jail. Six months later Superior Court Judge Albert Pickett sentenced Harris, who pleaded guilty, to 10 years in prison and 10 years' probation on charges of kidnapping, false imprisonment and criminal damage to private property.

Ronald Reagan's Sunday round was interrupted too. He returned to Washington DC after news of a fatal bombing at the Marine Corps headquarters in Beirut.

GREG NORMAN'S NOVEL WAYS TO FINISH SECOND – LESSON ONE

TOLEDO, OHIO, AUGUST 1986

Greg Norman was brilliant that year. The Australian completed the 'Saturday Slam' – he led all four major tournaments into the final round. He won only one of them, the British Open, but perhaps that's not unusual when compared with the proportion of third-round leaders who do win 'majors' (40-45 per cent). What was really unusual was how he lost the final major tournament of the year, when he was beaten by a miraculous shot in the US PGA.

First, let's quickly review the first three Grand Slam tournaments of the year.

After three rounds of the US Masters, Greg Norman led by one stroke with a score of 210. He was beaten by an incredible final round of 65 by Jack Nicklaus, but might have forced a play-off had he not gone off-line with a four-iron shot to the eighteenth green.

After three rounds of the US Open, Norman led by one stroke with the same score of 210. A last round of 75 let him down, and Norman finished equal twelfth. Raymond Floyd took the title.

After three rounds of the British Open, the second a brilliant 63, Norman led by one stroke with a score of 211. This was the one he won. It was his first major Championship success.

After three rounds of the US PGA tournament, Norman led by four strokes from Bob Tway with a score of 202. It was the most convincing of his four third-round leads in the major tournaments. It was also the most curious.

Norman started the US PGA with a course record 65 in the first round, but Tway eclipsed this with a third-round 64 on the Saturday. Tway, who had been nine strokes off Norman's lead at the halfway stage, was now four strokes adrift in second place. The tournament was also affected by the weather. Fog had delayed the start of the second day's play, and the end of the tournament was delayed till the Monday after much of Sunday's final round was interrupted by heavy rain.

With only eight holes to play, Norman still had a lead of four strokes. Then he double-bogeyed the eleventh hole, and Tway was only two behind. After the fourteenth they were level, both seven under par, and they matched each other for the next three holes – par and par, par and par, par and par – although Tway had to make some good recovery shots to stay level. The best was an inventive 'sand blast' from deep rough at the seventeenth hole, when he clipped the ball to within three feet of the hole.

At the 354-yard eighteenth, they both found the rough on the right with tee-shots that were planned to short-cut the dog-leg, but Norman's ball rolled on to the fairway and Tway's stayed in the rough. Tway hit a nine-iron from 130 yards, and the ball found a bunker, 25 feet from the pin. It was the first bunker Tway had been in all week, and it came at the worst possible time.

Norman's shot found the green ... at first. Then his ball rolled tantalizingly into deep grass. It seemed a better place than in a bunker.

Tway aimed to blast his ball somewhere near the flag. The ball came up and out, and hit the ground 20 feet from the hole. It began to roll ... toward the hole ... like a ball hit with a putter ... like the perfect shot ... and down it went.

After seeing that, Norman had to go for the hole. He changed his thoughts and changed his club – sand-wedge to pitching wedge – and his shot went eight feet past. He didn't need the return putt – he was assured of second place – and he missed that too. His round of 76 meant he lost by two in sheer statistics. Really he lost to a strange shot.

From there, Norman went on to six successive victories in September and October, and he cut his time on the US Tour short to display his brilliance in his native Australia. He was so strangely brilliant that year, that it took something bizarre from a bunker to beat him ... but Greg Norman's bizarreries were only beginning.

A SKINS TOURNAMENT

LA QUINTA, CALIFORNIA, NOVEMBER 1986

A book on strange golf stories cannot be complete without some reference to an early Skins tournament. The concept was introduced to the public in 1983, when four golfers, selected for high entertainment value and popularity, competed on a hole-by-hole basis for big stakes. To win the stake on a particular hole, a golfer needed to win the hole outright. If it was shared in any way, the stake would be carried forward until there was an outright winner on a hole.

Some people considered it to be a game-show format, contrived for television on a week-end – Thanksgiving week-end – when television needed a sporting attraction. The public certainly approved of the first Skins tournament. Television ratings were high, and people were enticed to buy property around the featured golf course, the Desert Highland at Scottsdale, Arizona. Of course, it helped to have competitors like Jack Nicklaus, Arnold Palmer, Gary Player and Tom Watson. These four all-time greats also contested the second Skins tournament.

I have chosen the 1986 Skins tournament as an example. The idea was still relatively new and the outcome demonstrated what could happen in a contest which rewards only those who win holes. There was no appearance money, and the golfers didn't want it any other way. They were confident enough to think they could earn more on the hole-by-hole arrangement.

In 1986, the four contestants were Jack Nicklaus, Arnold Palmer, Fuzzy Zoeller and Lee Trevino. The Skins tournament had moved to the PGA Stadium West course, designed by Pete Dye at La Quinta, about 30 miles south-east of Palm Springs. This was because most available property had already been sold around Desert Highland (1983 and 1984) and Bear Creek in Murretta, California (1985).

In the three previous Skins tournaments Jack Nicklaus had won a total of $295,000, including $240,000 with one birdie at the eighteenth in 1984. The following year, 1985, Fuzzy Zoeller collected $255,000 (£190,000) on his first appearance. Zoeller won $150,000 with one 15-foot birdie putt on the twelfth green. It was the sort of drama that American television audiences loved.

In 1986, the stakes were $15,000 (£10,000) on each of the first six holes, $25,000 (£16,850) on each hole from six to 12, and $35,000 (£23,600) for each of the last six holes. It was really 18 separate tournaments.

There was no outright winner on the first three holes. Palmer had a good chance at the second but missed a six-foot putt. Nicklaus rescued the third with a 17-foot birdie putt with Trevino certain to manage a birdie from close to the pin. The stake at the fourth hole was $60,000, and Fuzzy Zoeller sank a 12-foot putt for a birdie and the first skin.

Trevino won $55,000 at the seventh – two $15,000 holes with no outright winner and the $25,000 seventh – when he holed a wedge shot from 68 yards for an eagle. Palmer collected $25,000 with a birdie at the 552-yard par-five eighth. The first day's play ended after nine holes, with Nicklaus yet to win.

The following day, a Sunday, saw Nicklaus miss from five feet with a chance to win $100,000 at the twelfth. At the next hole, the stake now $135,000, Trevino and Nicklaus both missed three-foot putts, and Zoeller won the pool with a par. Nicklaus and Trevino both birdied the fourteenth, Palmer and Trevino birdied the sixteenth, and the stake rose to $140,000 by the seventeenth, where Zoeller's birdie two won the Alcatraz hole, even though he had a far longer putt to sink than Palmer.

They needed an extra hole to settle the $35,000 at stake for the eighteenth, and again it was won by Fuzzy Zoeller. He was the only winner that day. In total, Zoeller won $370,000 (£250,000) – a record at the time for one round of golf.

Zoeller, at 35, was at the top of his profession, playing against men 10 years his senior (or 20 in Palmer's case). He had emulated Horton Smith and Gene Sarazen by winning the US Masters at his first attempt, in 1979, and had beaten Greg Norman in a play-off for the 1984 US Open. Yet Zoeller had not played the best golf in this 1986 Skins Tournament. On the second day he bogeyed the tenth and twelfth, picked up at the sixteenth, and two of the holes he won were with pars. Nicklaus, meanwhile, the US Masters Champion, had a round of about 70 and would probably have won a stroke-play competition. But it wasn't stroke-play. It was a Skins tournament. And that meant one of golf's strangest outcomes – Jack Nicklaus ending a tournament with no winnings, despite an excellent round.

In January 1988, the Skins tournament was extended to the Seniors, whose drawing power that year included the 75-year-old Sam Snead. Two years later, at the age of 60, Arnold Palmer won $240,000 (£140,000) – the biggest cheque of his 35-year career.

The Skins tournament was established, soon to become normal.

GREG NORMAN'S NOVEL WAYS TO FINISH SECOND – LESSON TWO

AUGUSTA, GEORGIA, APRIL 1987

Three players were involved in the play-off for the 1987 US Masters. The most famous of the three were Seve Ballesteros and Greg Norman, both experienced in big tournaments. The third man was Larry Mize, who was claimed as a local hero. Mize had spent part of his childhood in Augusta but had vowed not to play the Augusta course until he had earned the right. Mize had yet to win on the US PGA Tour but had come close. In the 1986 Kemper Open he had led Greg Norman by two strokes with two to play, but lost after playing two balls into a lake on the sixth play-off hole.

Here, at Augusta, the three men tied on 285 after an exciting last round which saw half a dozen players in contention. For much of that last round, Mize looked the least likely to win, especially when he bogeyed a couple of late holes, but he birdied the eighteenth from eight feet and ended three under par. Ballesteros, playing behind Mize, ensured the same score with a par at the eighteenth.

Greg Norman went to the eighteenth green three under par after a birdie at the seventeenth. He was left with a 22-foot putt for a second consecutive birdie and the lead. He hit it well and was ready to leap victoriously into the air. He was sure it was in. He could feel it was in. But it wasn't.

The overnight leaders, Ben Crawshaw and Roger Maltbie, were still to come. Both needed birdies at the eighteenth to go into the play-off with Mize, Ballesteros and Norman. Maltbie

249

failed to sink a 35-footer, and Crenshaw missed from 20 feet.

It was after 6 o'clock when Ballesteros, Norman and Mize went to the tenth tee to start their play-off. All three players hit the green in two, and three balls sat within 20 feet of the hole awaiting birdies. Surely one of them would birdie the hole.

Ballesteros tried from 20 feet and hit the ball five feet past. Norman, short from 15 feet, tapped in for a par, and Mize was left with a 10-foot putt to win the US Masters. The ball broke left and missed the hole.

Somehow Ballesteros missed his return putt, so Mize and Norman went to the eleventh tee without him.

Norman hit his drive 25 yards further down the fairway than Mize, and Mize's second was a poor five-iron which left his ball over 40 yards from the hole, and to the right. Norman aimed for a safe part of the green, slightly to the right of the hole, where he knew he could get down in two putts. His ball came to rest 40 feet from the hole. The difference between 40 feet (Norman) and 140 feet (Mize) looked like the US Masters title.

Mize's shot was up and over a crest and on to a very fast green. The betting favoured him playing it into the pond at the back. He took out his sand-wedge and dropped his 140-foot shot a yard or two in front of the green so that it didn't run too quickly. It bounced across the green toward the hole, and the crowd, in unison, realized what was happening. Their voices rose in a roar, the ball went in the hole, and Mize raised both fists and jumped so high that, as he put it later, he could have dunked a basketball.

Greg Norman's putt broke away from the hole. The winner of the 1987 US Masters was Larry Mize, with a freak shot.

First Tway, now Mize.

Greg Norman was becoming a collector of strange finishes.

THE TOP STARS WALK OFF

MELBOURNE, AUSTRALIA, NOVEMBER 1987

When the experienced Russell Swanson eight-putted on the third green in the final round of the Australian Open, it was obvious that the organizers had a problem on their hands. Playing the third hole was like playing a hole on a Crazy Golf course.

Before that final round, Greg Norman had led the National Panasonic Australian Open field by seven strokes. His third victory in the tournament seemed guaranteed. Only something extraordinary could stop him winning on the fourth day of the tournament. That something was the pin placement on the third green.

The third hole at the Royal Melbourne course was a par four of 333 yards. The Royal Melbourne greens were usually fast and contained many subtle humps and hollows, and in the mid-1970s Lee Trevino vowed never to return to such difficult greens. This day, though, there was the added hazard of a north wind that varied between 35 and 50 miles per hour. More crucially, the pin had been placed in an up-slope position where it was vulnerable to the winds. Later investigation showed that an assistant greenkeeper had set the pin two yards from the intended position.

The first three rounds had produced some superb golf. Terry Price had shot a 67 for the first-round lead, but Greg Norman's 70 kept him favourite. Norman followed this up with two successive rounds of 66, both magnificent, and his three-round score of 202 gave him a commanding lead.

Then came the final round. It took Norman over an hour to play the first two holes. The problem was the queue forming on the third tee. At one point there were over 20 players waiting on the tee.

Spectators on the third green saw three hours of comedy rather than skill. Players discovered that putts would not stop rolling within four yards of the hole. To get down in four putts was a good achievement – many took five or six – and the players lingered on the green while they studied the baffling problem. Caddies attempted to mark balls only to find them still moving, perhaps rolling back down a slope after going up it. Larry Nelson's caddie touched the ball, and Nelson took a two-stroke penalty.

Brett Ogle was more fortunate than most. His putt went a foot and a half past the hole, but as his caddie went to mark the ball the wind blew it back into the hole. Mike Colandro putted next and could be forgiven for thinking luck was against him. He hit four successive putts – all from around 15 to 20 feet – and saw them all follow the same course. The ball ran round the edge of the cup for almost a complete circle and set off back toward his feet. Colandro sank his fifth attempt. He had been level par at the start of the final round. By the fifth hole he was eight over.

Ronan Rafferty and Sandy Lyle both refused to complete the third hole. The golfers on the third tee – the five waiting groups included leader Norman – walked off in support rather than risk humiliation on that green. The players were angry, the spectators were furious, and sponsors were confused.

The organizers considered the options available.

The 1985 Australian Open had been converted to a 54-hole tournament after a day had been lost to rain, but that decision had been criticized. Another option was a 71-hole tournament, eliminating the hazardous third hole, but this idea was soon rejected. That left only one option. They would have to switch the final round to the Monday and make sure the pin was correctly positioned on the third hole. But even that solution had problems, as many players had flights booked to New Zealand or Europe for their next tournament. A move to boycott the final round provoked a heated debate amongst the players. In the end they agreed to continue, although a few golfers pulled out to fulfil other commitments.

On the Monday Greg Norman clinched the title with a record 10-stroke victory. His 273 broke the Royal Melbourne course record by five strokes.

SAVING A CHILD'S LIFE

PHOENIX, ARIZONA, MARCH 1988

A man in Amish dress jumped into an outdoor swimming-pool.

Mary Bea Porter saw him in mid-air, fully clothed, about to hit the water. It distracted her from her next shot, a tricky one from the rough at the thirteenth hole at Moon Valley Country Club. She was on the LPGA tour, playing a qualifying round for the Standard Register Turquoise Classic, and her life was at an all-time low. It had been one thing after another – her husband's bankruptcy, divorce, debts, and her home and car gone – and now here was this strange scene.

Then she saw the child, lying face down in the pool. It was a boy of perhaps three years. She saw the Amish man pull the child out of the pool and hold him by the ankles, shaking him up and down.

Mary Bea Porter flipped off her shoes and ran toward the house, which bordered the rough on the thirteenth fairway. She faced a six-foot high fence. Wrought iron. Vertical bars. Nothing to climb on to.

'Do you know CPR?' someone asked.

Cardiopulmonary resuscitation.

Her caddie, Wayne, lifted her up. She put her right foot on top of the fence, jumped over, landed on two feet, stumbled forward and scraped her knee and her hand. The Amish man handed her the apparently dead child.

An Amish woman was on the patio, holding a telephone.

'What do I do?' she asked. She had not used a telephone

before. The Amish family were visiting from Pennsylvania.

'Dial nine-one-one,' said Wayne, the caddie, who was trapped on the other side of the fence. He could have got over next-door's fence but their Dobermann looked hungry for legs.

The child in Mary Bea Porter's hands was grey and had a flat stomach and chest. She had a five-year-old boy of her own, and knew she had to do something, even with no training.

She tried to clear the baby's mouth, in case he had choked. Then she hit him hard on the heart. She desperately sought a technique. She put her hand in his mouth, moved his tongue to the side, held his nose and blew into his mouth. She tried again. His heart began to beat. It was like starting a lawn-mower engine.

The baby choked and moved his eyes.

'Bring a blanket, or a towel,' shouted Wayne from the other side of the fence.

The emergency services were on the telephone.

'What do I do now?' the golfer asked them.

'Keep the boy on his side.'

She yelled this advice at the boy's father. It wasn't how women usually treated Amish men.

The ambulance crew needed the address of the house. Mary Bea Porter had to search for a bill or a letter before she knew.

The baby was being sick, expelling a very thick mucus. The rescue vehicles arrived. The boy screamed. The rescue team hugged everyone. The Amish were in shock.

Two women from a nearby house walked across to the scene. Mary Bea Porter had the child in her arms, her golf glove soaking wet, her clothes showing clearly that she was a golfer.

'Was it your ball that hit the little boy on the head?' one woman asked her.

'The baby drowned,' someone said. 'She saved his life.'

Mary Bea Porter returned to the golf course. Her threesome had waited a few minutes before letting the next threesome play through. Then they had continued as a twosome.

Wayne handed Mary Bea a club. It could have been a Coke

bottle for all she was concentrating. She hit a reasonable shot but it fluttered in the wind and landed in a bunker. She laughed. Well, there were more important things in life than golf shots ... things like life itself.

Her round of 76 was three strokes short of qualifying. It was typical of her golf. She had won one tournament during her first spell on the tour, in the mid-1970s, and had finished thirty-seventh in the women's money-list in 1975, but times had been hard since her return. In 1987 she had won only $955 (£600) in prize money in 21 tournaments. This year it was only marginally better – $420 (£250) in three.

Newspapers and television stations queued up for her story, and the LPGA, receiving a petition signed by 50 golfers, granted her an unprecedented special exemption into the Turquoise Classic. But Mary Bea Porter was emotionally and physically drained by the events. Her first-round 83 was almost embarrassing, and she failed to make the cut.

Meanwhile, three-year-old Jonathan Smucker was taken to John C. Lincoln Hospital and Health Centre, where he was found to be in good condition. He was transferred to St Joseph's Hospital and Medical Center for observation.

PROFESSIONAL TAKES 19 ON A HOLE

SYDNEY, AUSTRALIA, FEBRUARY 1989

Amateurs are often reassured when professionals take 19 for a hole, whereas professionals have a right to be smug when they hear tales of amateurs losing count after 50. Robert Emond's experience at the 1989 Australian Tournament Players Championship should therefore be put in the context of stories from the world of amateur golf.

A letter in *Golf Illustrated* (9 July 1909) described how an amateur had taken 97 for a hole at Windermere: 'It was a downhill hole, about 230 yards – quite possible to reach the green if you hit your tee shot. I didn't, nor did my partner, and his second found a whin brush to the left of the green. I played my second and waited. He had one smash, then another, and by the time I had walked up to the green had reached double figures. I told him to pick out, but he declared his intention of playing his ball out, and went on striking like a flail, and calling out each stroke as it was played till at 95 he found the green, having in the meantime cleared the whin brush quite away. And with that stroke he laid me a stymie, but I had 94 for the hole, so didn't worry over it. He holed out in 97, quite the biggest score I ever heard of, and I saw the whole of it.'

A second example occurred in 1912 in a qualifying round of a ladies' competition at the Shawnee Club in Pennsylvania. The number of entrants was exactly the same as the anticipated number of qualifiers for the later match competition, but there were special prizes for the best qualifying round, so that round had to be played. At one hole, a competitor hit her tee-shot into a fast-flowing stream just short of the green. Knowing she only had to complete the round to ensure qualification, she resolved to play out. Her ball was floating in the middle of the wide stream, and the only way to it was by boat. Her husband rowed the boat adjacent to the ball, while his wife slashed shot after shot with her niblick, showering him to saturation. She stuck to her task, and played shot after shot after shot, until she finally connected and put the ball ashore – a mile and a quarter downstream from the hole. Unfortunately, she had hit her ball into a dense thicket and it took her some time to find it. Then she thrashed a few more shots until she was safely in a clearing and could find a more direct way to the green. She holed out in 166, and the Shawnee club presented her with a special cup – for qualifying.

Travers and Crowell later suggested that this story may have grown in the retelling, but they agree that something of the kind did happen, and point out that the winner of the tournament was Mrs Caleb Fox, a pioneer woman golfer.

Another story that varies in the telling is that of Tommy Armour's 23 at the 1927 Shawnee Open. The following day's newspapers give his seventeenth-hole score as 11 rather than 23, but folklore suggests that Armour hit shot after shot out of bounds and the only thing in dispute was whether he was down in 21 or 23. Whatever the correct details, it is a strange story because Armour had won the US Open a few days before, beating young Harry Cooper in an 18-hole play-off. His 11 (or 21 or 23) came in the third round, and his scores were listed as 80, 71, 82 and 79. The most detailed account I could find of Armour's third-round débâcle at the seventeenth goes as follows: 'Whatever hopes Armour may have had of finishing somewhere went a glimmering when he hooked three drives out of bounds at the seventeenth. The hole cost an 11.'

At the 1938 US Open, Ray Ainsley was 'credited' with 19 strokes at the 397-yard sixteenth hole in the second round. It is still a record for the US Open. That year's tournament was at Cherry Hills, Denver, and Ainsley began with a round of 78 that left him equal twenty-fifth. Then, on the second day, he hit a good drive at the sixteenth but his five-iron shot hit the edge of the green and bounced back into a five-foot wide brook which contained a couple of inches of water. The ball drifted with the current back toward the tee. Ainsley chased it and started swinging. 'Ainsley stood in the stream, chopping away and then backing up to chop again,' wrote Tom Flaherty in *The US Open*. 'The scorekeeper stood over him like a referee, counting "seven, eight, nine". Finally the scorekeeper doubled up in laughter and he fell to the ground. Ainsley's playing partner, Bud McKinney, took up the count.' On a few occasions the ball teased Ainsley by jumping the bank before dropping down again. Eventually, he popped it out on to dry land, and spectators debated whether it was for 19, 22, or even 23. It made little difference to Ainsley, whose round of 96 (even with a 19) wasn't good enough to make the cut.

Ah, you might say, those anecdotes are from long ago. What about more recently? Has a professional golfer taken 19 for a hole in the last few years?

The answer is yes.

In the 1989 Australian Tournament Players Championship, Robert Emond had an 81 for his first round. His second round began at the tenth hole and he progressed well on the first nine. He was out in 36, which included birdies at the fifteenth, sixteenth and seventeenth. All was well until the first hole, which he was playing tenth. That first hole at Riverside Oaks was a 573-yard par five, and Emond, a 20-year-old rookie from Geelong in Victoria, began by hooking his drive into the water (one). He took a penalty drop (two) and hit a new ball along the fairway (three). His next shot put the ball on a bank at the front of the green, but it rolled down into more water (four). He removed his right shoe and sock and made two attempts to hit the ball out of the water (five and six) before picking up for a one-stroke penalty (seven). He dropped in the rough and hit it back into the water (eight), conceding another one-stroke penalty (nine). Flustered by now, he dropped another ball but it hit his shoe for a two-stroke penalty (10 and 11). He dropped again and hit the ball into water again (12) for another one-stroke penalty (13). Then he hit the ball to the fringe of the green and marked it (14). Unfortunately, as the ball was technically off the green, another two-stroke penalty was in order (15 and 16). Finally, Emond three-putted (17, 18 and 19).

In the circumstances, the rest of Robert Emond's round – he had a 90 on his card – was creditable but he failed to make the cut by 23 strokes. His 19 at the first dwarfed Adam Nance's 11 at the 152-yard fourteenth the previous day. Nance had hit four balls into a lake on the left-hand side of the green before landing one two yards from the pin and two-putting.

The tournament was won by Greg Norman, who came with a typical late charge – 70, 70, 69 and 67 – to pip Roger Mackay by two strokes. At the twelfth, in the final round, Norman's ambitious tee-shot came to rest over 300 yards away, right by the pin. He holed his putt for a stunning eagle.

GREG NORMAN'S NOVEL WAYS TO FINISH SECOND – LESSON THREE

TROON, JULY 1989

The British Open was back at Royal Troon, and with it came a novel four-hole play-off, a course record from Greg Norman, and a shot from one of the Ozaki-Faldo-Couples threesome that put a spectator in hospital. The latter came at the 577-yard sixth in the second round, when a ball struck a 46-year-old woman on the head while she was standing outside the ropes. Knocked unconscious, she was taken to Ayr County Hospital and detained until the following day. It was another reminder of golf's dangers. Earlier that year, Hale Irwin had required 16 stitches after being hit by a stray ball during the professional-amateur tournament preceding the Nissan Los Angeles Open.

After an outsider had led at the end of the first round – this time it was Wayne Stephens with a 66 – the pacesetter proved to be Australian Wayne Grady. At halfway, or what was assumed to be halfway, Grady was two strokes ahead of Payne Stewart and Tom Watson, the latter attempting to equal Harry Vardon's record of six British Open titles. Grady took a two-stroke lead into the final round too, but then had to contend with a phenomenal charge from Greg Norman. Norman finished his round of 64 well ahead of Grady and Watson, and had to wait over an hour for the leaders.

Norman's 64 started with six straight birdies. He dropped a shot at the eighth, the short 'postage stamp' hole, but was still out in 31. On the way home, Norman birdied the eleventh,

261

twelfth (from 45 feet) and sixteenth, just missing an eagle or two. After 72 holes, he was 13 under par, as were Mark Calcavecchia and Wayne Grady when they completed their rounds.

Mark Calcavecchia	71	68	68	68 —	275
Wayne Grady	68	67	69	71 —	275
Greg Norman	69	70	72	64 —	275

It was the first three-way play-off in British Open history. It might have been two-way had Calcavecchia's wife gone into labour during the tournament, for the American would have gone home for the birth. Instead, their daughter, Britney Jo, was born three weeks later.

The new play-off format had been a possibility since 1985. The idea was that they played the first, second, seventeenth and eighteenth in a four-hole stroke-play. Had it been 'sudden-death' Greg Norman might have won. He was the only one to birdie the first play-off hole; Grady and Calcavecchia had par fours.

Norman birdied the second too, but so did Calcavecchia (from 35 feet). When they reached the 223-yard seventeenth, their twenty-first hole of the day, Norman led by one stroke. He was left with a 12-foot putt for his par three, but missed it by a few inches. Calcavecchia safely managed his par, so he and Norman were all-square, with Grady two strokes back after a bogey at the seventeenth.

Greg Norman's drive at the eighteenth somehow bounced awkwardly into a bunker. Calcavecchia's drive wasn't exceptionally good but his second shot was one of those magical ones that Greg Norman was learning to conjure from opponents at such crucial times of a tournament. Earlier in the day, Calcavecchia had chipped directly into the hole from 60 feet for a birdie at the twelfth, and had played an eight-iron 161 yards to within four feet of the eighteenth hole in regulation play. Now he faced a difficult 200-yard shot from rough with the pressure intense. His five-iron was perfect, a few feet from the pin.

Norman had to take a chance, but his second shot found another bunker, and his third went out of bounds in front of the clubhouse. Grady earned his par four, Calcavecchia sank his birdie putt, and Norman conceded philosophically, even though the Gods now owed him three or four 'majors'.

A LARGE PLAY-OFF

ESTELA, PORTUGAL, FEBRUARY 1990

When a fierce southerly wind cut across the exposed Estela links on the final day of the inaugural Vinho Verdi Atlantic Open Championship, scores were high and the contest was close. Six players tied on 288, and five others trailed them by only one stroke.

Besides the six-way play-off, the tournament threw up other odd features, like the Royal and Ancient official studying club-head grooves for the first time. It was also a tournament of fluctuating fortunes. Eamonn Darcy was an early leader, but a course record of 67 gave Stephen Hamill of Northern Ireland the halfway lead. At the end of the third round American Ron Stelton was in front.

Then came the final round, which saw many of the leading players score in the high 70s. The only man to break par was Richard Boxall with a 71, but Ronan Rafferty's 72 earned him a place in the leading pack. Rafferty had been the leading money-winner in Europe in 1989.

The third-round leader, Ron Stelton, missed the play-off by one stroke after an 80, while Anders Sorensen was bunkered at the seventeenth when an outright win seemed likely. Sorensen had a 77, which meant the tournament ended with only one stroke dividing the top 11 players.

R. Boxall	71	73	73	71	—	288
S. Hamill	71	67	74	76	—	288
S. McAllister	71	71	72	74	—	288

R. Rafferty	72	70	74	72	—	288
A. Sorensen	68	73	70	77	—	288
D. Williams	70	71	73	74	—	288
S. Bowman	71	73	73	72	—	289
R. Drummond	70	73	70	76	—	289
M. Jimenez	73	68	72	76	—	289
S. Richardson	72	70	71	76	—	289
R. Stelton	70	69	70	80	—	289

The six men in the play-off went to the 404-yard tenth hole, where they formed two threesomes. In the conditions, it was a very difficult par-four hole. Anders Sorensen and Stephen Hamill were both too strong with their pitch shots, and bogeyed the hole in five. The third of their threesome, Stephen McAllister of Scotland, was short of the green after two shots with wooden clubs, but his pitch shot left him a 12-foot putt, which he duly holed for his par.

In the next threesome, Ronan Rafferty was bunkered with his second and then out of the running when his third flew over the green. David Williams put his tee-shot in the sand-dunes and that was virtually the end of his challenge.

Stephen McAllister's final opponent was Richard Boxall, the man with the best round of the day. Boxall continued his good form by reaching the green in two, the only one of the six play-off contenders to do so. He putted from the lower tier and the ball stopped 15 feet short. He missed his second putt, and McAllister celebrated his win.

Six in a play-off was unusual, but five bogeys at the first play-off hole was even more unusual. McAllister had won the tournament with a par-278 total and a par four at the first play-off hole.

GREG NORMAN'S NOVEL WAYS TO FINISH SECOND – LESSON FOUR

ORLANDO, FLORIDA, MARCH 1990

They say the 441-yard eighteenth hole at Bay Hill, a par four, is one of the PGA Tour's most difficult holes, and statistics back this up – an average of 4.56 during the 1989 Nestlé Invitational – but Robert Gamez made a mockery of statistics when he beat Greg Norman by one stroke to win the 1990 Nestlé Invitational.

Gamez was a 21-year-old rookie. He had been on the Tour for only a month or two, yet had surprised a few people by winning his first tournament, the first debutant to do so since Ben Crenshaw (in 1973). Gamez was to surprise a few more before he left Bay Hill.

In the final round he was competing for the lead with Greg Norman, Larry Mize and Curtis Strange. A par on the eighteenth would complete his score at 276, but that wouldn't win him the tournament, not unless Larry Mize and Greg Norman dropped shots on their last two holes. Mize was in the same group as Gamez, Norman in one behind.

Gamez hit a drive of 265 yards on the eighteenth hole and then chose a six-iron for his second shot. It is an intimidating approach as the green is flanked by an elbow-shaped pond and plenty of sand. Gamez watched Larry Mize play his second shot, then changed his mind about his club. Perhaps a seven-iron instead. His adrenalin was pumping, but the wind had changed slightly. He took a seven-iron from his brother Randy, his caddie, and prepared to play one of the great shots of golf.

It was 176 yards to the hole. The ball went high in the air and Gamez knew it would be close.

But how close?

Close enough for a birdie chance?

Close enough for a good shot at a birdie?

Or closer?

The ball bounced beyond the flag and sucked back into the hole for an eagle two.

The roar from the crowd reached Greg Norman, who was standing on the seventeenth tee.

Who's done what?

Norman heard over the walkie-talkie that it was Gamez, with an eagle at the eighteenth, and he quickly calculated that he needed to birdie one of the last two holes to earn a play-off. At the seventeenth, Norman missed a 10-foot birdie putt. At the eighteenth he missed a 15-foot birdie putt. At the scorer's tent he met Gamez for the first time and congratulated him.

Gamez	71	69	68	66	—	274
Norman	74	68	65	68	—	275
Mize	71	70	67	68	—	276
Allem	69	70	68	70	—	277
Strange	74	69	65	69	—	277
Hoch	69	68	70	70	—	277

This seven-iron shot by Robert Gamez, an eagle from 176 yards, was the longest finishing shot ever to win a tournament. It was far further than Lew Worsham's classic wedge from 104 yards in the 1953 Tam o' Shanter. And it was much further than the 126-yard wedge from the rough that brought Isao Aoki an eagle at the eighteenth in the 1983 Hawaiian Open and enabled him to notch the first Japanese win on the US Tour, by one stroke from Jack Renner.

Greg Norman had brought the best out of yet another golfer.

GREG NORMAN'S NOVEL WAYS TO FINISH SECOND – LESSON FIVE

NEW ORLEANS, APRIL 1990

Greg Norman was at his brilliant best with a late charge in the USF and G Classic at the English Turn Golf and Country Club. He gave the term 'Sunday player' a new meaning with a final round of 65 which included eight birdies, an eagle and three bogeys. Norman needed only 22 putts for his final round, and only 99 in the tournament, thus becoming only the fifth player to break the magical century. It required something miraculous to beat Norman in such form, and something miraculous duly appeared.

The opening day of the tournament was eventful. A strong wind blew over a hard, fast course, and golfers experienced difficulties. Hale Irwin was seven over after only four holes, and Mike Sullivan took 11 at the fifteenth, an especially problematic hole.

Rain and lightning caused a two-hour delay on the second day. When darkness ended play, 23 golfers still had rounds to complete, and the third round didn't start until 10.30 on the third day. After it, Greg Norman was five shots off the lead with a logjam around him. As a sign of something to come, he had played his seventeenth-hole tee-shot to within six inches of the pin before tapping in left-handed, and had birdied the eighteenth from 40 feet.

| David Frost | 71 | 70 | 66 | — | 207 |
| Brian Tennyson | 69 | 70 | 69 | — | 208 |

Corey Pavin	72	67	70	—	209
Mark O'Meara	69	69	71	—	211
Curt Byrom	76	66	69	—	211
Steve Elkington	69	70	72	—	211
Russ Cochran	72	69	71	—	212
Rick Fehr	73	69	70	—	212
Fred Funk	69	71	72	—	212
Gary Koch	70	67	75	—	212
Greg Norman	73	68	71	—	212

At the beginning of the week, South African David Frost had been an unlikely candidate for tournament leader – he had missed the cut in his last eight tournaments. On the final day he set off three couples behind Greg Norman, but no doubt heard news that the Australian was doing all sorts to the course. Norman eagled the fifteenth and birdied the sixteenth. Then, at the eighteenth, he dropped his two-iron second shot to within a few inches of the hole. It was some act to follow on such a difficult hole, and against the wind.

Frost arrived at the hole over half an hour after Norman. After an outward 38, he was five under par on the inward holes, and now needed a par four at the 471-yard final hole to meet Greg Norman in a play-off. It looked a problem when he put his tee-shot into a fairway bunker. His second, a three-iron, landed in a greenside bunker, not far from where he intended. He hoped he could get within a few feet of the hole with his third shot and escape with a par four.

Greg Norman was talking to the tournament director at the time. The hush descended for Frost's bunker shot. Norman did not watch it. He had no need. The familiar muffled roar from the crowd told him all he needed to know.

Again?

Yes, David Frost had holed a 50-foot sand-wedge shot to pip Norman by one stroke.

Tway, Mize, Calcavecchia, Gamez, and now Frost.

Some people talked about a jinx. Jim Murray of the *Los Angeles Times* suggested that if he were Norman he would give up golf and go into something fair, like fighting oil-well fires. Steve Hershey of *USA Today* thought it was too unbelievable for Alfred Hitchcock, and Hollywood would laugh at the script. It was preposterous that so many once-in-a-lifetime shots could happen to the same victim.

It wasn't easy to be philosophical about it – 'Even Plato and Aristotle would have a hard time dealing with Norman's funereal finishes,' wrote Dave Lagarde of the *New Orleans Times-Picayune* – but Norman seemed calm enough. He recognized that the breaks could come his way if he continued to play well. Around the same time, he won the Doral Ryder Open after a final-round of 62 and a chip-in at the first play-off hole, and in the 1990 Memorial Tournament he was declared the winner when rain wiped out the final round.

Greg Norman was the game's biggest money-winner at the time, and, with striking flaxen hair and blue eyes, captivating smile, overwhelming talent and good sportsmanship, he was one of golf's most admired men. There was, of course, a simple explanation for why he was losing to such miraculous late shots. It was because he was so good, always in contention, and others had to do something spectacular to beat him. Therein lies the attraction of strangeness. It doesn't affect only duffers. It can also happen to the best.

A SPORT FOR PRINCES?

LUDGROVE SCHOOL, JUNE 1991

It is rare that an amateur golf item is included in a British national television news programme, but it happened on Monday 3 June 1991, when eight-year-old Prince William, second in line to the throne, received a depressed skull fracture after being accidentally hit by a golf club at his school.

It happened at Ludgrove Preparatory School in Berkshire, where Prince William had been a pupil since the previous September. During the lunch break, when a number of boys were practising golf on the school putting-green, one child swung his club too hard and too far. Prince William, bleeding from a cut on his head but still conscious, was driven six miles to the Royal Berkshire Hospital by one of the Police Officers who give the Royal family continuous protection. The Princess of Wales, Lady Diana Spencer, drove from Kensington Palace to join her son, and the Prince of Wales, Prince Charles, was driven from Highgrove to the hospital.

Doctors at the Royal Berkshire Hospital ordered the transfer of Prince William to the Hospital for Sick Children, Great Ormond Street, London. The boy's mother travelled with him in the ambulance, and his father followed in his own car. At Great Ormond Street, neurosurgeon Mr Richard Hayward conducted a 70-minute operation to correct a depression of the skull just above the boy's eye. The cut needed 24 stitches.

The Princess of Wales cancelled an engagement in Yorkshire in order to remain at the boy's bedside, and Prince William spent two days in hospital before being released. He was told to take it easy for a while, but otherwise seemed to have no ill effects. As Prince Charles quickly pointed out, the boy who had swung the golf club probably felt much worse about the incident.

The Prince William incident provides some insight into how golf accidents occur. Three Newcastle-upon-Tyne researchers, writing in the *British Medical Journal* (22 June 1991), offer us more detail. Smith, Ling and Alexander studied 11 local children with golf-related head injuries. 'Nine of the children were injured when standing behind another child swinging a club,' they wrote. 'The head was struck on either the backswing or the follow through. Two children were hit on the head by golf balls struck by other children. In seven of the accidents the children had borrowed a golf club and were playing in either parkland or local fields. In one case the child had found the club in a field. Only one of the accidents occurred on a golf course; another occurred at the practice range of a course, and a third on a Crazy Golf course. On no occasion was play supervised by an adult.'

These researchers agreed with a 1980 finding that 'golf is the commonest cause of serious sports-related head injuries in children, despite it being a predominantly adult game'.

Sadly, a golf-related depressed skull fracture in a child is not strange. It is only strange if the child is someone you know ... or someone like Prince William, second in line to the British throne.

CHIP BECK BREAKS SIXTY

LAS VEGAS, OCTOBER 1991

Chip Beck's record-equalling round of 59 was his third in the 90-hole Las Vegas Invitational Tournament. It was played on the 6,914-yard course at the Sunrise Golf Club, which had replaced Spanish Trails as one of the tournament's courses. Sunrise was only a year old, with minimal rough and no trees, and golfers sensed that scores could be low.

Two weeks previously, Chip Beck, 35 years old and twice US Open runner-up, had helped the United States regain the Ryder Cup at Kiawah Island. One of Dave Stockton's two wild-card choices, Beck had won a vital singles against Ian Woosnam. He had also learned more about how other golfers handled pressure, something that would be needed at Sunrise, especially as the Hilton Hotel chain had offered a $500,000 bonus (£292,000) for a golfer breaking the magical sixty.

Like Al Geiberger, the original 'Mr 59', Beck started his record round from the tenth tee. A 40-foot putt for a birdie three put him in a good mood. It was by far the longest putt he would sink all day. After a par four at the eleventh, his second, he birdied six in succession. Indeed he had a 25-foot putt for an eagle at the 546-yard sixteenth, but needed two attempts. A par at the eighteenth meant he had gone out in 29.

He birdied the first from four feet and the second from 10, then parred the third. His first 12 holes had therefore included nine birdies, and he suddenly realized that he had a real chance of a round under sixty. He checked that the Hilton Hotel bonus was a real offer.

He sank a two-foot putt for a birdie at the fourth, which he was playing thirteenth, but missed a 10-footer at the fifth and a 20-footer at the sixth, settling for two pars. To break sixty, he had to do the last three holes in three under par.

He had a 25-foot putt for an eagle at the seventh, but needed two putts. It was still a birdie. Two more birdies would enable him to equal Al Geiberger's 59, and Geiberger was one of Beck's heroes.

His drive at the eighth left him an eight-foot putt for his birdie. Down it went.

Chip Beck moved on to his final hole, the 408-yard ninth, a par four and a likely one to birdie. His drive left him 157 yards from the pin. Taking an eight-iron from his caddie Dave Woosley, he hit his approach shot to within three feet of the hole. Beautiful. Then came the wait. He let his amateur partners play out – the professionals did not come together until Sunday's final round – and the longer Beck looked at the three-foot putt awaiting him, the longer it looked. Eventually, he steadied his shaking hands and made sure he put the ball into the hole.

People would say later that Geiberger's was the more astonishing round as it was completed in difficult conditions on a longer course, but Beck still had to cope with the pressures, and his round could easily have been even lower. He believed he was playing so well that day that he could have matched Geiberger's record on other courses.

After opening rounds of 65 and 72, Chip Beck ended the third day sharing the lead, but the pace was very hot in such a low-scoring tournament. His final rounds, 68 and 67, left him tied for third place, and his actual prize money of $78,000 (£45,500) was far lower than his $500,000 bonus. The tournament was won by Andrew Magee, who finished level with D. A. Weibring, 31 under par, and won the play-off at the second extra hole.

The unpredictability of golf is beautifully illustrated by contrasting Beck's fortunes with those of Mark Brooks in the same tournament. At the seventeenth, in the second round, Brooks thought his ball had lodged in a cherry-tree. Despite a thorough search by a local cherry-picker, which revealed eight balls (all belonging to others), Brooks took the stroke-and-distance penalty. Then, at the eighteenth on the fourth day, he had another unfortunate incident. Either his throw was wild when he tossed his ball to his caddie for cleaning, or the caddie misjudged it. Either way, the ball landed in a pond. Brooks took off shoes, socks and shirt, found 18 balls (all belonging to others) and paid the penalty for not completing the hole with the same ball.

Where there is one strange story, another is usually not far away.

A ROUND IN COURT

NOTTINGHAM, APRIL 1994

It had all begun at the Sherwood Forest Golf Club several years before. In August 1990, two members of the club wrote to the club secretary with claims that John Buckingham, a 57-year-old retired businessman, had cheated. The club committee investigated the claims and found them not proven.

In June 1991 Buckingham started court proceedings to claim libel damages from the two golfers. Buckingham said that golf was an important part of his life and his reputation had to be preserved. He believed there was an attempt to hound him out of the club, so he brought his case in an attempt to gain an apology.

The trouble stemmed from a club competition in which Buckingham, a ten handicap player, played with Reginald Dove and Philip Townsend.

Dove, who had played regularly with Buckingham for two years, had had no previous reason to doubt the other's integrity.

Townsend had played with Buckingham for 12 years.

'I trust him implicitly and have never had any cause to criticise his behaviour on the golf course,' Townsend said later in court, giving evidence on Buckingham's behalf. 'He is not the sort of man to cheat.'

Dove's first concern came at the eighth hole when Buckingham's ball came to rest behind a sapling. Dove reckoned that Buckingham attempted to move the ball forward, first with the sole of his golf-shoe and then with his instep. Dove discreetly told Townsend what he had seen. Townsend said he had seen nothing.

The next hole to feature in Dove's story was the twelfth.

Buckingham's ball disappeared into the rough and Dove searched for the ball.

'Then, to my amazement, I saw a ball sat on a tuft of grass like a coconut,' said Dove. 'There was no ball there when I went into the trees. I mentioned to Mr Townsend that I was convinced he [Buckingham] had replaced his ball. Again he [Townsend] seemed uninterested.'

At the next hole Dove had a similar experience. According to Dove, Buckingham's ball again went into the trees and then mysteriously turned up in a good position. In his letter to the club secretary, Dove described the scene: 'Mr Buckingham's shot was high and went into the trees. I went with him to look for his ball. I searched close to my trolley but then looked further away. I was somewhat surprised to hear Mr Buckingham say he had found the ball quite close to my trolley. It was very obvious Mr Buckingham had dropped another ball when my back was turned.'

Buckingham's story was that both balls were visible in the trees. Townsend supported this by saying that Dove admitted that he hadn't actually seen Buckingham drop a ball.

At the seventeenth Buckingham hit another shot into long grass. Dove followed him like a hawk in the belief that he was going to drop another ball. Eventually, when they had looked long enough for the ball, Dove told Buckingham he should take the shot again. Buckingham did. Reluctantly, according to Dove.

A nine at that seventeenth hole cost Buckingham his last chance of a prize. He finished with a 86 (net 76).

The second defendant in the case, Graham Rusk, was also pleading privilege and justification. Rusk told the court that he had been warned to watch Buckingham in the rough and the trees when he first joined the club in 1988. Rusk also recalled an incident in 1990 when Reginald Dove and himself were suspicious of Buckingham's actions in a bunker at the seventh hole. They thought Buckingham was moving his ball to get a better lie, but Buckingham's hands were hidden from view.

On another occasion, claimed Rusk, Buckingham had replaced his ball two inches to the right of his marker.

Dove and Rush sent letters to the club secretary but the management committee found the claims not proven. It is indeed very difficult to prove or disprove claims of cheating. What next? Will we have CCTV cameras in strategic places on golf courses?

Two other golfers claimed to have seen Buckingham cheat. One gave evidence that he had seen Buckingham bend down and place a ball in a position far away from where the ball had apparently gone. Another member gave evidence that he saw Buckingham very clearly crouch and move his ball in a match in 1988.

The jury of seven women and one man took four and a half hours to decide that Buckingham had not been libelled. The foreman of the jury took the unusual step of adding a rider to the verdict: 'We would like you to know that we are concerned that our decision might be perceived as *proof* that Mr Buckingham definitely cheated. This is not necessarily the view of the whole jury. However, as reflected in our verdict, we did not feel that Mr Rusk and Mr Dove acted maliciously.'

The judge thought they were a sensible jury (even though none of the jury played golf and the judge did).

'We have played every shot on this course several times over the past fortnight,' said the judge, who now knew Sherwood Forest as well as a local caddie.

THREE AMERICAN PRESIDENTS,
THREE WOUNDED SPECTATORS

PALM SPRINGS, FEBRUARY, 1995

When two former Presidents, George Bush and Gerald Ford, joined current incumbent Bill Clinton in a foursome at the Bob Hope Chrysler Classic it promised to be exciting for spectators. Ford assessed the situation correctly on the first tee when he suggested that the general public should take up positions *behind* the golfers. Indeed, plenty of ducking and dodging was in store for spectators.

Bill Clinton, at 48, still had time on his side to improve his game. A few months previously he had holidayed on Martha's Vineyard with the expressed ambition of completing a round in less than eighty. He managed an 82 on the first day of his stay but it was downhill thereafter.

George Bush, now 70 years old, had been an 11-handicap player in his prime but his goal now was 'just to get the ball in the air'. Gerald Ford, 81, was another who was probably past his best. The fourth member of the group was professional Scott Hoch, whose golf had one thing in common with Clinton, Bush and Ford – he had never won a major.

The foursome was joined by Bob Hope himself. The 91-year-old comedian travelled the course in a golf-cart and played at all the holes. He didn't keep a proper score and sometimes started a hole on the fairway.

The first tee was a portent of what was to come.

A nervous Gerald Ford hooked his drive into the crowd.

'Fore,' he yelled, almost before his swing had come to rest.

An equally nervous Bill Clinton sliced his first tee-shot into a bunker.

George Bush hit a reasonable first shot but his second shot resulted in the day's first casualty. Bush's drive rebounded from a tree and hit an elderly lady, Norma Earley, in the face. The impact broke her glasses and cut her across the bridge of the nose.

George Bush hurried across to the woman and offered sympathy while the tournament officials provided first aid. Norma Earley was taken away to hospital in a golf-cart. Her cut required ten stitches.

Bush made a birdie at the sixth hole, but at the fourteenth his ball struck another spectator. John Rynd was sensible enough to have turned his back on play. According to differing reports, the ball hit Rynd on either the back of the leg or the buttock.

'How's the wound?' Bush asked him.

'No blood, no problem,' the man replied.

Bush autographed the ball for him.

Gerald Ford then hit a spectator, Geraldine Grommesh, at the seventeenth hole. The ball drew blood from the spectator's left index finger but no stitches were needed.

Clinton erred in other directions, barely topping his ball with one tee-shot and landing another in a yard next to the fairway. Clinton had to check with tournament officials before picking up the ball and dropping it on the fairway.

If Hoch was worried about always being in front of the other golfers, it didn't ruin his game. His round of 70 was by far the best of the group (although it was a par 68 course). The personal battle between Bush and Clinton was more interesting. Bush (92) was delighted to beat Clinton, who pleaded that his 93 was his worst score for three or four years. Gerald Ford went round in 100. However, one observer pointed out that these scores did not include 'mulligans' (free shots).

The journalists loved it. They were able to ask questions like 'what sort of lies did we have from the President today?'

Bill Clinton can at least claim to have played with great golfers. In 1996 he went round with Greg Norman in Australia.

It was on a visit to Norman's Florida home, however, that Clinton tore the quadriceps tendon on his right knee when he slipped on the guest-house steps. Presidents always have strange golf careers.

GREG NORMAN'S NOVEL WAYS TO FINISH SECOND – LESSON SIX

AUGUSTA, GEORGIA, APRIL 1996

Greg Norman's first-round 63 at the US Masters equalled the course record and gave him a two-stroke lead. A second-round 69 extended his lead to four shots. A third-round 71 put him six ahead after 54 holes. Norman was well-placed to win the US Masters. At last.

Norman's closest rival was Nick Faldo, who had won back-to-back Masters in 1989 and 1990. Norman himself had added the 1994 British Open to his 1986 British title, but he still had to win a major in the United States. The stage was set for one of the most dramatic rounds in a major championship although there was no way of predicting that on the final morning. Norman, 13 below par, looked assured of the trophy with his six-stroke lead.

On the first tee Norman hit his drive into the trees. His second shot went into a bunker. A bogey sent him to 12 under par for the Championship. The lead was five strokes.

Norman and Faldo both made birdies at the second.

Two pars at the third.

Norman went over the green with his approach to the fourth and dropped a shot. The lead was four.

Faldo dropped a shot at the fifth after finding a bunker. A lead of five again with only 13 to play.

Faldo birdied the sixth. The lead was back to four.

Two pars at the seventh.

A par five for Norman at the eighth, but Faldo sank an

eighteen-foot birdie. Norman's lead was now three.

At the ninth Faldo missed a 30 foot putt for a birdie, but Norman missed a seven foot putt for par. Norman (11 under) led Faldo (nine under) by two.

The next three holes changed all that had gone before.

Norman missed a ten foot putt for par at the tenth and his lead was only one shot.

Norman missed a three foot putt for par at the eleventh and they were all square.

Then, at the twelfth, Norman hit his ball into water and finished the hole with a double-bogey. The lead was two shots again but the lead was now Faldo's. Four successive pars had gained Faldo five shots on his rival.

Faldo's lead stayed at two shots when both birdied the thirteenth and fifteenth and had pars at the fourteenth. Then, at the sixteenth, Norman hooked a shot into the lake and registered another double-bogey.

Faldo extended his lead to five shots at the eighteenth with a 20 foot birdie putt after driving into a bunker.

Faldo hugged his caddie and then went across to Greg Norman.

'I don't know what to say to you,' Faldo said. 'I just want to give you a hug.'

They hugged each other on the last green and Faldo set off towards his third green jacket.

Greg Norman took his disappointment with great dignity and spoke philosophically of his bad last round. He recognised that he had played badly and lost the tournament himself. He also recognised that Faldo had played very well in the final round. There may not have been miraculous shots of the calibre of Tway, Mize, Calcavecchia, Gamez or Frost, but Faldo's superb last round of 67 was a worthy tournament winner.

Faldo	69	67	73	67 – 276
Norman	63	69	71	78 – 281
Mickelson	65	73	72	72 – 282
Nobilo	71	71	72	69 – 283

A RECORD PUTT

ABOVE THE ATLANTIC OCEAN, SEPTEMBER 1997

If a golfer putts a ball eight and a half miles in 23 seconds, where is the golfer playing?

This may sound like a question from a Golf Studies examination paper but it was one that people were asking in September 1997.

The answer was 'on a Concorde flight from New York to Malaga'.

The United States Ryder Cup team were en route to Malaga, preparing to meet the Europeans at Valderrama, when they were challenged by the pilot to break the record for Concorde's longest putt. The previous best was 100 feet.

The coaching manual suggests that you putt as slowly as possible and give Concorde the maximum amount of time to travel at 1,330 miles an hour while the ball is still rolling. On his second attempt, Brad Faxon rolled a 120 foot putt all the way along the centre aisle and into a porcelain tea-cup which was lying on its side. His ball was travelling for 23 seconds. Therefore the ball must have travelled eight and half miles (plus an extra 40 yards for the length of the putt).

You might wonder why the golfers needed some distraction. After all Concorde was only in the air for 3 hours 25 minutes.

Nobody knew whether the omens were good or bad for the Ryder Cup. In fact they were not that good for Faxon. He lost two of his three matches and the United States lost by 14½ to 13½.

THE FIRST WINNING 59

LA QUINTA, CALIFORNIA, JANUARY 1999

When David Duval woke up on the last morning of the Bob Hope Chrysler Classic he decided he would need a 59 to win the tournament. He was seven strokes behind the leader, Fred Funk, and plenty of other players were in contention.

Duval started the 6,950-yard Arnold Palmer Course with three birdies, and managed further birdies at the fifth and the ninth. He reached the turn in 31 but it did not look good enough to win the 90-hole tournament. Then, coming back, he birdied the first three holes. On the outside Duval showed all his normal stoicism but on the inside he was really buzzing. He made par at the thirteenth before notching another birdie at the 569-yard par-five fourteenth. Still displaying no outward sign of emotion, his expression concealed by his trademark wrap-around sunglasses and a baseball cap, Duval proceeded to gain shots at the fifteenth and sixteenth. Two more birdies and he would have a round of fifty-nine.

At the par three seventeenth he faced a 20 foot putt for another birdie but left it short. His chance of a 59 seemed to have gone.

However, Duval was still fired up coming to the last hole and he hit an exceptionally long drive. Walking up the final fairway he was more concerned with his score than the possibility of winning the tournament. He was in the perfect mood to hit a superb five-iron which came to rest six foot from the final hole. He had a six-footer for the coveted fifty-nine. The nervousness set in.

He searched deep for his normal putting style, sank the putt and celebrated. Out of character, he punched the air and thrust his arm skyward. A broad smile swept across his face.

```
Par      453 435 444 – 36    453 453 435 – 36 (72)
Duval    342 425 443 – 31    342 442 333 – 28 (59)
```

Now David Duval had to wait to see how his nearest rival, Sandy Pate, fared at his last two holes. Pate needed one birdie to force a play-off.

'Are you going to the range to prepare for a possible play-off?' someone asked Duval.

'Yeah, I really need to work on my game,' he replied, to amusement.

Pate played his last two holes in par figures, so a play-off was not needed after all. Duval won by one stroke. A round of 59 was no longer totally strange – this was the third occasion on the PGA Tour – but this was the first time a professional had 59-ed the final round to win a PGA Tour competition.

SELECTED BIBLIOGRAPHY

Alliss, Peter, *The Who's Who of Golf*, 1983
Anderson, Robert, *Heard at the Nineteenth*, 1966
Anderson, Robert (editor), *A Funny Thing Happened on the Way to the Clubhouse*, 1971
Blackburn, Norman, *Lakeside Golf Club of Hollywood: Fiftieth Anniversary Book*, 1975
Blalock, Jane, and Dwayne Netland, *The Guts to Win*, 1977
Browning, Robert H. K., *A History of Golf: The Royal and Ancient Game*, 1955
Burnet, Bobby, *St Andrews Opens*, 1990
Clark, Robert, *Golf*, 1899
Cossey, Rosalynde, *Golfing Ladies*, 1984
Croome, A. C. (editor), *Fifty Years of Sport at Oxford, Cambridge and the Public Schools*, 1922
Darsie, Darsie L. (editor), *My Greatest Day in Golf*, 1952
Darwin, Bernard, *Green Memories*, 1928
Darwin, Bernard, *Golf Between the Two Wars*, 1944
Darwin, Bernard, *A History of Golf in Britain*, 1952
Dobereiner, Peter, *The Game with the Hole in it*, 1970
Dobereiner, Peter, *For the Love of Golf* 1981
Dobereiner, Peter, *Down the Nineteenth Fairway*, 1982
Dobereiner, Peter, *The Book of Golf Disasters*, 1983
Duncan, George, *Golf at the Gallop*, 1951
Evans, Webster, *Rubs of the Green*, 1969
Evans, Webster, *Encyclopaedia of Golf*, 1980
Farrar, Guy B., *The Royal Liverpool Golf Club*, 1933

Flaherty, Tom, The Masters: *The Story of Golf's Greatest Tournament*, 1961

Flaherty, Tom, *The US Open, 1895-1965: The Complete Story of the United States Championship of Golf*, 1966

Gibson, Nevin Herman, *The Encyclopaedia of Golf with the Official All-time Records*, 1964

Goodban, J. W. D., *Royal North Devon Golf Club, 1864-1964*, 1964

Grimsley, Will, *Golf: Its History, People and Events*, 1966

Guiney, David, *The Dunlop Book of Golf*, 1973

Hagen, Walter, *The Walter Hagen Story*, 1957

Hawkins, Rodney, *Golf at Letchworth*, 1985

Heager, Ronald, *King of Clubs*, 1968

Hobbs, Michael (editor), *In Celebration of Golf*, 1982

Hopkins, John, *Nick Faldo in Perspective*, 1985

Houghton, George, *Believe it or Not, That's Golf*, 1974

Keeler, Oscar Bane, *The Autobiography of an Average Golfer*, 1925

Kennington, Don, *The Sourcebook of Golf*, 1981

Kirkaldy, Andrew, *Fifty Years of Golf*, 1921

Knott, Cargill Gilston, *Life and Scientific Work of Peter Guthrie Tait*, 1911

Lang, Andrew, *A Monk of Fife*, 1896

Leitch, Cecilia, *Golf*, 1922

Longhurst, Henry, and Chris Plumridge (editor), *The Essential Henry Longhurst*, 1988

Low, John L, *F. G. Tait, A Record*, 1900

McCormack, Mark, *The World of Professional Golf*, 1967-

Macdonald, Charles Blair, *Scotland's Gift: Golf*, 1928

Marshall, Keith B, *This for the Half*, 1988

Masson, I. H., and M. H. Hill, *Littlestone Golf Club*, 1988

Nown, Graham, *Bye Bye Birdie: Great Golfing Disasters*, 1989

Ouimet, Francis, *A Game of Golf*, 1932

Player, Gary, *Grand Slam Golf*, 1966

Plimpton, George, *The Bogey Man*, 1969

Plumridge, Chris, *The Book of Golf Disasters and Bizarre Records*, 1985

Reid, William, *Golfing Reminiscences*, 1925

Rodrigo, Robert, *The Birdie Book: A Miscellany of Golf*, 1967

Sarazen, Gene, and Herbert Warren Wind, *Thirty Years of Championship Golf*, 1950

Scott, Tom, *The Concise Dictionary of Golf*, 1978

Snead, Sammy, and George Mendoza, *Slammin' Sammy*, 1986

Sommers, Robert, *The US Open*, 1987

Stanley, Louis, *Green Fairways*, 1947

Steel, Donald, and Peter Ryde (editors), *Shell Encyclopaedia of Golf*, 1975

Stewart, James Lindsay, *Golfiana*, 1887

Stringer, Mabel, *Golfing Reminiscences*, 1924

Travers, Jerome D., and James R. Crowell, *The Fifth Estate*, 1926

Tresidder, Phil, *The Golfer Who Laughed*, 1982

Trevino, Lee, with Robert B. Jackson, *Supermex: The Lee Trevino Story*, 1973

Watson, Geoffrey James, *Off the Tee*, 1963

Wethered, Joyce, *The Game of Golf*, 1931

Wind, Herbert Warren, *The Lure of Golf*, 1971

Wood, Harry B., *Golfing Curios and the Like*, 1910